THE ETHIOPIAN JEWS OF ISRAEL

Personal Stories of Life in the Promised Land

✡

To the Mendocino Coast Jewish Community

It has been a pleasure to present this
work to you in person.

Len Lyons

THE ETHIOPIAN JEWS OF ISRAEL

Personal Stories of Life in the Promised Land

✡

LEN LYONS

WITH PHOTOGRAPHS BY ILAN OSSENDRYVER
FOREWORD BY ALAN M. DERSHOWITZ

JEWISH LIGHTS Publishing

Little by little, even the egg can stand on its legs and walk

ETHIOPIAN PROVERB

Contents

▦

DEDICATION *Page 8*

ACKNOWLEDGMENTS *Page 9*

FOREWORD *Page 10*

PREFACE *Page 12*

SANBAT SALAM *Page 15*

FROM KING SOLOMON TO OPERATION SOLOMON *Page 19*

CHAPTER I RELIVING THE EXODUS *Page 33*

CHAPTER II FIRST HOME AWAY FROM HOME *Page 63*

CHAPTER III THE NEW PEOPLE OF THE BOOK *Page 69*

CHAPTER IV DEFENDING ISRAEL WITH OUR BLOOD *Page 96*

CHAPTER V IN GOD WE TRUST *Page 111*

CHAPTER VI SINGING A NEW SONG IN A NEW LAND *Page 142*

CHAPTER VII GETTING ORGANIZED *Page 166*

CHAPTER VIII PROFESSIONALLY SPEAKING *Page 206*

EPILOGUE *Page 234*

GLOSSARY *Page 236*

NOTES *Page 238*

SELECTED BIBLIOGRAPHY *Page 239*

To Maxine, with love and gratitude.

My greatest joy is the life we have created together.

Acknowledgments

My first expression of appreciation goes to Maxine, my wife. Without her ideas, advice, intuitions, and loving support, this work would not have been begun, much less completed. She also participated in more than half the interviews. Second, this book would not exist were it not for the warm and trusting welcome we received from so many Ethiopian Israelis who opened their homes and their hearts, sharing with us their unique and life-changing experiences.

For their invaluable assistance in the early stages of this project, I thank Barbara Ribakove Gordon, Lisa Schachner, and Judy Wolf. Thanks to Stuart Matlins of Jewish Lights Publishing for his faith in my work and his commitment to publishing the results. For a beautiful and dignified book design, I am grateful to Gary Chassman of Verve Editions and to Kari Finkler.

Photography is a key element of this book and intimately conveys the seriousness, beauty, and diversity of the Ethiopian Jewish community in Israel. Ilan Ossendryver captured these qualities in a people he cares for deeply. His cheerful nature and tireless efforts equal the excellence of his work. For the photos of Ethiopia, I am grateful for the assistance of Zippi Rosenne of the Beth Hatefutsoth Archive and of Barbara Ribakove Gordon and Mazi Melesa of the North American Conference on Ethiopian Jewry. Art Leipzig and Mike Lieman graciously allowed us to use their historic photos of Ethiopia, while Menemsha Films was kind enough to make available stills from the film *Live and Become*. This book is enhanced by the original map created by Tagist Yosef, whose advice and friendship are as delightful as her artwork.

For their careful reading of the manuscript and insightful editorial comments, I thank my daughter Gila and my friend Alan Lobovits. For helping me keep a healthy perspective through it all, I am grateful

to my son Ami. Thanks to Lyla Nathan for a critically important reaction to my work in progress. For her professional editorial skills and genuine interest in this material, I am deeply grateful to Karyn Slutsky. Michael Shiner provided generous help in obtaining research materials. I have been inspired and enlightened by my colleagues on the Ethiopian Jewry Committee of the Jewish Community Relations Council of Boston. For opening their homes during my extended trips to Israel, my heartfelt thanks to Ronit Schwartz and to Amos and Janet Gino, Danny and Lisa Grossman, David and Rosalyn Moss, David and Oshra Nachman, and Chaim and Dalia Tadir. Thanks to Moshe Hazut for his gracious assistance with our work in Haifa.

I am indebted to Tehitina Assefa and Yuvi Tashome for their talents as interpreters and for being delightful traveling companions, to Alma Book for her sensitive transcriptions from Hebrew and many good ideas, and to Elias Gebrehiwot and Tayech Workalemahu for their transcriptions from Amharic. I was also fortunate in that nearly everyone we met during our travels for this project enthusiastically helped us enlist the support of others in the Ethiopian community, especially Shlomo Berihun, Batia Eyob, Eshetu Kebede, and Avraham Neguise.

I am deeply moved by those who offered financial support for my fieldwork: Marcie Hemmelstein and the Caylon Foundation; Errin Siagel and Teresa Koster; Saul and Anne Siegel; and Jonathan Slavin. I offer my sincere gratitude to many individuals at Hebrew College of Newton, MA: to Nathan Ehrlich and Rabbi Art Green for their critical and timely support; and to David Chivo and Judith Segal for creating the Ethiopian Jewry Research Archive, which will house my original materials, including the recorded interviews on CDs, transcriptions of them into English, photographs, and videotapes

FOREWORD

BY ALAN M. DERSHOWITZ

This is a beautiful book about a beautiful people in a beautiful country. It powerfully illustrates the racial and cultural diversity of the Middle East's only democracy. Israel's Ethiopian Jews are quickly becoming an increasingly important part of the Jewish nation's experiment in multiculturalism. In this important and edifying book, we meet the wonderful individuals and families who contribute so much to Israel's success. We see young sabras and old Ethiopians trying to adapt to a new environment. We see soldiers, scholars, rabbis, farmers, tradespeople, mothers, fathers, grandmothers, and babies, all of whom have three important things in common: they are black Africans from Ethiopia; they are Jews; and they are Israelis.

It has not always been easy to make them Israelis. Bringing them from Ethiopia was always a challenge. In the beginning it was difficult to get them out. Later it became difficult to get some of them in. I have been privileged over the years to work with a team of extraordinary lawyers, from both Israel and throughout the world, who have pressed the Israeli government to absorb Jews of color from Ethiopia and other places. Led by Joseph Feit and the Honorable Irwin Cotler, we have filed lawsuits, helped raise money, pressured leaders, and argued in the court of public opinion in favor of increased immigration into Israel.

The effort, not yet completely successful, has been well worth it. I will never forget seeing a group of newly arrived immigrants from Ethiopia during their first hours in their adopted country. It was like a time warp. People from deep in the third world were now becoming comfortable in the first world. Individuals who had never seen a flush toilet, a water fountain, a computer, or an airplane had been flown to a modern technological state.

I recall meeting a woman with a cross emblazoned across her forehead. She wanted to know how to get it removed and replaced with a Star of David. I saw a group of old Ashkenazi women from an assisted living home who had made beautiful black dolls wearing Israeli blue and white costumes with Stars of David. They were handing them to the arriving children. I saw confusion and joy on the faces of the new immigrants. I imagined my own great-grandparents arriving from Poland to the Lower East Side of New York and then realized how much more of a culture shock this immigration must be.

Israel has managed to absorb Jews from the most far-flung corners of the world—from the former Soviet Union, from India, from South Africa, from the former Yugoslavia, from Yemen, from Iraq, and from many more places. Israel is a sanctuary to the world's oppressed and persecuted Jews, as well as a home of choice for many who want to live the Zionist dream. The tapestry is bright with colors. The music, food, clothing, dance, and ambiance reflect its eclectic sources. The youngest generation represents genetic mixes previously unheard of in the world. It is all part of a great experiment in ingathering Jews from around the world to their traditional homeland. The result is one of the most creative, energetic, interesting, and surprising places in the world. May it be blessed with peace so that its diverse people can live up to their unlimited potential.

"And it shall come to pass in that day, that the Lord shall set his hand again

the second time to recover the remnant of his people,

which shall be left from Assyria, and from Egypt, and from Pathros, and from

Ethiopia (Cush)... And He shall assemble the dispersed of Israel

and gather together the scattered of Judah from the four corners of the earth."

— Isaiah 11:11-12

PREFACE

In 2003, my wife and I were blessed with an opportunity to host Ethiopian Jews from Israel in our home. These students were participating in a partnership between Boston and Haifa. Hearing their unique and powerful stories, I became intrigued and moved by the inspiring saga of the Ethiopian Jews, their dramatic escape from Ethiopia to Israel, and their heartfelt longing to become Ethiopian Israelis. Over the next months, we met many more Ethiopian Jews through their visits to Boston and on our trip to Israel. I had never met people like them—so reserved, attentive, deeply thoughtful, and in whom respect for another is carefully noted and authentically given. Before long, I began to feel attached to the individuals I had already met and involved in the quest of their community to feel at home in their new homeland. And so this book began with the desire to capture in personal terms the reality and the feel of their lives some twenty years after the first large wave of immigration to the Promised Land.

From the start, I knew I wanted to present their story as much as possible from their own perspective and to include their accomplishments and successes as well as their well-publicized struggle to function as equal participants in Israeli society. I once explained this goal to an American Jew who actively supports the Ethiopian community in Israel, and he asked me a challenging question: Why isn't an Ethiopian Jew writing this book? My instinctive answer is one I still stand by—through the use of portrait photography and interviews, they *will* have written this book indirectly.

The conversations represented here took place between spring 2004 and winter 2006. They are organized as eight chapters, or themes, to give shape to the story. The conversations were free form, and what our subjects have to say often overlaps or merges with other themes. The occasional repetition of key ideas attests to some common perceptions and concerns throughout the community. These eight chapters are preceded by an account of my worshipping with the Ethiopian Jews and then a narrative that provides the context for their Jewish identity and mass immigration to Israel.

After being warned that Ethiopians are very "private," it was

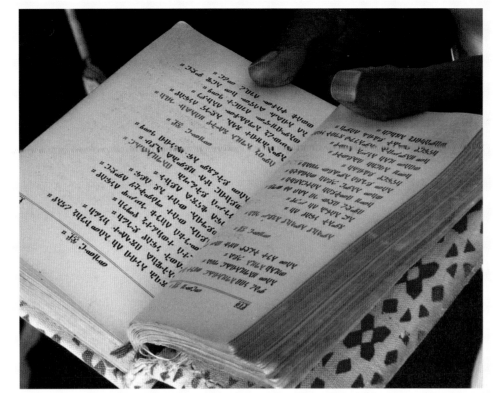

a welcome surprise to see how willing people were to talk personally and at length. One person led us to another, or on to several others, until there were more willing participants than we had time to speak with. The subjects are not a representative sample of the Ethiopian Jewish population of Israel as a whole. This is not a work of social science in any respect; it is a documentation of a human endeavor from the perspective of those constructively engaged in it. Our subjects are very honest about the poverty, crime, lack of literacy, and disaffection within their community, but they are not those most afflicted by these conditions. A book focusing on those who suffer in the margins of Israeli society would be an important but very different kind of project. The individuals interviewed in this book are actively and constructively engaged with Israeli society and eager to speak to their community's concerns.

The most important qualification I brought to this book is a love of listening. My fascination for the unique and moving stories of these courageous Jews never waned. We interviewed people in the language they chose as most comfortable for them. Bilingual interpreters facilitated the conversations requiring Hebrew and Amharic—about two-thirds of the total. After transferring all the recorded interviews onto CDs, I employed different bilingual staff to transcribe them word-for-word into English. The interviews as they appear in this book are condensed and edited to make them readable, but what you will read are the speakers' own words and opinions.

The transliteration of Amharic terms in this book may vary from other texts. For example, a *kess*, or priest, may also appear in English as *qes*. Ethiopian flat bread, *injerra*, is sometimes spelled *injera*. I have used the transliterations I have found most common in print. Hebrew transliteration is seen in English more frequently, but there are still differences in spelling; for example, I use *halacha* for rabbinic law, but other books may use *halakha*.

Ethiopians refer to each other by their first names. They do not use "family names" as we know them in English, although Ethiopian Jews are adopting them in Israel. Thus, I refer to them as they refer to themselves. It is not overly familiar for me to refer to Shlomo Berihun as Shlomo, or to speak about Dr. Seffefe Aycheh as Dr. Seffefe. When Dr. Seffefe sends me e-mail, he adheres to his own custom and addresses me as Mr. Len.

My hope for this book is that it provides a sensitive, honest, and respectful representation of the Ethiopian Jews who appear in its pages. The greatest pleasure of this work has been getting to know them.

SANBAT SALAM

■

In an imprecise but meaningful way, the research for this book can be measured in words, thousands of words in hundreds of conversations. There were more than sixty in-depth interviews that were translated, transcribed, and studied carefully—all of which gave me great insight into the Ethiopian Israeli experience. However, the most enlightening single experience for me was a distinctly and uncomfortably nonverbal one.

As part of my research, I decided to attend Saturday morning Sabbath services at Ethiopian synagogues as often as possible. The Ethiopian Jews had been a religious community in their native land, and if I wanted to learn about their transition to life in Israel, one key to understanding the community was to worship with them on the Sabbath. In the villages of Ethiopia, the sanctity of the Sabbath had been central to their lives. When they are asked what surprised them the most upon their arrival in Israel, a very common answer is that they were shocked to discover that Jews violated the Sabbath routinely and conspicuously; for example, by driving their cars.

My first Sabbath service was spent at the synagogue of Kess Avihu and his father, Kess Malke, in Ashkelon. A *kess* (priest in Amharic; pl. in Hebrew *kessim*), is the title given a spiritual leader. Because my interpreter observed the Sabbath strictly and did not live in Ashkelon, she could not accompany me. I spoke only a few phrases in Hebrew and not a word of Amharic, so I planned to communicate with hand signals and smiles. And, if I was lucky, perhaps I would find someone in the congregation who spoke English.

The synagogue is a bright, modern building on a cul de sac in an Ethiopian neighborhood of small houses and apartment buildings. The service had begun at 4 a.m., the standard starting time for Ethiopian

Jewish Sabbath prayers. I walked in at about 7:30 to a full sanctuary of more than one hundred worshippers. The room was bright, airy, and dignified in its decor. The men stood in long, polished wood pews; women in traditional white wraps and colorful headscarves sat behind a screen that segregated them physically, but not visually.

As the only white person in the room, it did not take long for me to become an object of widespread attention. I was wearing my *tallit* (prayer shawl) and yarmulke; the other men wore a yarmulke or some other type of head covering, but only a few wore a *tallit*. Everywhere I turned my gaze, a pair of eyes was focused on me. There were nods of welcome here and there, a smile, lips soundlessly mouthing *Shabbat shalom*, or the Amharic equivalent, *Sanbat salam*. Some watched me stealthily, instantly averting their eyes when I noticed them, as if to say, "Sorry, I couldn't help staring at you."

The two *kessim* and five or six elders stood in the center of the room on a raised platform surrounded by worshippers. A few religious school students in their early teens occasionally joined them and then returned to their seats in the congregation. Everyone in the room faced the ark that held both the Torah and the Orit—the thirty-nine books of the Hebrew Bible translated into Ge'ez, an ancient Ethiopian language and precursor to Amharic. The *kessim* and elders wore turbans and white robes pulled

over their shoulders, and they leaned on long canes with flat hand rests. Without pause and without books, they were reciting prayers in a plaintive chant from memory. I could tell from the sound of the words that it was Ge'ez, not Amharic. The *kessim* typically lead the four-hour Sabbath prayer service entirely from memory.

A few men in nearby seats reached out to shake my hand. *Shabbat shalom. Sanbat salam.* Another man came over to me, handed me a prayer book in Hebrew, and opened it, pointing out the *Amidah*, the prayers that I knew. He spoke to me in Hebrew, but he soon realized his mistaken assumption and smiled politely but with some degree of amusement. He seemed to trade a meaningful look with a friend. I looked at each of them and used hand signals to say, "Sorry. I know you can't figure out who I am." I wished I could tell them.

The *kessim,* some men in the congregation, and all the women recited prayers with palms raised to the sky, fingers moving subtly, as if gently touching something invisible raining down from heaven. Blessings, perhaps. Every so often, the women would ululate for a short period of time: *el-loo-loo-loo, el-loo-loo-loo, el-loo-loo-loo.* It seemed that these exotic sounds must be correlated to something in the prayer text, but it would have to remain a mystery until a later time. Several times during the prayers, men and women would individually leave their seats, walk to the front of the sanctuary and kneel before the ark, pressing their foreheads to the floor. Then they would rise and back away with great solemnity. I was entranced and, equally, lost.

The prayers, the sounds of ululating, and the individuals kneeling before the ark continued for more than an hour. Afterwards, the *kessim* led a small procession to the ark and removed the Orit, a large leather-bound volume, and brought it back to the platform in the center of the sanctuary. Kess Avihu read in Ge'ez from the Orit, and Kess Malke provided a running translation in Amharic. When the Orit was returned to the ark, the service was over.

People came toward me, curious and welcoming. They gathered around me, shook my hand, and spoke to me, waiting for my response, which could only be *ani lo m'daber ivrit* ("I don't speak Hebrew"). They offered a few words of English, generously trying to help. My answers produced only puzzled looks. I had expected to stand out, but the feelings of embarrassment and inadequacy that welled up inside surprised me. I felt a desperate need to explain who I was, what I was doing in Israel, and why I had come to their synagogue. I wanted to apologize. They were obviously trying to reach out to me, but I could neither understand them nor express myself. The idea of leaving immediately, fleeing, suddenly seemed appealing, but my hosts did not give me a chance to act on it.

As the congregation began to file out the back door, several men motioned for me to follow them, and one took my arm. We entered a courtyard behind the synagogue where there was a small building designed to look like a *tukul,* a circular hut with a thatched roof, typical of homes and synagogues in Ethiopia. People seated themselves on benches at narrow, low tables, the men in the center of the room, the women on the periphery. At the head table, facing the others, were the *kessim* and the elders. The table was piled high with round and square breads, some heavy and dark, others light and fluffy. Another table had bottles of soda, juice, and homemade beer called *tela.* Kess Malke held up two loaves and pronounced a long blessing in Ge'ez.

The congregation responded, the *kessim* tore the breads, and men began to pass the pieces around on paper plates. After the bread was passed to the elders at the head table, a plate was brought to me. Then paper plates piled with chunks of blessed bread were passed around the *tukul* to the other men and to the women.

After the blessed bread had been eaten, whole loaves were passed around and people began tearing it into chunks and dipping the pieces into a brown bean paste, several bowls of which were on every table. *"Harif?"* I asked. Because I don't like spicy food, I made sure to include that word in my scant Hebrew vocabulary. They nodded and scooped big gobs of the dip onto each piece of bread. They urged me to try some, using the universal hand signal for "just a little bit." To avoid offending them, I pretended to accept by touching the bread to the paste, but so lightly that it did no more than produce a faint brownish stain on my piece of bread. I took a small bite. In less than a minute, I was sweating and felt as if something was burning a hole through my tongue.

After a while, people began to leave and I followed them out to the front of the synagogue. I shook hands with many men; women smiled at me and nodded but did not approach me. I could tell they were inviting me to return, and I nodded enthusiastically. Then I had to leave them, cross the street, and get into my car. I started the engine and slowly drove away. Families were walking together toward the large apartment buildings. They walked erect, flowing white robes and black faces standing out proudly against the stone buildings. In the rearview mirror, I could see a few men and women watching me drive away. I felt my stomach sink, convinced that they now regarded me as the shocking white Jew who flagrantly violated the Sabbath. There was no way to tell them who I was and what I was doing in their midst. My frustration and sense of inadequacy returned even more strongly.

Then, suddenly, while stopped at a traffic light on a deserted street in Ashkelon, I realized I had experienced something that brightly illuminated the Ethiopian Israeli experience for me. In greatly diminished form, I had brushed up against what the Ethiopian Jews felt when they came to Israel. Unable to understand their environment, unable to communicate, to explain themselves, they felt disabled, misunderstood, weakened, and inadequate at every turn. What I had endured was barely a glimpse of that reality, because I could drive away and in minutes return to my world of comfort and familiarity. When the Ethiopian Jews arrived in Israel, they could never return to the world they knew. Even though they were with other Jews, after years of longing for just this Zionist *aliyah*, they felt unexpectedly and deeply lost. While they were happy to be in their spiritual homeland, in many ways they did not feel at home. They had to learn how to speak, how to act, how to dress, and how to work. Most painfully, they felt they were being told by the rabbis and many other Israelis that they also had to learn how to be Jews.

Even a momentary awareness of how it feels to be a Jewish stranger in a strange Jewish land deepened my understanding of how much strength and dignity it takes to make the journey from being an Ethiopian Jew to being an Ethiopian Israeli. Many Jews in Israel, North America, and Europe have been supportive of this process, but the most powerful resource available to Ethiopian Jews is their own community, each other. They know it will take hard work. Their talents, perseverance, and deep-seated instinct for caring about each other are the greatest reasons for optimism.

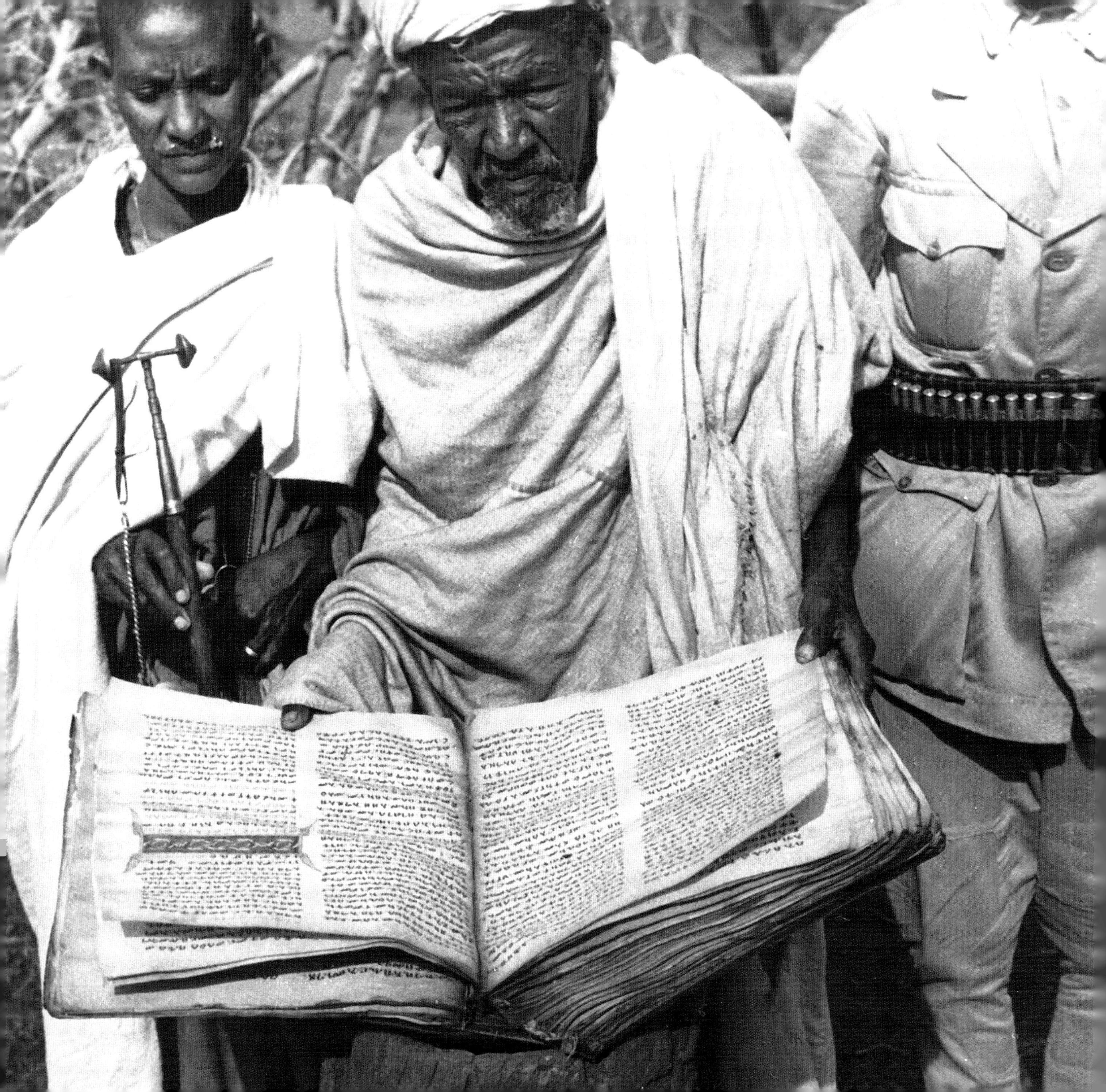

FROM KING SOLOMON TO OPERATION SOLOMON

The exodus of the Ethiopian Jews from their native land and their mass immigration to Israel is a unique historical event. No other cultural or ethnic population has relocated virtually at light speed from a rural, nonliterate culture surviving on subsistence farming and crafts to an urban, high-tech society where they were welcomed to fulfill their religious destiny. In 1977, there were about 100 Ethiopian Jews in Israel; by 2007, there were more than 100,000 Ethiopian Israelis. From their perspective, "exodus" and "immigration" are inadequate terms. As Ethiopian Israeli lawyer Itzik Dessie expressed it, "I would rather not speak of immigration; I prefer to speak about *aliyah.*" *Aliyah,* a purposeful "going up" to reside in Israel, had been a long-held dream for Ethiopia's Jews that was passed down from generation to generation over the centuries. The pursuit of that dream came at a high cost, paid for in thousands of deaths and the shattering of families. Its realization has been partial and elusive, for the Ethiopian Jews are engaged in a long and difficult struggle to become fully integrated Israelis. For them, the Promised Land has yet to fulfill its promise.

Most of this book is devoted to the profound challenges and inspiring accomplishments of the Ethiopian Israelis, as told in their own words. The brief historical narrative that follows sets the stage for their stories by focusing a spotlight on their Jewish origins and the circumstances that enabled them to escape from Ethiopia and come to Israel.

JEWISH ROOTS: MYTH AND HISTORY

The Ethiopian Jews have their own traditional account of how Judaism came to them in their land of origin. They trace their ancestry back to the legendary union of the Queen of Sheba (Makeda) and the biblical King Solomon. The Hebrew Bible records their fateful meeting (I Kings 10:1–13; II Chronicles 9:1–12) as a simple visit by Makeda to Solomon's court, where she presents him with exotic gifts. But in the Ethiopian tale of the nation's origins, a compilation of oral history known as the Kebra Negast (the Glory of the Kings), the meeting of Solomon and Makeda led to a union of historic impact.

The Kebra Negast tells of the young queen who seeks to learn how to govern from the wise king; she submits to his instruction and succumbs to his charm. At a celebratory banquet, he wines and dines her into a slumber and awakens her with romance and seduction. That night, Solomon dreams that the royal line will be continued through their child. He sends Makeda home but tells her she must return their child to him for a royal education. Years later, Makeda dutifully sends young Menelik to Jerusalem to be raised according to the teachings of Israelite law and to be educated in the court of his father. When the time comes for Menelik to leave Jerusalem, Solomon anoints him king of Ethiopia and provides him with an entourage from his court. Menelik, however, is given a secret mission by God: to take with him the Ark of the Covenant, transferring it to the city of Aksum. Tradition holds that the Aksumite Empire (fifth century BCE–seventh century CE) became the seat of Menelik's power, the new Holy Land, and, eventually, the nation of Ethiopia.

As late as the twentieth century, most Ethiopians—both Christians and Jews—accepted the Kebra Negast as the authoritative account of their nation's beginnings. In 1955, for example, the revised Ethiopian constitution affirmed that the emperor of Ethiopia, Haile Selassie, was a descendant of King Solomon and Makeda, the queen of Sheba. Haile Selassie, who reigned from 1930 to 1974, referred to himself in official documents as "The Lion of Judah." Through the lens of this pivotal document, the presence of Israelite influence seems clearly visible very early in Ethiopia's history.

Sacred Hebrew texts also point to Judaic influence in the Horn of Africa centuries prior to the advent of Christianity. The *Tanach* (the Torah, Prophets, and Writings) contains nearly fifty references to the land of Cush and the Cushites. Cush became identified with Ethiopia through the Septuagint, a third-century translation of the thirty-nine books of the *Tanach* into Greek by Jewish scholars in Alexandria who rendered Cush as "Aethiopia" (Greek for "sunburned faces"). During the time of Moses, the Kingdom of Cush dominated a vast region that included southern Egypt and stretched into parts of Sudan and perhaps northern Ethiopia. This is the context for the assertion that Moses, during his sojourn in the south of Egypt, marries a "Cushite woman" named Tzipora (Numbers 12:1). Prophetic writings of the seventh century BCE also speak of Hebrews in the land of Cush (Isaiah 11:11; Zephaniah 3:10; and Psalm 87:4).

There is no independent evidence to suggest that Cush meant anything more specific than "south of Egypt," but in their sixth-century translation of the Hebrew Scriptures into Ge'ez, the Ethiopian Christians followed the Septuagint. The Ge'ez translation of the Septuagint is called the Orit (similar to the Hebrew *oraita*, meaning "the law"). Thus, the Orit, the sacred text of both Jewish and Christian sects in Ethiopia, perpetuated the identity of biblical Cush and "Aethiopia."

A TANGLE OF RELIGIOUS IDENTITIES

The possibility that Israelite influences were present at a very early date can be seen in the way early Christianity was practiced in Ethiopia. Christianity became the official religion of ancient Ethiopia following the conversion of the Aksumite emperor Ezana in 330 CE.

The religious practices of these new Christians included observing the Sabbath on Saturday, circumcising male children on the eighth day after birth, constructing churches in three concentric circles in accordance with the Torah's instructions, and performing sacrifices based on the ritual in the Temple in Jerusalem. Additionally, Christians would not eat the meat of a pig. They referred to the days of the week in the Hebrew tradition of First Day (Sunday), Second Day (Monday), and so on, and they called Friday *arb* (in Hebrew, *erev*), for "evening" of the Sabbath.[1]

The distinctive nature of early Christianity in Ethiopia was its profoundly "Judaized" character. The Ethiopian historian Getatchew Haile writes: "In short, the Jewish influence in Ethiopian Christianity seems to originate from those who received Christianity and not from those who introduced it. In short, the Jewish elements were already entrenched in indigenous Aksumite culture when it adopted Christianity."[2] Historian James Quirin, who has written extensively on the Ethiopian Jews in Ethiopia, states simply, "Ethiopia was Jewish before it was Christian."[3]

However, religious distinctions were murky and tangled in this region, and as Steven Kaplan, the distinguished historian of the Ethiopian Jews, warns, "Attempts to reconstruct the history of the

[Ethiopian Jews] on the basis of external ideas of 'Jews' and 'Judaism' versus 'Christians' and 'Christianity' obscure far more than they illuminate."[4] The most accurate word to characterize religious life in ancient Ethiopia is *syncretistic*, a bringing together of multiple elements—Israelite, Christian, and pagan.

PATHWAYS TO ETHIOPIA

The influence of the Torah and Israelite customs in ancient Ethiopia is clear, but explaining how they were brought there is a matter of educated conjecture. There have been a variety of theories proposed. One is that a contingent of the biblical Exodus from Egypt traveled south, toward Cush, instead of east, toward Sinai. Another theory is that the Judaic influence came by way of a small Jewish community that was known to have developed in Elephantine in southern Egypt in about 600 BCE. It has also been proposed that the flight from Jerusalem after the destruction of the First Temple in 584 BCE was the source. However, the explanation historians believe to be most likely is that the influence came by way of trade with outposts of Israelites who lived across the Red Sea in the region of southern Arabia or Yemen (see map). There were well-established Jewish communities there; in fact, Rabbi Akiva was reported to have visited one in the second century. As a result of trade, Israelite customs and religious practices are likely to have crossed the Red Sea into ancient Ethiopia.

Who were the bearers of Jewish influence, and how did they leave their imprint? Did they intermarry with East Africans, creating a genetic link with the nation of Israel? Or did they simply introduce Israelite ideas and practices that took hold in the local population?

Most historians believe that those in the Aksumite Empire who adopted Judaic ideas and practices were groups native to the Horn of Africa, such as the Agau people. No one has been

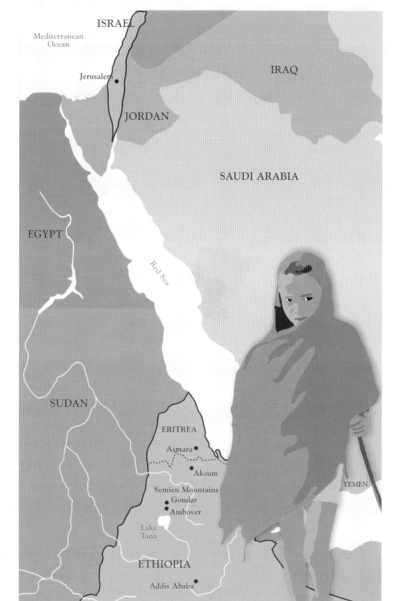

able to find differences in body type, skin color, physiognomy, or other physical features between today's Ethiopian Jews and other Ethiopians. In 1999, a study compared the DNA of Ethiopian Jewish men in Israel and Ethiopian men in Addis Ababa and concluded that the biological evidence supports the view that the men in both groups descend from the same ancestry.[5] It is out of the Aksumite-Ethiopian stock that the Ethiopian Jews arose as a distinct group, religiously and culturally.

Despite their intertwined early traditions, the Christians and Jews of Ethiopia soon split, with the Christians eventually isolating those who resisted Christianity. How did animosity evolve out of the blended religious environment of ancient Ethiopia, where everyone was a descendant of the wise King Solomon and the irresistible Queen of Sheba? The Kebra Negast dates the beginning of hostilities between the Christians and Jews of Aksum to the early part of the sixth century during the reign of Emperor Ella-Asbeha (also known by the biblical name Caleb, signaling his claim to a relationship with King Solomon). The Aksumite emperor fought with the Judaic communities of southern Arabia, driving a wedge between Aksum's Israelite-influenced Christian subjects and those who practiced Israelite customs but rejected Christian doctrine.

THE DEVELOPMENT OF THE FALASHA

From the sixth century, when the Aksumite Empire began its decline, to the fifteenth century, the window looking into the history of Ethiopia is opaque. As famously expressed by Edward Gibbons, "Ethiopia slept for a thousand years, forgetful of the world by which it had been forgotten." The nation was a loose and decentralized entity that produced no lasting documentation of its affairs. In addition, the rise of Islam in northern Africa served to isolate Christian Ethiopia from trade with surrounding nations, eliminating external records that might have shed light on this obscure period. Much of what is known comes from the oral history recorded in the legends of the Kebra Negast, which did not concern itself with Ethiopia's Jews except incidentally.

Nevertheless, there were several well-known references to Ethiopian Jews in literary sources. One reference appears in the writing of Eldad Ha-Dani, a traveler of uncertain identity whose *Sefer Eldad (The Book of Eldad),* composed in the late 9th century,[6] mentions Jews "beyond the rivers of Cush." As the name Ha-Dani (the Danite) indicates, the author portrays himself, as well as the Jews in Ethiopia, as members of one of the Lost Tribes. Another legend contributing to the idea of a Jewish "nation within a nation" appears in the Kebra Negast, which tells of Queen Yodit (Judith), a ruthless tenth-century ruler who was described as *ayhud.* The term *ayhud* was used pejoratively (and ambiguously) to describe several different groups who were unwilling to accept Christian doctrine, but *ayhud* has often been interpreted as referring to Jews in particular. Yodit was said to have raised a brutal and powerful army that vanquished the Christian forces and allegedly destroyed many churches, slaughtering their clergy and rulers in a fearsome rampage. Another well-known traveler, Benjamin of Tudela (Toledo), wrote during the twelfth century that "across the Red Sea" from Yemen (roughly the region of Ethiopia), there were Jews "not subject to the rule of others, and they have towns and fortresses on the tops of mountains."

During the twelfth through the fourteenth centuries, the Amhara rulers to the south mounted frequent attacks on the relatively autonomous *ayhud,* certainly including Jews, who managed to maintain a fragile independence. The rugged landscape to which the Jews had retreated provided them with some protection. They lived in the Semien Mountains and in the Lake Tana region, where the inaccessible terrain made them difficult to attack. With the ascension of Emperor Yeshaq early in the fifteenth century, the status of the *ayhud* was radically altered. Yeshaq elevated the conquest of Christian heretics and Jews to the highest priority of his regime. His purge of the religious "deviants" resulted in violent deaths and forced conversions among Jews and other non-Christians. The most profound and far-reaching consequence of Yeshaq's victory over the *ayhud* was the decree that denied them the right to own land. Yeshaq is said to have proclaimed in 1416, "He who is baptized in the Christian religion may inherit the land of this father; otherwise let him be a *falasi.*"[7]

Yeshaq's decree was very likely the first historically noted use of the Ge'ez word *falasha.* In this context, *falasha* meant "landless," but its connotation broadened to include "stranger," "immigrant," and "outsider." Falasha also became the accepted name of Ethiopian Jews by their advocates elsewhere in the world, who seemed unaware of its pejorative connotations. In fact, the Ethiopian Jews referred to themselves as Beta Israel (House of Israel), a term that we know was in use during the 1700s and possibly much earlier. The real problem for the Falasha (or Beta Israel) was not what they were called, but their landless status, which had severe and enduring socioeconomic consequences. The prohibition against land ownership in an agriculturally-based economy drove the Jews of Ethiopia into their roles as potters, metal workers, weavers, masons and tenant farmers. These roles meant not only that the Beta Israel would be impoverished, but

that they would also become an ostracized caste. Working with metal and making tools, for example, were viewed as despicable activities, for it was widely believed that people who worked with fire had access to "the evil eye" and could cast spells. The Beta Israel were afflicted with other epithets, including *buda* (sorcerer) and "hyena" people. In addition to casting evil spells on Christians, the Beta Israel were superstitiously thought to transform themselves into hyenas at night, when they would roam the countryside and kill Christians. Innumerable Ethiopian Jews were attacked or killed well into the twentieth century whenever unexplained misfortunes afflicted their neighbors.

JEWISH IDENTITY DEFINED

The point is often made by historians that the Ethiopian Jews must be understood to have evolved within the context of Ethiopian history, and not solely looked at from the perspective of Jewish history. During the fourteenth and fifteenth centuries, for example, forces acting upon the region's Christian leaders led to shaping some of the prominent characteristics of Ethiopian Judaism as it was practiced into the twentieth century. During this period, the church in Egypt began to pressure Ethiopian royalty and its clerics to abandon Israelite-based practices, especially the observance of the Saturday Sabbath. The emperor acceded to this demand and did not tolerate any resistance

from the clergy. Those priests and monks who refused to give up their Judaized practices had to flee for their lives. One of these, a monk known as Abba Sabra (*Abba* was a term of respect), sought refuge among the Beta Israel in the Semien highlands. Along with a disciple, Sagga Amlak, Abba Sabra was responsible for transplanting the monastic tradition from Christian Ethiopia to the Beta Israel, where it took root and flourished well into the twentieth century. Whether these holy men abandoned Christianity and joined the Beta Israel is unclear, but there is no doubt that the monastic tradition—unique to the Ethiopian expression of Judaism—became deeply entrenched in Beta Israel life during this period. Because of their superior literacy, the monks defined to a great extent the prayer liturgy that endures in the traditional Ethiopian Jewish practice to this day.[8] It was the monks who trained the priests (*kessim* in Hebrew) and set the example for piety, which was the true measure of one's religious status for the Ethiopian Jews.

It was during the sixteenth century that the Beta Israel, for the first time, were defined as Jews by a rabbinic authority. The Spanish-born Rabbi David ben Abi Zimrah of Cairo, known as "the Radbaz," was asked to decide upon the status of a child born to a Falasha slave and her Egyptian master. The Radbaz knew enough about Ethiopian Jews to state in his response that they did not follow the Oral Law, not because they rejected it, but because they did not have access to the

Talmud. He judged that the Falasha were descended "from the tribe of Dan" and that the woman's offspring was Jewish.[9] The Radbaz's decision proved to be a historic precedent, for in 1973 the chief Sephardic rabbi of Israel, Ovadiah Yosef, referenced it when he authenticated the Jewish identity of the Beta Israel. Two years later, the chief Ashkenazi rabbi, Shlomo Goren, issued a similar judgment. With these decisions, the right of the Ethiopian Jews to immigrate to Israel and to be eligible for citizenship under the Law of Return was assured. But before their Jewish identity could lead them to Israel, the Beta Israel and Jews elsewhere in the world had to become aware of each other.

EUROPEAN AND ETHIOPIAN JEWS: A MUTUAL DISCOVERY

The existence of the Ethiopian Jews came to the attention of the Jews of Europe through the work of Christian explorers and missionaries. The adventurous Scottish traveler James Bruce spent roughly two years with the Falasha in the remote villages around Gondar during the 1770s. A competent linguist and researcher, Bruce was able to learn a great deal about them and about Ethiopia (then known as Abyssinia). He was the first to note that the Ethiopian Jews considered themselves to be descended from King Solomon and the Queen of Sheba, and that they referred to themselves as Beta Israel, while others called them Falasha. He returned to England in 1774 with valuable Ge'ez manuscripts, such as the Song of Songs and Ethiopia's national epic, the Kebra Negast. Bruce published an account of his journey in 1790 in a five-volume work, *Travels to Discover the Source of the Nile.* The work was sufficiently popular to spread its news beyond scholars, and eventually it came to the attention of Protestant missionary organizations.

In fact, Christians took much more of an interest than European Jews in the discovery of Ethiopian Jews, as their impoverished circumstances and lack of education made them seem like promising targets for conversion. In 1838, the London Society for Promoting Christianity Among the Jews worked with Ethiopian emperor Theodore to secure the right to conduct missionary work, sending Samuel Gobat from Switzerland, Martin Flad from Germany, and Aaron Stern, a converted German Jew, to work with the Falasha. However, the missionaries met more resistance than they had expected. They converted an estimated forty individuals per year, counting the dependent children of the converts,[10] a very meager harvest in view of the estimated Beta Israel population at the time of between 150,000 and 200,000.[11]

Although the Protestant missionaries did not succeed in converting many Beta Israel to Christianity, their presence had important consequences for the Ethiopian Jews. It prompted the Beta Israel to respond by organizing the first attempt to leave Ethiopia for the Holy Land. In 1862, an influential religious leader, Abba Mahari, led a contingent of an unknown number of Ethiopian Jews on an ill-fated attempt to walk to Jerusalem. The fear of forced conversion was one motivation, but they were also convinced, under the influence of Abba Mahari, that the time for redemption had come.[12] Most of the expedition perished of disease and starvation before they reached the Red Sea, and the others turned back.

Another more important consequence of the missionary activity was the awakening of interest in the Beta Israel among the Jews of Europe. In 1864, the German rabbi Azriel Hildesheimer, after studying the decision of the Radbaz and the scholarly writing of a few Europeans of his own time, published a plea in the *Jewish Chronicle* for a Jewish mission to Ethiopia. The call was answered by Joseph

Halevy, a Polish Jew from Turkey who contacted the Alliance Israelite Universelle in Paris and offered to lead such an expedition. With the support of the Alliance, Halevy left for Ethiopia in October 1867 and returned a year later, a champion of the Falasha whom he admired for their faithfulness to their unique practice of Judaism, despite the hardships it invited. He published a lengthy account of what he learned and a few years later translated one of the original Beta Israel writings, *Te'ezaza Sanbat (Commandments of the Sabbath),* into French. Jewish organizations, however, failed to respond for a variety of reasons, such as the plight of Jews in Eastern Europe and deteriorating conditions within Ethiopia, where a new emperor, a devout Christian, discouraged contacts between the Falasha and supportive Jews from Europe.

Of course, it is crucial to understand the major features of the Ethiopian Jewish practice that the European visitors confronted in the Gondar and Lake Tana area of northwestern Ethiopia. Above all, the tradition adhered to biblical practices, especially the sanctity of the Sabbath, an emphasis on the laws of purity related to menstruation and childbirth, animal sacrifices as prescribed by the Torah, and a conscientious separation from Christians. Because of their isolation, they had been ignorant of the Talmud's existence. This meant that they knew nothing of post-biblical holidays, such as Hanukkah and Purim; nor did they know that animal sacrifice, the separation from the community of

the mother after childbirth, and other Temple-related rituals had been abandoned by Jews elsewhere. For all but a handful of educated individuals, their isolation also meant that until the shocking arrival of these European Jews in their villages, they did not know that there were other Jews, much less that they were white.

At the turn of the century, Jacques Faitlovich, a Polish Jew living in France who was a student of Halevy, entered the life of the Beta Israel and changed the direction of their religious life, unintentionally setting the stage for their *aliyah.* If there is a (non-Ethiopian) hero of the Beta Israel story, it is this dedicated individual. Faitlovich not only studied what Halevy had to teach him, he also learned Amharic and Tigrinya, the language of Tigray, which had a substantial Beta Israel population. Faitlovich saw the Beta Israel as a unique Diaspora community in need of education and support. Funded by Baron Edmond de Rothschild, Faitlovich, only twenty-three years old, first visited the Ethiopian Jews in 1904. Until his death in 1955, he devoted his life to advocating for their needs in Ethiopia, educating them about rabbinic Judaism and connecting them to the wider Jewish world.

Faitlovich's plan was two-fold: first, to find young and talented Beta Israel men, send them to centers of Jewish learning in Europe and Palestine where they would become educated, and then have them return to teach their own villages about rabbinic Judaism; second, to raise funds and guard their welfare in Ethiopia to the greatest extent possible. Since modern Israel was four decades away from its birth, he naturally had no thought of their mass immigration. Yet everything he tried to accomplish prepared them for that opportunity. Equally important, Faitlovich secured support for the Jewish identity of the Beta Israel from sources with impressive credentials. He convinced forty-eight rabbis from several countries to sign a statement testifying to the Falasha's Jewish identity, and he also exacted an endorsement from the influential Rav Kook in Jerusalem. Pragmatic as well as principled, Faitlovich lined up funding from the Jewish Agency for his Jewish schools in Ambover, Gondar, and Asmara. The parents and grandparents of some of today's Ethiopian Israelis attended these schools to learn about rabbinic Judaism. Faitlovich internationalized the cause of Ethiopian Jewry by stimulating a "pro-Falasha" movement in the United States. American Jews were to become instrumental politically and financially in the efforts to bring the Ethiopian Jews to Israel.

Faitlovich's goal of creating Beta Israel religious scholars and teachers faced many stumbling blocks. Parents had a natural resistance to allowing their teenage sons to travel far away for years of study, and the youngsters who were sent were prone to loneliness and illness. The preoccupation of most Ethiopian Jews with day-to-day survival was another barrier to turning their attention to a new religious orientation. Nevertheless, Faitlovich's seeding of the population with scholars bore fruit over time. By 1950, there was a cadre of teachers who mastered not only rabbinic Judaism, but several languages. Two of them, Taamrat Emanuel and Yona Bogale, played a major role in promulgating Jewish learning among a small but crucial core of the Beta Israel population.

With the creation of the state of Israel in 1948, Faitlovich began to think not of immigration, but of Israel's taking responsibility for helping the Ethiopian Jews. In 1954, with the help of the Jewish Agency, he opened a teacher-training institute in Asmara with more than fifty Beta Israel men and women enrolled in its first year. The following year, twenty-seven of these students went to study at Kfar Batya in Israel, where Faitlovich, suffering from a serious illness, had the pleasure of greeting them before his death in October 1955. After Faitlovich's death, activism in Europe and America on behalf of the Ethiopian Jews continued, but at a decreased level.

THE TIDE FLOWS TOWARD ISRAEL

Thanks to Faitlovich, the Jewish Agency, and pro-Falasha activists in America and Europe, a small percentage of Ethiopia's Jews became more educated and interconnected with the rest of Jewry. It cannot be emphasized too strongly that this growing awareness was shared by only a tiny fraction of the population. Travel between villages, where most of the Jews lived, was difficult and dangerous. With an extremely low literacy rate and a decentralized Jewish "community," there was no simple way to communicate, much less teach people the laws and practices of rabbinic Judaism and convince them to give up their own traditions. For example, animal sacrifices at Passover continued in some villages into the 1970s.

Education aside, daily life remained difficult and, at its worst, fraught with danger. In 1958, a contingent from the Beta Israel community gained an audience with the Emperor Haile Selassie to present its grievances. The complaint listed unfair burdens placed upon Beta Israel tenant farmers and craftsmen, named many Jews who had been murdered and synagogues that had been burned to the ground because of accusations of "sorcery," and lamented the fact that "we . . . have been living in this country since time unknown, and nevertheless, we are viewed by the Christian population as a foreign race."[13]

What drove the Jews to the exodus, or more accurately "escape," from Ethiopia was a combination of their growing awareness of Israel and the deteriorating conditions in Ethiopia. Emperor Haile Selassie had become increasingly unpopular and out-of-touch, and in 1974 he was overthrown by Marxist rebels. A communist committee known as the Derge ruled Ethiopia, and it briefly looked as if the situation of the Beta Israel might change for the better. The communists immediately overturned the prohibition against land ownership by Jews and other minorities. However, they subsequently nationalized the farmland and eliminated all private ownership. Moreover, the government soon passed laws that discouraged and in effect punished religious observance. Many Ethiopian Israelis remember when the market day was changed to Saturday to force the Beta Israel to violate the Sabbath or forego their meager income from sales of pottery and metal work. The Derge's authority was transferred to the dictator Haile Mariam Mengistu, whose regime was particularly stringent with Jews because of the Yom Kippur War and Ethiopia's ties to the Soviet Union. Among other measures, the regime prohibited the teaching of Hebrew, forced Jewish schools to close, and cut off diplomatic relations with Israel. Mengistu was also unpopular with other factions of the Ethiopian population, and anti-communist rebel militias soon coalesced to fight against Mengistu's army. Both sides forcibly conscripted soldiers from the countryside, including defenseless Beta Israel men and boys, many of whom were never heard from again after being pressed into service. Given the Beta Israel's increasing awareness of Jews in Israel and their spiritual attachment to Jerusalem, the oppressive conditions in Ethiopia were enough to tip the balance in favor of escape, even with its dangers and uncertainties.

The first wave of the *aliyah* began to gather momentum in 1977 from the northeastern province of Tigray to Sudan, where, according to reports that filtered back into Ethiopia, the Jews were able to connect with Israeli agents who arranged for their travel to Israel. This was made possible on the Israeli side by the decision of Prime Minister Menachem Begin to act on the rabbinic pronouncements of 1973 and 1975, which had confirmed the Beta Israel's Jewish identity and their right to settle in Israel. Next, the Jews of the neighboring Gondar province found their own routes to Sudan, which were dangerous and sometimes deadly. They traveled on foot at night with little food and no armed protection. Each route, each time period, presented its own frightening scenario. The exodus began as a trickle of refugees and gathered momentum over the next six years as Ethiopian Jews streamed into the refugee camps of Sudan by the thousands. They lived among thousands of Christian and Muslim Ethiopians who were also fleeing Mengistu, poverty, and hunger. Despite the overwhelming dangers, the number who reached Israel traveling independently is impressive. In fact, even before the airlifts of Operation Moses, there were already 7,000 Ethiopian Jews who had made it to Israel.

Family dislocation was particularly traumatic. There were many situations where families could not travel together, for they were large (from six to nine children was typical) and the span of ages was great. Because they could move the fastest, teenagers were sent first. Parents planned to come later with small children, but in many cases they could not leave, or they were caught and arrested. Four to five thousand died en route of hunger, of violence from soldiers or *shiftas* (robbers who roamed the countryside), and from disease in the refugee camps of Sudan. In Israel, beginning in 1985, a religious

holiday, Yom Hazkarah, is observed annually on the twenty-eighth of the month of Iyar (coinciding with Jerusalem Day) to memorialize those who died trying to reach Israel. In some cases, family members who were thought dead had in reality been trapped in refugee camps or had hidden in other countries and turned up years later. In more than a few cases, survivors found that their spouses had remarried, and it was common for teenagers to live in Israel as orphans until parents arrived many years later. Many of the Ethiopian Israelis interviewed in the following pages left their families as teenagers and were reunited with them as adults.

In addition to the secretive individual journeys, the exodus had its high-profile milestones that made the evening news. The first of these was not intended to be made public. Operation Moses (November 21, 1984–January 5, 1985) rescued 7,000 Jews from Sudanese refugee camps via clandestine flights through third countries, until an Israeli official mistakenly leaked the story to the news media. This embarrassed the government of Sudan, which had been looking the other way, and the operation ended abruptly. About 600 of those left behind were flown to Israel months later in Operation Joshua, an American-sponsored airlift negotiated with Sudan by Vice President George H. W. Bush.

From 1985 to 1990, Ethiopia made emigration illegal and its attempt punishable by substantial and often brutal prison terms. Stories of jail time, torture, and death were well-known and have since been documented, but even that did not stop the flow entirely. Over those five years, about 2,000 managed to reach Israel, often using false papers, pretending to attend universities elsewhere, or other subterfuges. By this time, the lure of Israel was strong and even Jews whose circumstances were favorable in Ethiopia saw their future only in terms of the Jewish state. By 1990, Mengistu was under siege by rebel forces, which were gaining ground, and for strategic reasons the dictator revived diplomatic relations with Israel. Legal immigration began and word spread quickly that the Israeli embassy in Addis Ababa was the launching pad for Israel. At this time, the remaining Beta Israel and even the descendants of Beta Israel who had converted to Christianity during the nineteenth and early-twentieth centuries (known now as the Falas Mura), abandoned their homes and possessions, flocking by the thousands to live in the slums of Ethiopia's capital in the hope that they would be brought to Israel. Most of the 20,000 who arrived in 1990 and early 1991 walked from their villages as far as hundreds of kilometers away. They were sick, malnourished, and without the means of supporting themselves. While awaiting an unknowable departure date, they were "rescued" in place by the Jewish Agency, the American Jewish Joint Distribution Committee (JDC), the North American Conference on Ethiopian Jewry (NACOEJ), and the American Association for Ethiopian Jews (which became the Israel Association for Ethiopian Jews in 1993). Israel began negotiating with the Ethiopian government for a faster rate of immigration, but by the early spring of 1991, the rebels began closing in on Addis Ababa, dictating a new urgency to all concerned.

Sporadic gunfire could be heard around the city; and the fear of all the activists and planners in Israel and America was that the Ethiopian Jews could become victims of the violence that threatened to overwhelm Addis Ababa. In May, Mengistu fled to Zimbawe, and the victory of the rebels appeared assured. Through negotiations between Israel, Ethiopia, and the United States—and the transfer of $35 million to Ethiopia's treasury—a deal was reached that allowed Israel to perform a spectacular rescue aptly named Operation Solomon. On May 24–25, 1991, more than 14,000 Ethiopian Jews were processed through the embassy, bussed to the airport, and flown to Israel within thirty-six hours in unmarked jets with the seats removed to accommodate as many as 1,000 passengers who took nothing with them but the clothing they wore. Three thousand years separate the legendary progenitor of the Ethiopian Jews from the spectacular rescue operation that bears his name; but it took only fourteen years, from 1977 to 1991, for this Diaspora community to relocate most of its members and begin life anew in its spiritual home.

■ ■ ■

In 2007, the number of Ethiopian Israelis is just over 100,000, but the exodus is not over. In fact, within a year of Operation Solomon, Jews were discovered to be living in the Quara region of Ethiopia, which was geographically remote and politically isolated from the rest of the country. By 1993 several thousand Quaran Jews had been brought to Israel, but 2,000 others who lived in lower Quara were left behind.

Another group that remains is far more numerous. Between 15,000 and 17,000 Ethiopian Jews continue to live as refugees in Addis Ababa and Gondar. These are the Falas Mura, recent returnees to Judaism whose ancestors converted to Christianity in the previous century (usually to escape discrimination) but whose Beta Israel relatives have since moved to Israel. Like the Jews who swarmed into Addis Ababa in 1990, the Falas Mura left everything they owned in their villages in the hope of emigrating. They live near facilities known as "compounds," which are feeding stations, schools, centers for Jewish worship, and, for 300 lucky people each month, a departure point for Israel. From 1990 to 2005, NACOEJ operated the compounds, but in the wake of difficulties with the government of Ethiopia, the Jewish Agency for Israel inherited their management. Late in 2005, NACOEJ was still working in Gondar, but the government of Ethiopia required the compound in Addis Ababa to cease operation, leaving the Falas Mura there with virtually no support.

In addition to the incomplete exodus, the absorption of the Ethiopian Jews as equal partners into Israeli society, which is the focus of this book, looms as a daunting challenge. In view of their history and relatively short time in Israel, their accomplishments have been stunning. In less than thirty years, the vast majority has fast-forwarded from a lifestyle that resembled the Middle Ages to a society at the cutting edge of the computer age. Differences in family dynamics, language, education, and especially in the way they practice Judaism make it a tough fit. There is certainly discrimination based on cultural differences, religious background, and lack of education, but to what extent discrimination is based on their being black is difficult to assess. In the next section of this book, Ethiopian Israelis themselves address the topic frequently. The rate of unemployment and poverty are high: according to some data, more than 60 percent of them live below the poverty line. The Ethiopian Jews have long seen Israel as their spiritual homeland, but so far as everyday life is concerned, many still feel like outsiders. Their quest to make Israel a home in which they feel at home is challenging, dramatic, and inching its way toward success. As a well-known Ethiopian proverb says, "Little by little, even the egg can stand on its legs and walk." At this point, it is best to let them tell their stories for themselves.

RELIVING THE EXODUS

They came from Ethiopia on foot after weeks or months of walking. They stowed away on steamers sailing the Red Sea. They maneuvered using false passports and visas through third and fourth countries.

They took off from hidden runways in the middle of the night. Most profoundly, the Ethiopian Jews flew to Israel on the wings of an age-old dream. Returning to Zion had been a cornerstone of Ethiopian Jewish thinking for centuries. It was the theme of their largest annual festival, Sigd. On Shabbat (the Sabbath), Ethiopian Israelis remember their parents and grandparents teaching them that Israel was the Land of Milk and Honey, that Jerusalem was a refuge offering peace and holiness, and that it was where they belonged. Rabbi Yosef Hadane, chief rabbi of the Ethiopians in Israel, describes his community's exodus from Ethiopia as a miracle not unlike the ancient Hebrews' exodus from Egypt.

What lies beneath the surface success of Operation Moses, the great rescue operation from the refugee camps of Sudan (November 21, 1984–January 5, 1985) and the journey of those who came earlier on their own, is the suffering and loss that haunt the Ethiopian community. It is an undercurrent of pain and sadness from which they cannot escape. As epidemiologist Dr. Seffefe Aycheh expresses it, "So many of them buried their relatives along the way, it gives them a kind of moral trauma every day."[1] More than 4,000 died en route to Sudan, some at the hands of pursuing soldiers and thieves, and some from starvation. Others were lost as they waited in the disease-ridden refugee camps. The dead totaled nearly one-fifth of those who set out on the journey. It is rare to find a family without at least one member who perished in the exodus. In 1985, at the urging of the Ethiopian community, the rabbinate declared a religious holiday, Yom Hazkarah, to memorialize those who were lost trying to reach Israel.

In 1991, when Operation Solomon brought more than 14,000 Ethiopian Jews into Israel in thirty-six hours, their reception took a different kind of toll. Although the journey itself was not an ordeal that challenged their survival, the absorption infrastructure was overwhelmed. Those who were accustomed to living among their own relatives in Jewish villages were housed in overcrowded trailers and in hotels among strangers. When they first arrived, Israelis greeted them with food, flowers, and photographers; but as the task of integration began to demand money, effort, and patience, the warm reception cooled off.

While the exodus of the Ethiopian Jews was a success of epic proportions, the goal of that endeavor—to live as Jews in the Holy Land—remains a dissonant mix of fulfilled and broken dreams. For all Ethiopian Israelis, no matter when they arrived, the memory of their individual and collective journey still plays a role in their perceptions and emotional life. After experiencing the danger, deprivation, and thousands of deaths that accompanied their journey to Israel, the elusiveness of real integration and full acceptance of their Jewish identity is that much harder to bear.

What this first group of subjects has in common is that they readily recall in vivid detail what Shagau Mekonen calls their "journey of suffering."

Shagau Mekonen

"We learned there was a camp of soldiers on the main road.

The guides told us that we could only pass it in complete darkness on a very difficult path with rocks and trees all around.

It was on a hillside, and you couldn't see anything.

While we walked in the dark, I was trying to make my way, and as I went through a very narrow pass,

I heard a scream. I heard the scream, and then . . . silence. At that moment, I was told to stop in my place,

and we had no choice but to use flashlights to see what was happening.

Suddenly, only two steps in front of me, there was a cliff, and someone had just fallen over it."

Shagau Mekonen is a head teacher at Yemin Orde, a celebrated youth village of 600 students, about half of them Ethiopian teens who are in need of a supportive environment. He and his wife, Geula, live on its verdant grounds overlooking the Mediterranean in a small apartment bustling with their four children and their toys. Shagau seems to manage them as happily as a gardener tends his flowers. He recalls his exodus from Ethiopia with the vividness of trauma. As he says, it would take a full day to tell about each day of a journey that has become emblematic of the sacrifice and suffering of the Ethiopian Jews for the sake of reaching the Holy Land. In Israel for twenty years and a religious man, Shagau aspires to use his skills as an educator to help his community succeed in its struggle to integrate.

Shagau Mekonen was raised in a religious family in the province of Gondar, the middle child of eleven. His father was a farmer and sewed clothing to make enough money to feed his large family. Shagau's mother died when he was two, and he was raised by his stepmother and elder sisters. Their village was tiny and remote. The *kess* would come to visit only once in a while, but religious practice, passed down informally from parents, was central to their lives. "In Ethiopia, religion wasn't based on doing *mitzvot* (commandments)," he explained. "It was based on the belief in God, the Holy One, blessed be He." Although the performing of *mitzvot* was not the test of an observant life for Ethiopian Jews, that does not mean their behavior was unrestricted. On the contrary, there was virtually no deviation from strictly keeping the Sabbath and holidays. Shagau's adherence to a religious code remains, but it has been transformed from the Ethiopian expression of Judaism to the Israeli rabbinic model. Second only to Sabbath observance was the aspiration of all the families in Shagau's village to reach Jerusalem. Shagau arrived in Israel on December 26, 1984, at age fourteen, old enough to preserve in frightening detail his family's clandestine escape from Ethiopia via Sudan.

Were you aware of Israel when you lived in Ethiopia?
It was talked about all the time. Starting at age thirteen, the dream was constantly to get to Israel. In Ethiopia "Israel" meant Jerusalem. Jerusalem was supposed to be like a meeting of heaven and earth, something magical—in fact, something I'm still waiting to see! And it's important to emphasize that going to Israel was thought of as something you could do in a flash, something that wouldn't even take a day of traveling.

What was Jewish religious practice like in your village?
Shabbat really was the only part that was followed according to *halachic* [rabbinic Jewish law] ritual observance. On that day, we didn't do any work whatsoever. As a shepherd boy, I was forbidden from taking a staff, and I had to prepare my food in advance for Shabbat. Therefore, Shabbat was really the most important thing in Ethiopian Judaism, next to Jerusalem.

There was no candle lighting or a *Kiddush* [blessing over wine] of the kind we have today. But there was special bread that was prepared for Shabbat. My father was one of the oldest people in the neighborhood, so on Shabbat all the neighbors—it wasn't a big neighborhood—would always bring us their bread. Shabbat is observed like a big family, all the families are together.

Was there reading from the Orit [the Hebrew Bible in Ge'ez]?
The Orit was read when there was a *kess*, which was not often. There were certain prayers that everyone knew. My father knew a lot more than me. But there were certain prayers that were always taught to the children. There was nothing organized that they would teach you. The teaching was from father to son, and that is the way that it continued. Therefore, the respect and reverence were much more preserved. There were no questions. It wasn't like "What will happen if I do this or don't do that?" There were no questions. It was just "Yes, that's what you do. That's what you have to do."

Can you tell us about the journey to Sudan?
As I said before, we thought we would get there quickly, but it was a very long journey.

"My father had no food to give the guides, so he promised them…
our horse and donkey when we arrived."

I call it the journey of suffering. Each day of the journey would take me a day to tell you about. It's hard to just talk about pieces of the journey but I will try.

Each of us in the family had a role. At the age of thirteen, in Ethiopia I was thought of as responsible. My role was to guide the horse that my mother was riding on with her baby of eight months whom she carried on her back. That was my main task.

When we left our village, it was good timing because the Mengistu regime [1974–1991] was not controlling our area. The rebels [fighting Mengistu] had already come in. They let us leave, and the Christian neighbors did not take revenge on us. So we left during the day, not the night [as most Ethiopians were forced to do]. For the first week, there were no problems because we were in the area of the rebels. When we crossed over to the area controlled by Mengistu, we had to lie and say we were fleeing because we didn't want to live under the rebels' regime. The soldiers accepted this. My father's sister lived in that area of Gondar and we went to her place.

My father had decided that we should not travel on Shabbat. But it wasn't just our family involved in this group. The group decided they had to travel on Shabbat, so we said to my father that we [our family] cannot remain alone without the others. We didn't have a choice. It was a difficult decision for him. He made a vow that if we could get to Jerusalem with God's help, he would mend the transgression of traveling on Shabbat. We arrived at my aunt's home and stayed there for a week. It was during Passover [in Amharic, Fasika], so we celebrated all of Passover there, from the seder on. After Passover we continued, and my father's sister joined us.

At this point, we could only walk at night because of Mengistu's control of the area. There are a few nights that I can't forget. We hired guides who were non-Jews because they knew the local people. They knew what to do. At night, the local residents would come and say, "We'll help you," but, actually, they would come to steal anything they could—equipment, chickens. They would even try to take babies and young children because they could sell them.

After the descent when someone walked off the edge of a cliff, the family got separated. I was alone with my mother, and we couldn't find the rest of our family. I tied the horse to a tree and told my mother, "Don't get off the horse until I find someone." I went looking and found my older brother. His task was to protect the horse that was leading the group, so everyone was with him, all the family. This includes all the uncles and aunts. This is a night for which my family remembers me [for reuniting them].

When we got near the border of Sudan, we were dying of thirst. There was no food left. We didn't know whether we were going to make it at that point. My father had no food to give the guides, so he promised them that he would give them our horse and donkey when we arrived.

The guides didn't have their own food?
No, they ate from our food. We had one horse and three donkeys for the journey. When we arrived at the border, everyone said to my father, "Don't say anything; they've already forgotten about the donkey." But my father said, "No, I promised. When they are ready to leave us, I'll give the donkeys and the horse to them." And he did, so we were left with only one donkey.

At the border of Sudan, the guides left us, but not before they threatened our lives. They even said to my older brother, who was very tall, "Let's see from how great a distance we can shoot you"—threats like that. My father said, "Don't say anything; don't answer them."

How did you get to the refugee camp?

We reached the valley between Sudan and Ethiopia, and there we waited hours upon hours until the Red Cross came to pick us up. They put us in trucks, the kind they put cows into in Israel. At the refugee camp, they fenced us in. No one could exit or enter. They closed us in with ropes, and there were guards. I didn't know if this was Israel or not. Then we were told that this isn't Israel, and that in fact we are not even supposed to say we are Jewish. The first night it rained, and the earth turned into mud all around.

Can you tell us about your family's experience in the refugee camp?

These are stories that are very difficult to tell—stories about diseases, about the people who died. We had to just watch it and not cry because you could not cry about every person who died. We were all sick, except for my oldest brother. And the baby that I told you about, whom my mother carried on the horse that I was responsible for, he died. I remember the very day that we buried him. We went at about eight or nine in the morning, but we couldn't return that day because more people kept coming to the field because they had people that had to be buried. We couldn't leave. Burial is very important in Ethiopia, it's also important to us in Israel. It's our tradition to accompany the dead. It doesn't matter if you knew the person or not.

There is also a tradition in Ethiopia that a stone used to cover a grave cannot be one that is taken forcefully out of the ground. It has to be a stone already on the surface. But in Sudan, there weren't any stones left on the surface. It is still very difficult for me when I go to a cemetery.

Were you healthy during your time in the refugee camp?

I had some illness in my chest. I couldn't breathe; I couldn't talk. I have to say, there was one night where everyone thought I was about to die. In Ethiopia, there are these people who are like fortune-tellers, and they were there, saying yes, I was going to die. One night, they said to my family, "If Shagau survives a certain amount of days, he will live, and if not, he will die." When I saw all my family sitting and crying, I remember feeling that I had crossed over to the other side. I asked them what happened. They told me, "You don't know how you almost left us; we thought we had lost you." But I didn't remember anything about it.

To go to a doctor in the camp was a danger. We believed they could give you a shot and kill you. My father decided not to send me to the doctor, and that I should die in the tent rather than in the infirmary. But somehow, it became known that there was a Jewish doctor who worked there, so my father went to meet him. My father knows how to count the generations [i.e., he knows everyone in families: aunts, uncles, cousins, and cousins' cousins].

He is good at that, so he found a relative in common with the doctor. He asked this doctor if he, and only he, would take care of me. So he agreed. He gave me three shots every day for a full week. After that, thank God, I overcame the disease.

How did you get from the refugee camp in Sudan to Israel?

They took us to a forest at night, and suddenly I saw white people. They didn't speak. Not one word. The plane we saw wasn't an Israeli plane. Suddenly we heard, "They are Jews, they are Jews." It was an Israeli commando. They just picked us up and put us on the plane. We knew, okay, now it's definite. We were on our way to Israel. The first thing I remember about the plane ride, as a child, was that they gave us big bananas for breakfast. We had seen bananas at home, but not that big. Until this day, I am still looking for such big bananas.

We stopped in another country, Italy or France, I didn't know which. And there we boarded an Israeli plane with a *Magen David* [Star of David]. But we still were not sure we were going to arrive until the plane landed. The translator said to us, "Okay. Now you are really in Israel. You can bend down and kiss the ground." I remember we prostrated ourselves and kissed the earth. It was a scene that cannot be forgotten.

They took us to the absorption center in Ashkelon, and two days later they took us to Netanya and put us in a hotel. I remember there were mirrors everywhere. Suddenly, I could see myself moving. We had mirrors in our village in which we could see our faces, but not big mirrors where you see yourself move. They told us we were not allowed to leave the hotel. We didn't know if it was day or night. The only thing we knew was when it was meal time.

How did you observe Shabbat, which I know was so important in your village?
We finally got outside of the hotel, and that's when the breakdown started. Suddenly, we were seeing people drive their cars on Shabbat. The hotel was close to the beach, and people were swimming—on Shabbat! My father was asking, "How could this be?"

How are things different for Ethiopians who are coming now? Is it a different experience than when you came?
I think that for the first immigrants, it was more important to learn the language right away, to be absorbed into the culture. As new immigrants, we wanted to be Israeli in every way. Today, there is more of a desire to keep our own traditions. I also think that we received special treatment from the Israelis, because we were the first ones to arrive in Israel. It was a big news event. Ethiopian Jews, black Jews, came to Israel. The hope was very high.

We hear that many teenagers identify with African Americans. Why do you think this is happening?

It is unfortunate, but I understand why they identify with them. There are more Ethiopians making *aliyah* and they [Israelis] are not so fond of us anymore. Therefore, the feeling of the Ethiopian youth is, "What is wrong with me?" The Ethiopians don't connect with the Israelis, so they connect to people of color. Also, everyone knew their place in the family in Ethiopia—the father, the mother, the children. Respect was everything. When we came here, they took away the responsibilities of the parents by sending the children to boarding school. It feels like everything was broken and you can understand where all the problems start. They didn't give the parents enough tools to cope with a new country, a new mentality, different behavior. But today, they are starting to give them these tools because they see before their eyes that the dream is falling apart. When I talk to the families of my students, I say, "You are his father, you are his mother. Folks, this is your child, even though he studies here with me." [In Ethiopia, few Jewish children went to school; when they did, the school was responsible for their performance academically and behaviorally.]

What do you personally hope to be doing five years from now?
First of all, I want to raise my children. Besides that, I don't know what I will be doing. I want to advance in a career and to continue to be involved in education. Education is the most important thing for our community, and I believe that is where I can contribute the little that I have to offer.

Takele Mekonen

"We were in Tiya, a refugee camp at the southern border of Sudan.

After one month, people started dying of dysentery. I told my friends we had to get out, or we would die.

So we sold everything the Red Cross gave us—butter, flower, soap, clothes, everything. We sold it to families.

There were not only the Jews there, but thousands of Christians and Muslims.

We saved our money and paid a truck driver to take us to Gedarif. We had to pay a bribe because the Sudanese

government did not allow refugees to come to Gedarif. They were supposed to remain in camps

at the border, but I knew if we stayed there, we would die."

Takele Mekonen displays a photograph from the early 1970s of his father, Sibhat, armed to escort Jews from his small village past non-Jewish areas into the city of Gondar. In Israel, Takele uses a different tactic to ensure the community's well-being. "Education is the key to success without doubt," he says. Takele is the director of Fidel ("Alphabet" in Amharic), a nonprofit group focused on improving the elementary school environment for Ethiopian students. In the Fidel offices, located in the hectic commercial district of downtown Petach Tikvah, Takele's conference room is stacked floor-to-ceiling with books and materials for teachers. Fidel trains and supervises mediators who bring elementary school teachers and Ethiopian parents together to improve primary school education for the children. "What Fidel is achieving is fantastic," Takele explains. "When we started, the matriculation of the Ethiopian students from high school was around 17 percent and now it is 46 percent. There were only a few hundred university students when we started; now there are 3,000 Ethiopian university students in Israel."

Takele grew up in Woyniyeh, a Jewish village about fifteen miles from Ambover. His parents were exceptional in sending all six children to school, but they both died of illnesses when he was nine, and he was brought up by an uncle. To attend elementary school, he walked for several hours each day to Ambover with a small group of children ages seven to fourteen. In 1981, at sixteen, Takele set out on a dangerous and secretive nocturnal journey to the refugee camps of Sudan. In this conversation, he talks about how the Sabbath and other holidays were observed in Ethiopia, about the complex intrigue that enabled him to escape the deadly camps of Sudan, and finally about what he is trying to accomplish for the Ethiopian Israeli children.

Can you tell us about your home in Ethiopia and the circumstances of your leaving for Israel?
It is an amazing story about our family's house in Ethiopia, which was built around a large tree. For fifty years we lived there, and each generation kept expanding the house with the tree as its center. When we left Ethiopia, the neighbors burned our house and the tree. Why would they do that? Many people could have lived in it. It was a fine house. We just cannot understand it.

When I left, I had just finished high school. I was sixteen. My scores were very good, so I realized I could have gone to the university in Addis, but I decided to come to Israel. We were about twenty-five people: fifteen boys, five girls, and five adults. We heard about Sudan, but we didn't know where it was or where Jerusalem was. You would just go and believe that you will get to Jerusalem, that's all. We hired three guides to take us from our village. The guides were very afraid themselves, because it was the first time they brought anyone from our area. We walked at night, maybe for five or six hours at a time, and never in the daytime. We slept in the forest. We were worried about these guides; they were not Jews, so we didn't trust them. The boys slept in shifts, so someone was always watching the guides because one of them wanted to talk to the girls. We were very tense about that. I think I slept a lot while we walked, sleepwalking. We walked in a chain.

Did everyone survive the journey?
Yes, thank God. We all got to Sudan, but the guides took us only to the border, where we paid them the rest of the money. The journey took twenty-four days. We paid one-third in the beginning, middle, and end of the trip. Two of the guides were fantastic. After we paid them,

they talked to the Sudan border guards for us, and a Sudanese policeman came and took us to the refugee camp. Of course, they didn't know we were Jews because many thousands of Ethiopians were fleeing the Mengistu regime at the time [late 1970s]. Mengistu was forcing teenagers to be soldiers.

And how did you get out of the camp? This was long before Operation Moses.
We were in Tiya, a refugee camp at the southern border of Sudan. After one month, people started dying of dysentery. I told my friends we had to get out or we would die. So we sold everything the Red Cross gave us—butter, flower, soap, clothes, everything. We sold it to families. There were not only the Jews there, but also thousands of Christians and Muslims. We saved our money and paid a truck driver to take us to Gedarif. We had to pay a bribe because the Sudanese government did not allow refugees to come to Gedarif. They were supposed to remain in camps at the border, but I knew if we stayed there, we would die.

After six or seven hours, the driver dropped us in the middle of Gedarif at five o'clock in the morning. We saw some lights at a gas station, so we went there and asked them if there is some place where Ethiopians live. We could speak a little Arabic at that time. They told us there is a shelter and a coffee shop owned by an Ethiopian woman. We went there and she accepted us. She brought all of us food and water and gave us a place to stay. She was fantastic. I don't know what she is doing now or if she is still alive. She was a Christian, and a very good mother. She told us we could stay with her, and when we have money, we can pay her. She even arranged some jobs for us. I don't have her photograph, but I could draw her face from memory. After we earned some money, we rented a room in another shelter, a larger place, and we were there for two months before we connected with an Israeli agent. He sent most of our group to Israel in the next month, but he asked me and two friends to remain to help bring others, and we did. I stayed for a year, pretending I was Sudanese and working with the Israelis. My job was to bring other people to them so they could take them to Israel, and to give out medicine in the camps to fight malaria and dysentery.

You took on a lot of responsibility for a teenager.
I was seventeen by then. Do you know what it means to be seventeen years old in Ethiopia? It means you are married, you have a child; you have responsibility. Children in Ethiopia know how to manage their lives; they are not young. Jewish life is not easy, so we are more mature at an early age. You have to be a survivor. For me, this was a challenge. So I went back to the camps to give out the medicine. It wasn't

allowed, but nobody asked you what you were doing. I looked Sudanese and wore a *jalabiya* [robe] or *kafiya* [head scarf]. We worked very hard to bring a lot of people to Israel. I think in that one year, my group brought around 1,500 people. The Israelis knew exactly which families were Jews. We knew who to send first. If there was a woman who was ill or with a sick child, we brought them immediately. We also documented which people died.

How did you know who was Jewish in the camps?
For you it seems like a big problem, but for us, we knew the families and which villages they came from, and which ones were the Jewish villages. We contacted other coordinators who knew exactly who was planning to come on the next trip from Ethiopia to Sudan. We were always planning; my group did a fantastic job. There were five or six of us. We had money to give out. We gave the *kessim* [priests, spiritual

leaders] and the *shemagleoch* [elders who are called upon to settle disputes] extra money in case people started to quarrel. They would keep the peace. We had to be cautious all the time. Some difficult or angry people, even if they were Jews, could destroy everything. In fact it was a Jew who exposed us to the Sudanese government. My picture was being circulated, so then I had to escape from Sudan.

How did you find out about that, and how did you get out of Sudan?
I went to see a movie just to relax, because it was very tense work. While I was there, policemen came to our shelter. The woman who rented to us had her own house and my friends were sitting there with her. We were like a family. When the police arrived, she saw what was happening and told my friends to run out the back door. So they escaped, but I didn't know anything about it. After the

movie, I went to a restaurant and then to my shelter. The woman waited for me at the front door, and she called my name, "Ibrahim"— that's what I was called. She told me I had to escape, so I was in shock. My friends didn't leave anything, no notes to me, they had to run. So I took some clothes and my shoes and I went to a small hotel.

How did you finally get to Israel?
My team used to meet every week or two with the Israelis outside of Gedarif. We had a secret meeting place and I thought I would go there, but I wasn't able to get there on Tuesday night, which is when we would meet. Another group of Ethiopians came to Sudan; some of them were my friends from Gondar. I told them they had to be very cautious. I took them to the secret meeting place at night so they could find it when the time came. When they found out it was time, I went with them and we met one of my Israeli contacts who had a big Land Rover. We were going to Khartoum and then to Israel, but there was more room in the car, so we went back to Gedarif to bring out a few more people. We finally got to Khartoum, stayed two nights, and then flew to Israel through Greece. That is how I got to Israel.

Tell us about Ethiopia, your home, and what you remember about religious practice there. Can you recall what Jewish celebrations were like in your village?
The Jewish Sabbath—wow! It was fantastic.

The whole village came together to go to the *bet knesset* [synagogue]. When I was young, the *kess* in our *bet knesset* was the grandfather of Nigist Mengesha.[2] There was praying by the *kessim* in Ge'ez. We did not know what the prayers meant, but we prayed anyway. There was also reading in Ge'ez from the Orit [the Bible in Ge'ez], which sometimes the *kess* explained in Amharic. But as a child, you pray with everyone else even if you don't understand it. After the prayers were finished, the mothers in the village brought special Shabbat bread called *berakate*. *Berakate* means to bless, like *bracha* [blessing]. *Berakate* is the bread for a blessing, and the *kessim* would bless it before the meal. It is a big, round bread, which they would make in the ground in a *taboon* [a domed oven]. They would throw wood into the *taboon* until it became coal, then take some leaves from a special tree and wrap the bread, and then bake it on the coals on Friday night. It would stay hot all through the Sabbath. When the prayers were finished on Saturday, the *kessim* would bless the *barakate*.

Did you study or hear Hebrew when you were a student in the 1970s?
Sometimes. We went to a Jewish school in Ambover. We had Hebrew lessons, and we learned the *alef bet* [alphabet] and basic conversation. On Shabbat, we went back to the village where the *kessim* prayed sometimes in Hebrew as well as in Ge'ez. Some religious leaders had been sent to Israel, to Kfar Batya, to study, and

they returned to us as teachers. Some even wore a *tallit* [prayer shawl], and they knew the *Amidah* [standard Hebrew prayer]. I remember that the *kessim* were fascinated with the *tallit*, but most didn't use it. There were sometimes prayers in Hebrew, but not usually.

What do you remember of the Sigd festival?
Everyone came together for Sigd. The sons of the *kessim* would carry the Orit, usually on their heads. It was always someone close to the *kess* because it was a very great honor. We came out from the *bet knesset* with the Orit on the heads of the boys and the *kessim* led us up the hill. After the *kessim* came the *shema-gleoch*, the boys, and after them the women. We went to the top of the hill and prayed. Each woman carried a stone on her head. They would curse the stones and afterwards come down from the hill and would throw them away. As if they were throwing away their sins, like *tashlich* on Rosh Hashanah. Then, when we came down from the hill, there was a big feast and singing and dancing.

The Sigd ritual seems to have had many different meanings. What did it mean to you?
One meaning I remember from the *kess's* explanation is that we have to pray for the return to Jerusalem. That was the main message. They also said that Sigd gathers all of the Jews together, unites them to discuss and to share our lives as Jews, as a community. Especially in the 1980s, the message was also to pass down beliefs to the

children. There were special events for the children and for students. There was singing, sometimes a drama in which everyone participates. Sigd unites the community.

Now that you are in Israel, Sigd is still celebrated in Jerusalem, even though the community is already there. Why is Sigd still observed?
From my point of view, it is a way that we can pass on the tradition to our children, to preserve the tradition. The children are very proud of the *kessim*. In the last two to three years, I have seen a big change in the celebration in Jerusalem. It used to be very different from the way it was celebrated in Ethiopia, but in 2003 it was more authentic. The *kessim* came with the Torah, leading the people, and they went to a hill overlooking Jerusalem. The *kessim* explained the prayers. There was no talking. But they invited some politicians. I didn't like that, because the politicians are always saying, "We brought you!" I hate that.

It will be difficult to keep up this tradition without training more kessim.
Unless the younger generation gets organized on this issue, it will be lost. That will be a disaster for us, for a whole generation. They cannot train new *kessim* without schools, and the rabbinate will not fund those schools. The *kessim* have to do it themselves, and it is too difficult.

Can you assimilate and still preserve your traditions or will the youth want to behave like the native Israelis?
At first you try to be an Israeli, act like an Israeli, but then you understand that it is not the right thing. A lot of my friends are married and want to do something for their children to preserve the tradition. Even if they are not religious, they keep Shabbat, they pray with their children, they dress as they dressed during the holidays in Ethiopia, especially the women. This is a very powerful statement for the children. I saw the children and parents together at Sigd. The Ethiopian Jews have very good roots, and that is the way we grow. My daughter Liat is ten. And my son Edab is four; we try to speak Amharic with them. We explain how to celebrate things in our tradition. We take them to my grandmother and they speak with her in Amharic. My grandmother still dresses the way she did in Ethiopia. You have to continue this, I think, for the next generation. Assimilation doesn't give stable citizenship to any immigrant in the world. People need their roots. We need integration, but not assimilation.

What is the main problem that the Ethiopian community has with the educational system in Israel?
The Israeli schools should have a multicultural curriculum. They have a very good policy that gives respect to the different ethnic groups, but the policy is not usually implemented in the field. That is a problem for us and for other communities, like the Russians. There also should be Ethiopian teachers. They could be important role models.

Learning is one of the great accomplishments of the Jewish people historically. Teachers were respected. Unfortunately, the salaries and status of teachers are very low now. We have to give teachers power and dignity.

Can you explain the essence of what you are trying to accomplish through Fidel?
We try to bridge the cultural gap between the parents and the schools so they can communicate about the young students. There are seventy trained mediators in 300 schools, but it's not enough. There are 30,000 Ethiopian school children. The challenge is to train more mediators. The schools want them, and they write to the Ministry of Education. We have copies of these letters. But we aren't getting enough funding. It is a year-long training, and then they must be paid when they work. The majority of funds now come from the American Jews—from the federations, especially the New York Federation, the Moriah Fund, and the New Israel Fund. We also try to get the municipalities to have better integration in education. In Netanya, there was one school that had 70 percent Ethiopian students next to another school that had only two. The students should be dispersed more evenly. We try to influence that. We also have a club in Tel Aviv for school dropouts where we try to get them back into education. That is the key. The educational opportunities will determine what happens to the Ethiopian community in the future.

Sigal Kanatopsky

"We felt like we could not disappoint our father, even though he had died.

We had to be the best in everything.

He had a very difficult life in Ethiopia. He was a merchant, and so we didn't see him a lot.

He went for a week or two weeks and then came home. He paid a lot of people to bring us from Ethiopia to Israel,

and he didn't have the privilege to enjoy it after he suffered in Ethiopia and on the journey.

So we feel like we have now a religious responsibility not to disappoint him."

Sigal Kanatopsky, a graduate of Hebrew University in international relations, is working toward a master's degree in African studies. Her goal is to work in an African country to improve its relationship with Israel. While pursing an advanced degree, she works as the outreach coordinator for Yemin Orde, the youth village for students in need of support. Her husband, David Kanatopsky, whose family emigrated from Russia, is a counselor for the twelfth-grade students and studies education at Oranim College. They have two children. In this photograph, Sigal's late father, Melessa Zegewe Wovee, whom she calls the most influential person in her life, appears to be looking over her shoulder, as if guiding the way she conducts her life in Israel.

Sigal Kanatopsky seems to have been destined for a life of crossing borders and boundaries. It took her family two years to travel from Ethiopia to a Sudanese refugee camp, and at last to Israel, where they arrived in 1983. Sigal was then five years old. At twenty-six, she was among the first Ethiopian graduates of Hebrew University in Jerusalem. Sigal crossed another boundary in her marriage to the son of Russian Jewish immigrants, David Kanotopsky. Marriages outside of the Ethiopian Israeli community are rare, and in our conversation, she speaks of its challenges and consequences. As a first step in her career in international diplomacy, Sigal helps others cross cultural boundaries. She works summers with the Elijah Cummings Youth Program, sponsored by Senator Elijah Cummings of Maryland along with the Jerold C. Hoffberger Leadership Development Program. The program brings American inner-city students from Maryland to Israel for one month. Sigal helps the Ethiopian Israeli and African American teens learn from each other about pluralism, democracy, and the effects of racism.

What do you remember about your journey to Israel?
We lived in the small Jewish village of Wolkiet near the border between Gondar and Tigray. The Tigrayan Jews were the first to come to Israel in the early 1980s. I think we knew about going to Israel through Sudan from the Tigrayans because we lived so close. The whole journey of my family took about two years, counting the time in the refugee camp. There were twelve of us, my aunt's family and mine. In those days it was forbidden for any citizen to leave Ethiopia. There was a very big famine at the time, so a lot of refugees were escaping to Sudan, not just Jews. We went from village to village and sometimes stayed for months. We behaved like other refugees, like we were not Jewish. For the last part of the trip, we walked for three months to reach Sudan, three months by foot, and sometimes we had nothing to eat or drink. But even as children, we knew we were not allowed to complain because we were going to Jerusalem, the Holy Land that our parents and grandparents dreamed of. We traveled at night only; it was too dangerous to travel in the day. My father would go first to check the way with my older brother, and when my brother came back, we would continue. I remember some scenes clearly, like when thieves caught us and took our money.

What was it like when you reached the camp?
At the Sudan border, we met Israeli agents who asked us very specific questions to find out if we are Jewish or not. They asked our family name and which village we came from. There were certain villages where Jews lived. They asked what our occupation was. They [Ethiopians] considered Jews a very low level of society, so we were only allowed to do "Jewish work" [metal work, tenant farming, or pottery-making and other crafts].

We were in the camp for a year or a year and a half. There were very, very hard conditions. We almost lost one of my brothers there. There was a lot of disease and hunger. A lot of the Ethiopian Jews lost their relatives in the refugee camps.

Do you remember your first impressions of Israel?
The first night we spent in an eight-story building, an absorption center. When we woke up in the morning, we were shocked. We saw that we are in the middle of a city, a lot of traffic, and a lot of white people.

Maybe the elders knew that Jews in Israel were white, but the kids, no. On our first Shabbat in Israel, we were outside of the absorption center, close to the main road, and there was a lot of traffic. Jews driving on Shabbat! For

us it was a big shock. We saw that they were not keeping Shabbat. This was something we were not ready for.

What was Shabbat like in Ethiopia? Do you remember what your Jewish practice was like?
We were born into a very religious society. There was not any option; there are no secular people. In the center of the village, we had a synagogue, and every Shabbat everybody went to synagogue to pray. Everybody. No one stayed at home. We dressed in white clothes, the

whole community, and after the prayers we would come back home. We had a Shabbat lunch, together with the whole family. And Shabbat was the day that we got a speech from the *kessim*, our rabbis, about Shabbat and how it's a holy day and we need to keep Shabbat. After Shabbat lunch, it was time for the children to hear a story about Jerusalem, the Holy Land, the wars, and about the river of honey.

Can you tell me about the Elijah Cummings project?

The purpose of this project is to bring twelve high school students from the African American community to Israel to learn about Israel. Not the Israel that they see in the news, but about the real Israel. We travel with them from north to south. Every year we have one or two white children, but the majority is African American, and Christian. They travel with twelve Yemin Orde kids—Russians, Ethiopians, and Israeli-born. Each one of them has to do a personal presentation about different topics, like their church or synagogue, or racism. You

can see a lot of common things between the Ethiopian kids and the African Americans. Each one of them speaks about her feelings and experience of racism. It's amazing to see how they change their minds about Israel and Judaism and also about the Israeli-Arab conflict. They have no knowledge about it, except what they see on television. They learn from each other.

You're married to an Ashkenazi Jew. Do you and David experience racism as a mixed couple?

This was not new for my family. Two years earlier, my older sister married a Yemenite man. But one of my aunts said, "Oh, Sigal, such a good girl. It's a shame she is marrying a white man." It was also hard for David's grandmother. She was from the United States and I don't think she ever knew an Ethiopian before. But now we are very good friends, and we visit her often. When I met David, I was in the army. One day he drove me to Golani Junction and we talked about Ethiopia because he had experience being a counselor at an absorption center for new immigrants. We became friends, and he would come to my house like any other friend.

Since many of my friends were Israeli-born, not Ethiopian, it was not surprising to my family. They just knew him as David, his own personality. They didn't judge him as a white person.

When you are on the streets, outside of Yemin Orde or your family environment, do you experience a difference in the attitudes of people you meet?

Yes. People look at us because it's unusual for them to see a mixed couple. I was very angry, but David told me I shouldn't be because we can understand why people would stare at us.

I know that it's unusual, but I don't understand why people would not be polite, and just stare at us. People feel free to ask us, "Where did you meet?" and so on. I didn't even know them before. Why should I tell my personal story to someone I meet on the street?

Do your own cultural differences have an effect on your marriage?
We both came to the marriage with a lot of understanding of each other's culture. He worked with Ethiopian immigrants, and I grew up in Israel, so we were ready for this. When we have issues, we resolve them. Our goal is to respect each other's cultures. We go to Ethiopian family events and to David's family's events, and this isn't something we fight over.

Other than being part of a mixed couple, have you experienced racism in Israel?
Yes, in the army. I tried to prove myself, first as a woman, and then an Ethiopian woman. It was two missions combined. I remember the time I decided to go to the officer's course. I had a conversation with the commander for women, and she asked me, "Which kind of course do you want?" I told her the one for a communications officer. She asked me why, and I said, "Because I heard it's very difficult, so I want to try it." She said, "You know that a lot of Ethiopian girls before you tried and they failed. I suggest you to go to another course, an easier one, and that way you can make sure you will finish." She never met me before, and she didn't know

what my ability was. I felt so angry with her. I don't know if I took the course because I wanted to or just to prove to her that I can succeed.

It was a half-year course in communications equipment. It was very difficult, but I completed it successfully and became an officer. There were a lot of people who said, "Wow, you're Ethiopian, and you finished this course. And you're an officer. Wow." Surprise. Yeah, I'm Ethiopian, and I'm an officer. So?

What is the strength in your family that enabled you all to be doing something positive?
I think that our father was the main influential person in our life, before and after he died. He died from an illness a year and a half after we came to Israel. We felt like we could not disappoint our father, even though he had died. We had to be the best in everything. He had a very difficult life in Ethiopia. He was a merchant, and so we didn't see him a lot. He went for a week or two weeks and then came home. He paid a lot of people to bring us from Ethiopia to Israel, and he didn't have the privilege to enjoy it after he suffered in Ethiopia and on the journey. So we feel like we have now a religious responsibility not to disappoint him.

How did your mother influence your attitude toward being in Israel in general?
To not pity yourself because you are without a father or because you do not have enough money to buy clothes and so on. To say "Thank God" for what you have and go on.

And what do you want to pass on to your children?
I want my children to grow up with a knowledge of Ethiopian culture, I feel like this is my responsibility, not anyone else's. Hebrew and everything else she can study outside the home. So the first language I speak with my daughter Shachar is Amharic.

How much Hebrew does your mother know after twenty years? Does she feel part of the Israeli culture now?
She can make very basic conversation and take care of herself if she goes to a clinic or to the bank, but that's all. I think one thing that makes her feel Israeli is seeing her kids integrated. It's not just my mother; it's all the Ethiopian elders. But even if the situation here is not good, they don't want to go back to Ethiopia. Here they have had troubles, but if you ask them, "What if you could have the best situation in Ethiopia now, would you want to go back?" They would say, "Absolutely not."

already introduced by their growing up in a modern society so unlike the background of their parents. Alienation from their parents, along with unemployment and racial discrimination, contributes to the high crime rate

immigrants ages seventeen to twenty-seven a subsidized 1,000 hours of Hebrew, academic, and vocational training.[3] Another supplementary program designed partly for Ethiopians wanting more education after

among Ethiopian youth and the stress on the family. Proponents of the boarding school system insist that having the teenagers at home is more stressful, and that the schools ultimately benefit youth by preparing them more effectively for Israeli society.

Some schools uniquely address the needs of Ethiopian students. One of them, Yemin Orde, is mentioned in many of the interviews in this book because a large percentage of their graduates are among the most engaged with Israeli society. Yemin Orde is not just a school but a nurturing educational environment; this youth village is home to about 600 students, more than half of them Ethiopian. The school's mission is to educate and nurture the self-esteem of high school students whose families are unable to do so. Its fabled director, Chaim Peri, who retired in 2006, was a combination of folk hero and mentor to the Ethiopian community. More than a few graduates return regularly and see the community there as a second home.

Not all of the young immigrants fit neatly into a school population; some arrive just over the high school age limit. While a few in this group will have gone to a high school or a university in Ethiopia, the great majority will have had little or no schooling. To address this problem, the Jewish Agency's KEDMA program offers

high school is called Atidim (Futures). Atidim is a joint project of the Ministry of Education, the Jewish Agency, and the Ethiopian National Project, along with other foundations. In 2005, the program served 7,700 children and young adults in fifty locations. Students range in age from thirteen to thirty, and include Ethiopians who have completed army service and want to go on to a university.

In higher education, the picture is growing brighter. Some schools, notably University of Haifa, have special programs to enroll Ethiopian students under guidelines that accommodate their educational background. The Ministry of Education subsidizes university education for Ethiopian students. The key is to motivate students to take advantage of the programs. A major obstacle to doing so, however, is the knowledge that jobs for Ethiopian Israelis are still a rarity, even for those with a university degree. Nevertheless, between 1996 and 2006 the number of Ethiopian university students grew from a few hundred to a few thousand. Academic equivalence to the Israeli population is still a long way off, but the new People of the Book have begun a promising chapter of educational achievement.

Aviva Tashome

"I first tried to get funding for a program to give Ethiopian kids a preschool experience from the municipality and

some nonprofits. They told me, 'No—you can't do that.' They didn't think I was capable because

I didn't have enough training and education. They told me other city organizations were already providing this, but I

didn't believe they were. So I decided I would do it myself. I opened the preschool in my apartment.

There were only ten kids. Many very nice individuals donated toys and supplies.

Then the nonprofit organizations saw what I was doing on my own and they became more interested."

We were introduced to Aviva Tashome by her daughter Yuvi, one of our interpreters. In 1996, Aviva was taking a class in storytelling and was assigned to go into an elementary school to practice on the children. What she found alarmed her. She noticed that the Ethiopian children, even in elementary school, were less skilled at taking advantage of classroom activities than others, and she understood why. Israeli children attend preschools where they acquire skills and experiences that enable them to participate more successfully than the Ethiopian kids, whose families cannot afford preschools. Aviva organized the women in her Ashkelon neighborhood, raised money, and started a preschool. By 2006, her Open Gates school had a staff of five, thirty preschoolers, and a waiting list of another thirty. With the encouragement of the mayor's office, Aviva has started to look for another building to expand the school. Another benefit of the program is that some of the mothers of these toddlers are now free from childcare and have found work. (Photographs of Aviva Tashome's classroom appear on pages 70 and 71.)

The Beit Tzipora Centers

Not many Ethiopian children have the advantage of an enriched preschool environment like Aviva Tashome's

Open Gates program. For the majority in the elementary grades, extra help in academics is essential for keeping up

with the native Israeli children. One successful program, Beit Tzipora, the Centers for Study and Enrichment,

provides after-school programs in Ashkelon and Kiryat Malachi for 1,000 children. Founded by Marion and

Elie Wiesel in the mid-1990s, they named the school in memory of Elie Wiesel's younger sister,

Tzipora, who died in Auschwitz. The volunteers *(shown below)* are dedicated Ethiopian college students or

religious high school graduates fulfilling their national service obligation.

At Beit Tzipora in Kiryat Malachi, the children participate enthusiastically, although one boy seems more attentive to the camera than to his teacher.

The AMIT High School of Kiryat Malachi

AMIT (Americans for Israel and Torah) operates sixty-two religious schools serving 16,000 students

from kindergarten through twelfth grade.

Founded in 1925, AMIT's purpose is to strengthen Israel by educating young people, including those from disadvantaged ethnic groups, so they can realize their potential. The AMIT Junior and Senior High School in Kiryat Malachi has a conspicuous commitment to the Ethiopian Israeli community, which comprises 4,000 of the city's 22,000 residents. This AMIT school has a 60 percent Ethiopian population, a demographic bemoaned by many in the Ethiopian community who favor a more even distribution of Ethiopian students across Israel's schools. But in Kiryat Malachi, this is the school of choice for Ethiopian parents.

The school administration has had to give serious thought to accommodating the Ethiopian students' needs without undermining their confidence and self-esteem. At the time of the annual Sigd festival, the faculty helps the Ethiopian students put together a play for the school about their *aliyah*, while other students staff an information booth to educate their classmates about Ethiopian Jewish culture. Students falling behind are given extra time to complete assignments, and they are offered tutoring. For the most talented students, there is a program through which they can take advanced courses at a local college. Of the twenty-six students at this high school who take college courses, ten are Ethiopian.

There is no shortage of challenges, and poverty is one of them. In *AMIT Magazine* (winter 2006), a teacher reports on visiting the home of one child who was skipping school. She found a household where there was not only very little food, but no refrigerator. The teachers and staff sometimes raise money to provide basic

supplies for students from impoverished families. Yet 55 percent of students receive high school matriculation certificates from the Kiryat Malachi AMIT school—close to the national average of 61 percent for Israeli high schools. Given the demographics, the matriculation rate is impressive.

We were invited to roam the AMIT school grounds, short of interrupting classes, and take pictures. It was a crisp, sunny January day and we chose to stay outside. The photographs on these pages show the school's upbeat and well-integrated social environment. We photographed students as we found them in the schoolyard—walking, talking, hanging out together. Although we sometimes asked students to face the camera, we never grouped them artificially.

High School Students in Haifa

The Neveh Yosef Community Center hosts a party for recent high school graduates, most of them Ethiopian students. The Center serves a multiethnic, low-income community living on the slope of Mount Carmel.

On the rooftop of the center, some of the boys at the party demonstrate the influence of America and rap music. The black T-shirt worn by the boy third from left has a large image, hidden in this photo, of deceased rap artist 2Pac Shakur. The affinity for rap among some Ethiopian teens is bemoaned by the older generations.

High school seniors in Haifa (from left to right) Antanesh Tega, Ephraim Gavro, Aklile Kebede, and Alganesh Tagani.

"People see Ethiopian kids as problems, but it's difficult for us. We have to prove ourselves just to be considered equal to Israeli kids. I think we have more responsibility than Israeli teenagers. Besides having to adjust to Israeli society ourselves, we have to help our parents adjust. For us, there's still respect for parents. The Israeli kids can say to their parents, "No, I'm not going to do this." We don't do that. I want the Israelis to know that the Ethiopian community is trying to help themselves. The Israelis think that we're just waiting for others to come and help us. But it's not that way." —Ephraim Gavro

"There were only three other Ethiopians in my elementary school, and I'm the only one in my high school. If you're the only Ethiopian in a group, you feel like you're representing your people. When you grow up socially in a non-Ethiopian environment like I did, but you get an Ethiopian education in your house, you have a conflict about how to behave. It affects your personality. You don't know how to act. I think it's important for Israelis to know that we come from a culture that is very conservative compared to Israeli society, which is pretty open minded. I love that very much, but we need understanding from the Israelis that it takes us time to adjust. We are in conflict, the kids with their own families." —Aklile Kebede

Avtamo Malkan

"It feels like we are running a race in this society. We are always trying to catch up with the native Israelis. People are

going to have to tell themselves, 'Okay, we have a lot of problems, but we need to move on.'

The best way for the teenagers is to work with themselves first, to have a solution from inside of them.

It can't be some guy on the outside saying, 'Hey, look, I'm going to change you now, do things for you, and you will be

fine.' After that guy quits, the Ethiopians are going to be left hanging in the air.

I won't say we don't need help. But I believe the best help is going to come from inside."

At age nineteen, Avtamo Malkan is a vibrant, creative, and outgoing young man with a past punctuated by personal loss. Born in Asmara in 1985, he came to Israel in the Operation Solomon airlift of 1991 with his mother, an older sister, and his stepfather. The family was housed in a makeshift absorption center, or "caravan," in Akko. Immigration did not change his life for the better. His stepfather left the family, his mother committed suicide, and Avtamo and his sister were adopted by an aunt who had been in Israel since 1984. Avtamo refers to the time he spent at the youth village Yemin Orde as "four years of love," describing it as a kind of salvation. In addition to academics and an orthodox religious environment, Avtamo began to learn about and value his cultural heritage.

One of his greatest concerns is the number of Ethiopian youth who are involved with drinking and using drugs, and he tries to distance himself from those influences. Avtamo sang in the choir at Yemin Orde and has music in the back of his mind as a possible career. He keeps a journal of song lyrics, and his verbal talent is easy to spot, as he spoke in English with ease and confidence. His immediate plans are to attend *mechina* (military leadership training) in preparation for his army service.

Eden Argau and Yarden Mashasha

"I did not have self-confidence as a child. What affected me most was that my parents did not speak Hebrew. . . .

They were not educated, and they came from small villages. They didn't even know about a bath and a shower

because you would bathe in the river and go to the bathroom outside. So all the changes were very

extreme for them. I remember that I didn't want to bring my parents to the parent-teacher conferences because

I was embarrassed that they didn't know Hebrew." —Yarden Mashasha

■

"We had a huge house in Addis and a television—we had everything. We still own the house in Ethiopia; my father

decided not to sell it. Here, we live in a small apartment. . . . I miss my friends.

I've been in Israel for six years, but I am still in touch with them. I always write to them to ask,

'What's up? What's going on in Addis?'" —Eden Argau

These two University of Haifa students highlight the diversity of backgrounds that are masked by what appears to be a monolithic community. Yarden Mashasha *(left)* grew up in a small village in the Gondar province. When she was four years old, her family walked for weeks to reach Sudan and spent months in a refugee camp. They were airlifted to Israel as part of Operation Moses in 1984. Eden Argau arrived in 1998 as a teenager on a direct flight from Ethiopia's capital city, Addis Ababa. Her father was a high school principal and a Christian, married to her Jewish mother. Their experiences of Israel are filtered through very different lenses.

While the Ethiopian community in Israel may appear monolithic from the outside, there are many striking divisions within it. Eden and Yarden, both University of Haifa students in their mid-twenties, highlight the differences in the experiences of two individuals who, as Israelis, seem so similar. Both are from large families. They live together in Open Apartments, a multiethnic experiment in housing that includes native Israelis, Russian immigrants, Ethiopian Jews, and Arabs. Both were officers in the army, and they describe themselves as religious. Each pursues a career in people-oriented fields—Eden in education and Yarden in human resources management. But their perspectives are altered by their ages at the time of *aliyah*, and by the different environments in which they were raised in Ethiopia.

Eden, you came to Israel from Addis at sixteen. What do you remember about making aliyah?
Eden: The truth is that since my father was a Christian, he didn't want to go to Israel. It was hard for him to leave because he had a good job and a lot of friends. But my mother wanted to very much. It was her dream. All of us—the kids—we wanted to go very much, but not to Haifa, not to Netanya. We wanted to make

aliyah to Jerusalem, so that's where we went. My father did agree to come finally, and we wouldn't have left without him. After we got to Israel, he converted, and he really is happy. He goes to our synagogue regularly.

What was it like for you when you arrived?
Eden: I didn't know a word of Hebrew, not even *shalom*. In the beginning I felt that I had no connection to Israelis, and I felt lost. Really lost. I went to *ulpan* [intensive Hebrew class] with all the family to try to learn Hebrew. After *ulpan*, I was accepted to a boarding school because I was only sixteen and wasn't allowed to enter the university. But I already had a high school diploma from Ethiopia. I was in boarding school with Ethiopians who had never been educated, and everything was being taught at a low level. It felt like I was there for no reason, so I thought, okay, I'm going to get a job, and then I'll go to university after that.

Yarden, what was it like for you, and what do you know about your family's decision to make aliyah?
Yarden: I came from a village in Gondar where there is a totally different mentality. The Ethiopians in Addis are more open-minded and educated. They lived in mixed communi-

ties and had already seen white people. My father told me that we came here because of our religion. Our *kessim* [priests] would tell the people about Jerusalem and that we must go. Their reasons were ideological, Zionist. They didn't describe to them what Israel was like, what the houses look like, but only that it would be a good place, a place where everyone was Jewish. I don't think they even knew that there were white people. There are some people who came here for economic reasons, but my family was one of the wealthy families in our village, so it wasn't our economic situation. We sold everything we had and came with what we could carry.

Since you were only four when you arrived, do you feel like a sabra [native Israeli]?
Yarden: Yes, very much. I started school at an Israeli kindergarten. But I still have a very strong connection to the Ethiopian community. There is a split between the people who stick with their Ethiopian identity and don't connect to Israelis, and the others who consider themselves to be only Israeli and no longer Ethiopian. I am in the middle.

You explained why you lacked confidence in school. What was life like for you and your friends outside of school?

Yarden: There were times when the kids would give up a lot to help our parents. For example, we would go with them to a doctor or to the bank. I was just a little girl. What did I know about banks to explain it to them? I would have to explain everything to them in front of everyone, but I wanted to go out and have fun like the Israeli kids. There were times that I was really angry about being Ethiopian. My parents have by now adjusted very well to Israeli society.

What about discrimination? Were you aware of it as a teenager?

Yarden: There was an attitude that Ethiopians are "less than," or inferior, to Israelis. This attitude lowered my self-confidence during high school. In the army, I was an officer in a unit where there were no other Ethiopians. People would ask how I got that far. I never looked at myself and said, "I'm an Ethiopian," or "I'm inferior." It was only when I looked at myself in a mirror and saw the colour of my skin that I was aware of my Ethiopian-ness.

Eden: I don't feel inferior to the Israelis, but sometimes the Israelis make me feel like I am different. It's very common to meet Israelis who say, "You poor Ethiopians." Once I had a job where a Russian immigrant had this attitude. So I said to her, "I'm a Jew. So what if I am black; I am an Israeli. Why are we *miskenim* [worthy of pity]? We have a different mentality, we have a different language, we have a different culture, but we are still Jews."

What is your attitude toward dating? Is dating native Israelis common? Does it cause conflict with your parents?

Yarden: My parents have been in Israel for twenty years and only recently are they starting to accept boyfriends who are not Ethiopian. It started with them getting beyond the matchmakers who came to our house. The second stage was when I could bring a boyfriend home that I could still break up with, that I didn't have to marry! And the third stage was to bring someone home who they didn't approve of. My parents would be worried about a mixed marriage because they think an Israeli boy would not understand me. There is the concern that in a moment of weakness, something about me being Ethiopian would come out. It's not only the boy, but his family. If they think she is inferior because her family is Ethiopian, then that would be hurtful to her. But there are different attitudes in the Ethiopian community about who you can marry, just as there are in the other Middle Eastern communities.

What are your personal goals?

Yarden: I am studying education, and I plan to work with youth because in my opinion, that's where everything is going wrong. Ethiopian youth tend to identify more with Jamaican or African American culture than with Israeli culture. They listen to rap music because it's black people singing about racism. They don't even want to go into the army, many of them. The years between being a child and being an adult, this is the age when you can influence them.

Eden: My dream is just to help my community. And, really, our community needs help.

Emebet Adago

"Family life used to be everything in our tradition. But here, it's the kids who are bringing the parents everywhere,

to the doctors or translating for them wherever they go. They are very dependent on their kids.

Instead of having someone who can show them the way, the children have become those who are showing and

teaching. In the past, you could not talk disrespectfully to your parents like Israelis. You would come and

kiss their feet. As much as parents try to tell them, there's a certain shut-down attitude, especially from kids who grew

up here. People who came at my age, who remember Ethiopia, understand the adults.

We do a lot better than the kids who were born here."

When Emebet Adago arrived in Israel as a five year old, she was given the name Malka, which means "Queen," as does her Amharic name. Like many Ethiopian Jews in her generation, she changed her name back to the one that expresses her roots. We met Emebet at a former caravan site in Givat Hamatos, a poor area in the southeast corner of Jerusalem where as many as 800 Ethiopian and Russian immigrants once lived in duplex mobile homes. The caravans are now government housing for poor families from many ethnic groups. Along with several Israelis, Emebet works for the Good Neighbors project at a community center for young children. Inside, her trailer is cozy and colorful. A single space, serving as kitchen and living room, is draped with Indian fabrics, and a string of beads separates the living room from the bedroom.

In the interviews for this book, there were many emotional moments, but none were more intense than when Emebet told us of an elementary school principal in Ashdod who made the Ethiopian kids take a separate recess from the Israeli kids. The image brought her to tears. No one spoke for several minutes; we were all trying not to cry. Emebet was hoping to enroll in Hebrew University in fall 2004, where she planned to study international relations. In the summer of 2006, we learned that she was at Hebrew University, but not as a student. She was working as a security guard checking bags for explosives at the main entrance to the campus. Emebet has not given up. She applied for Atidim, an academic support program designed to make university education more accessible to immigrants.

Emebet Adago came to Israel through Cairo in 1990 with her mother, step-father, and a younger sister. They lived in an absorption center for three years. A housing shortage caused by the huge waves of immigrants from both Ethiopia and Russia during the early 1990s forced them to remain in the absorption center for three years. They were finally able to rent an apartment in a poor neighborhood of Netanya, where they still live. While her mother was attending *ulpan* to learn Hebrew, Emebet's stepfather became seri-ously ill and committed suicide, a fate that befell an unusually high percentage of that generation. Emebet attended boarding school at Yemin Orde. Her counselors there convinced her to participate in the Teens for Tzedek (charitable work) pro-gram, a joint project with students from Haifa and Boston. The group devoted weeks to helping Ethiopian kids at a sum-mer camp in Israel and then flew to the United States, where they volunteered at a food bank. "It was one of the best experi-ences of my life," she said. "It gave me the experience of making a difference. Even if we only changed the reality a little, it meant a lot to me."

When you changed your name from Hebrew back to your Amharic name, was your mother happy about it?
Yes, and she was also happy that I was learn-ing how to read and write Amharic. When we made *aliyah*, I didn't know how to read or write. My brothers did, but I was just ready to enter school when we came, so I didn't learn Amharic in Ethiopia.

How did the Israelis accept you?
Most Israelis were nice, but there were a few things said in the neighborhood, you know, *kushit* [Hebrew equivalent to "nigger"] and so on. At first, we were hurt by it, but you learn. After we moved into the apartment, I attended a religious elementary school. Slowly, where we lived became an Ethiopian neighborhood. In the beginning my mother was in *ulpan*, but then my stepfather got sick and she still had young children, so she couldn't study. Her first years here were the hardest years of her life, I think. Still, she doesn't speak Hebrew, but she can understand and can get by. She lives in one of the toughest neighborhoods in Netanya. A lot of young people have gotten into bad things, like crime and drugs.

Does your mother regret coming to Israel, because

it has been so difficult for her?
Never, never! She always says, "Thank God that I was brought here." She always thanks the government, too. No, she does not regret it.

What does the community's poverty contribute to the problems children are having with school and socially?
It has a very big influence because you're in a neighborhood where most of the parents aren't working. I went to a boarding school after ele-mentary school, and my mother didn't want me to go because I helped a lot in the house. But I had finished eighth grade and to continue in high school you had to pay for the studies and this was very difficult, but if I went to study in boarding school, Youth Aliyah [a division of the Jewish Agency] would pay for it, so I went. I spent the first year mostly crying. I wanted to be home. A friend and I left the school and returned home, but we went back. This school, Yemin Orde, turned out to be wonderful for me. It's a beautiful place. It really shaped me. Many of the Ethiopians who are successful graduated from Yemin Orde.

Have you experienced racism?
As much as you become close to Israelis, they will remind you that you're Ethiopian. When I

was a soldier in the army, I had a job teaching in Lod. A woman walking in the street asked to pass, so I let her pass. And she started to speak rudely to me. So I asked her, "Why are you talking rudely to me?" She said, "Listen to me. You're Ethiopian, and when you see me, you lower your head." What chutzpah! My color should change everything? I don't deserve any less respect. I heard recently about the principal of a school in Ashdod who separated the recess of the Ethiopian kids from the others. It hurts . . . if a principal of a school does something like that, if *he* is the example of things like that . . . I have to strengthen myself.

Where do you find your strength?
From my mom. She believes in me. There's a stereotype that when a kid goes to boarding school, even if the kid is good at home, she will get into trouble at boarding school. I remember my mom saying to my brothers, "I know her, and I believe in her. She won't change." That strengthened me, even in the most difficult times. When I know that there are people who believe in me, I can succeed.

If you could advise the government how to improve the situation for youth, what would you say?

The government should support things like clubhouses and activities that will interest youth. A lot of kids are wandering in the streets because they are bored; they don't know what to do with themselves. And the schools need to have a lot more faith in the Ethiopian students. As a soldier, part of my job was teaching, and I saw that if a child is not doing well, they say the child needs testing, that he needs to go to a psychologist, that

he has a learning problem. But maybe the problem is with the teachers and the education system. That is something that has to be considered. I saw recently a TV show about an organization that is retesting kids who supposedly have learning disabilities. They discovered that they were fine, no learning problems.

Does the role of women in Ethiopian culture make you feel confused about pursuing a profession?
It's not that way anymore. Parents support learning so that you will have a career. It doesn't matter if it's a son or daughter. My family expects a lot from me, and it's not any less than from my brothers. They know that this is a time to advance for the Ethiopian children and our generation. They don't expect girls to get married, have kids, and stay at home like it was before.

Would your family object to your dating an Israeli?
My mom had several cousins who married *ferenjim* (white Israelis). But me, personally, I think it would be easier for me to be with an Ethiopian. I'm still not totally Israeli. A big part of me is Ethiopian, and I want someone who will understand that and respect it.

Mazi Melesa

"... when I finish my studies and I'm trying to set an example for my little sister that getting an education

is the best thing, what if she sees that I don't have a place to work after all my years of study?

What kind of example is that?

She'll say, 'It's a shame, why did you do all that studying?

I'll take another path.'"

When we met Mazi in 2004, she was the elected chairperson of the Ethiopian National Students' Organization, which represents the interests of the 2,300 Ethiopian Israeli university students. The organization monitors and at times protests Ministry of Education policies that affect Ethiopian students adversely. The organization also tracks Knesset policies affecting employment and racism. Mazi believes emphatically that education is the key to integration. Mazi was then a senior at the University of Haifa, planning to graduate with a degree in occupational therapy. She was not optimistic about finding work in her field. Many Ethiopian college graduates wind up with jobs in the service sector, such as security guards or cashiers; if they are more fortunate, they find work in a professional capacity with the Ethiopian population. As it turned out, Mazi was offered a job close to her heart: working in the New York headquarters of the North American Conference on Ethiopian Jewry (NACOEJ).

Mazi grew up outside of Addis Ababa in the village of Nazeret, where her father owned a coffeehouse and an inn. At nine years old, she learned that she was part of a Jewish family and that they would move to Addis Ababa in hopes of making *aliyah*. In our conversation, she described what it was like to prepare for emigration, never knowing if or when it would happen, and then to drop everything and rush to the Israeli embassy as the news spread by word of mouth that the planes were flying that day. After arriving as part of Operation Solomon in May 1991, the family moved into an absorption center in Netanya for three years, until they were able to buy an apartment there. Mazi attended a secular boarding school, Neveh Hadassah, where there were very few Ethiopian students, and she served in the army before enrolling in the University of Haifa. As the director of the Ethiopian University Students' Organization, Mazi's perspective on what happens when a university student enters the larger society is both enlightening and disturbing.

What were you told about Israel, once you learned you would be immigrating?
As they say, it's a land of milk and honey, where everything is sparkling, a land of dreams. Everything is good, and there are no problems, and so on. My parents were born in a village near Gondar and they learned the stories of Jerusalem and being Jewish from our forefathers. But then they moved to a village outside of Addis Ababa where we were the lone Jewish family, except for my father's brother's family. Our parents kept it a secret from us because it would have been dangerous if people knew that we were Jewish.

How did you prepare to leave on Operation Solomon?
My father made an application with the Israeli embassy. When it was accepted, that's when we moved from Nazeret to Addis near the [NACOEJ-operated] compound so we could study Hebrew. We never knew when we were going to leave; no one promised us a date. It could happen any time. Or maybe not. There was a civil war in Ethiopia, and one morning we heard from a Jewish family that it was time, the *aliyah* had begun. We had to go to the compound immediately. We didn't bring anything with us but the clothes on our backs. We didn't say goodbye to our friends. We went immediately. Everyone was pushing to get inside the compound. It was very frightening for me because I was only twelve then. Everyone was pushing. The buses were taking people from the embassy to go to the airplanes, and I was afraid we would never get to go. After many hours, we got inside. We finished all the necessary paperwork. It was an exciting moment. Everything happened really fast. Suddenly we were in a jumbo military jet. They took all the seats out of the airplane, so we sat on the floor. We were all scared and excited.

What was the first moment like when you arrived?
Oh, we all sang "Heivenu Shalom Aleichem" when we arrived. When we got off the airplane, we saw our parents kneel down and kiss the ground. So all of us kids kneeled and kissed the ground. We knew they had dreamed of going to Jerusalem for many years, so it was a special moment for them to be in the Holy Land. It was very moving to see everyone kiss the ground.

Were you surprised by what you found in Israel after that first moment?
No, I was still young. For me, everything was nice, and shiny, and great. With time, I've grown up and have become educated and integrated with Israel society, and I've discovered difficulties. Yes, there is a huge gap between

what was told to us and what's here. But it took time for me to see this. *Aliyah* is hard for every immigrant. You have to learn the language, make friends who aren't Ethiopian, and there are problems. Suddenly, though, I felt in my heart that I'm an Israeli in every way, but when I got close to some Israelis, I felt they didn't look at me as Israeli. That was surprising because I was expecting a certain kind of unity, a feeling that everyone would be together.

They don't see you as Jewish?

I don't know about "as Jewish." Some people, even if they know I'm Jewish, they still see me as an Ethiopian. The only place I didn't feel this was in the army. But beyond this, I felt the discrimination in some places, especially when I was younger and tried to look for work. Even though I knew they were still looking to hire someone, they wouldn't take me.

How did that make you feel?

It made me feel very sad. That you feel part of the country, you serve the country in the army, you feel part of everything, and at the moment that you need to integrate, there is no reciprocation from some people in the society.

Did that feeling influence your decision to become an activist?

Very much. That's what motivated me. I see that the community needs us, a young generation who'll make a change here. I understand that there's a lot of work to do, and we can do

it. After several years now, the Ethiopian community isn't so quiet. They aren't causing an uproar, but still they sit with their kids and tell them, "You have to fight for your rights."

There's no better way to advance than to get an education. We went to the Ministry of Education to oppose a budget proposal a year and a half ago. They wanted to cut back the funds for Ethiopian education and this made us very angry. So this got us all out to fight; otherwise there is no way to be heard. It was in the papers, and it was on television. In my opinion, the media will always look at the things that aren't good in the community, and that's what they'll portray. The successes they won't publicize.

What is the biggest problem facing Ethiopian students in Israel?

The very large number of graduates who can't get jobs is very frustrating. There's a big push to get educated, but we don't see Ethiopians integrating into the job market. It's very discouraging. In my case, for example, when I finish my studies and I'm trying to set an example for my little sister that getting an education is the best thing, what if she sees that I don't have a place to work after all my years of study? What kind of example is that? She'll say, "It's a shame, why did you do all that studying? I'll take another path." We have to find the solution to the problem of unemployment. It's true that the economic situation is tough not just for Ethiopians, but in general. So the situation for us is com-

pletely awful. People have studied so hard and after they earn their degrees, they are guards at the central bus station or waiters.

I understand what you're saying about employment after a degree. But what about the educational system and obtaining higher education?

Ethiopian children don't get a good education. The percentage that finishes high school with a diploma is very low. We want to increase the number. The government has to study this and find out why there are so few children passing the *bagrut* [matriculation exam]. If they don't have a good score, there will be no way they can continue their education in academia.

Also, we have a test called "psychometrics" [aptitude test], which they use to decide if you can go to law school, or be a nurse, or get higher education. You can take it when you're eighteen or when you finish the army service. We think this cannot really tell them about our ability because the test is designed for the backgrounds of Europeans, not Ethiopians. It is culturally dependent. Unfortunately, this test closes the door to many young Ethiopian students. The score is not meaningful.

The University of Haifa was one of the first to open the door to Ethiopian students, even if we don't get a high enough score on that test. There are other universities, like Tel Aviv University and Hebrew University, which are not so good about opening their doors. My scores were not high on the test, but Haifa gave me the opportunity, even without the right score. I finished the university in very good standing. Once you get in, there's no special accommodation for Ethiopian students. They have to study like everyone else. They have the same exams. The government gave a great opportunity to the Ethiopian students by giving university scholarships for all of us, so we have the chance of getting an education. But the government also needs to find a solution for the problem of employment after we graduate.

What do you think is the root of the unemployment issue—racism or something else?
It's complicated. It's true that the economic situation is tough for everyone. It's still a fact that I see only a few Ethiopians integrating into the job market. The community has a stigma that is hard to overcome.

In terms of Ethiopians needing help, we've heard that many families have become dysfunctional and stressed. Have you experienced that, or have you seen it?
Yes. We came from homes [in Ethiopia] where parents are like gods. Respect? We couldn't even talk to them unless they spoke to us first. We give a lot of respect to adults in general. When we came to Israel, all that went; it just went! The kids see how the Israeli kids behave to their parents, how they are rude to them, and that's what the Ethiopian kid learns. Then he comes home and acts like his Israeli friend. The parents can't accept that. And that's the problem: the parents and their children don't

have a connection. There's no communication between them.

In Ethiopia, the father was someone you gave a lot of respect to. In Israel, the family doesn't listen to him. He doesn't have his credibility. I see it in my house with my father. He had a lot of standing, and now he's afraid to reprimand. We have to work at it from two directions—the parents and the kids. To the parents, you have to tell them that they're not in Ethiopia anymore, and the norms are different. You have to explain what the kids are going through, what their challenges are. And you have to talk to the kids to explain the position of the parents.

A lot of the Ethiopian youth seem to like rap music. Do you think they identify with African Americans or their culture?
I think that happens when a person hasn't found himself in society. They're looking for something to feel close to, and in rap they've found something that accepts them. They find a certain identity with being black, with coming from Africa. We—the national student organization—try to lead them to our own culture, where we came from.

What are the aspects of Ethiopian Jewish culture that you would focus on?
We are proud of our culture, which is an outstanding culture and has aspects that aren't in Israeli culture. When we need to act like Israelis, we act like Israelis. I have to be part of

society. But I choose what I want to take; I don't take everything from Israeli society. We keep the respect for family, for elders, and the community, our way of speaking. Also, we have patience in our culture.

Your fiancé is of Ukrainian background. Have you experienced negative attitudes as a couple?
Not from our families. My father completely supports this. My fiancé's parents are the same. They are warm and respect me completely. The only thing they are concerned about is that we understand each other's cultural differences. They don't have any problems with skin color. I've never heard anyone in the Ethiopian community say not to marry a white person. Sometimes they worry about not being able to talk to the family [in-laws] because of cultural differences, but not because of race. On the Israeli side, though, there is some racism, unfortunately. It's really wrong to think like this. It's wrong for Israel's future. Of course, people look at us. We are special because I am black and he is white. But we are human beings like everyone else. I don't know what they are thinking… maybe, "How can he go with an Ethiopian woman?" Unfortunately, some people think like they did 100 years ago. You have to tell everyone the reality.

(In May 2006, Mazi and Albert Pilip were married in Israel. They live in New York, where Mazi is working for NACOEJ and Albert is a doctor.)

CHAPTER IV

DEFENDING ISRAEL WITH OUR BLOOD

The Israeli army is not only a defense force but also a force for integrating the country's many ethnic groups, bonding everyone to the same national experience.

While some alternative national service options exist for ultra-religious young men and women, more than 90 percent of high school graduates—male and female, rich and poor, immigrant and native—experience the same training and compulsory military service. Therefore, the Israel Defense Forces (IDF) provides the most widespread arena in which Ethiopian Jews can become more fully Israeli.

In the decade following Operation Moses (1984–1985), there was a honeymoon period between Ethiopian youth and the IDF. While the new immigrants struggled to perform as equals in the classroom, where their lack of academic background and Hebrew language skills impeded them, it was a very different story on the battlefield where their patriotism, bravery, and physical stamina were natural assets. In short order, they earned a reputation as superb fighters, and by the late 1980s the number of Ethiopian Israelis in elite combat units was disproportionately high. In the officer selection process, some alleged discrimination, but most Ethiopian recruits from 1985 to 1996 saw the army as a welcoming institution. They felt appreciated and believed that by defending the nation they could repay their debt to Israel for helping them reach the Holy Land.

But by the late 1990s, there was a falling out. It began with the notorious Blood Scandal, which shook the Ethiopian Israeli community to its core. The army requires all incoming recruits to donate blood; in fact, most of the country's emergency blood supply is donated by soldiers, who go to the blood banks as a group with their fighting units. The Ethiopians participated wholeheartedly, convinced that contributing to the blood supply was deeply symbolic of their unity with the Jewish people. Then, on January 29, 1996, the daily paper *Ma'ariv* published a shocking revelation: since 1984, the blood bank, under the direction of public health officials, had been throwing out the blood donated by Ethiopians. The Ethiopian Israeli community had endured many blows to their dignity, but none produced a more explosive reaction than this one. The reason for the policy was fear of HIV exposure, which was known to be more widespread among the Ethiopians than native Israelis. Although blood is routinely tested for HIV, the virus can remain undetected for six months after initial exposure. Thus, officials decided that the level of risk was still too great. To avoid offending or stigmatizing the Ethiopian soldiers by refusing their donations, the blood was drawn but then secretly discarded. The Ethiopian community felt insulted, rejected, and stigmatized; they also felt patronized

because their own community leaders had not been consulted. Their outrage boiled over.

The director of the blood bank explained its actions in a *New York Times* article (January 29, 1996): "We thought that singling out an ethnic group and sending them home [from the donation center] would be more offensive and embarrassing." The same article also quoted a female Ethiopian Israeli soldier: "When they tell me that since 1984 they have been spilling the blood, it feels like the army means nothing, that I'll never be part of Israel, because my color is black and my blood is contaminated. It really hurts."

Though normally cautious in their political activities, the Ethiopian community burst into violent protests in Jerusalem, attracting more than 10,000 demonstrators. The police were overwhelmed and resorted to water cannons, tear gas, and rubber bullets to protect the office of then prime minister Shimon Peres. The Peres government conducted a comprehensive investigation, and the director of Magen David Adom (Israel's Red Cross) resigned. Although the genuine remorse expressed by officials helped assuage some of the anger, the long-term consequence of the Blood Scandal has been that today's Ethiopian youth are much less enthusiastic about military service than those who came before them. And since the rate of HIV infection remains comparatively high among Ethiopian Jews, the blood bank's policy has been revised to accept donations only from those who immigrated before 1974.

However, there are encouraging developments in the military; for example, the burgeoning corps of Ethiopian Israeli career officers. Ethiopian soldiers have increasingly been promoted in rank, not only because of their ability to command in the field, but also because of their academic achievement and intellectual competence. The army needs fighters, but it also needs planners in logistics, budgeting, and materials. A recent study acknowledges that the army is still not sufficiently tapping the talents of the Ethiopian Jews because of discriminatory attitudes, but the direction is a positive one. As the number of Ethiopian university graduates grows, the IDF is benefiting from their academic achievements, and there are now more than 200 Ethiopian Israeli officers.

In this chapter, we meet two officers who have risen in the ranks because of their expertise and "people skills." Gidon Ayech (shown above) is one of them. We also hear from a national hero who stopped a terrorist bombing in Jerusalem and miraculously survived weeks in a coma to become a spokesperson for the IDF. The photograph of Captain Gidon Ayech on this page, shot at a military base, has a poignant backdrop. Are there any other armies that post a sign on the exit gate saying "Go in Peace"?

Johnny Berhanu

"I am still trying to integrate. This is something that is tested all the time.

In the army, they do not make distinctions between who is Israeli and who is Ethiopian.

But when I leave the base and I go somewhere without my uniform, I'm stuck again,

and I have to handle it again."

Part commander and part listener, Lieutenant Johnny Berhanu has one of the army's most unusual jobs. He works with special needs soldiers. "These are people who have a difficult time fitting into the system," he explains. "I interview every soldier who has emotional or learning difficulties. I give them support and encouragement, try to find the right unit for them, and offer guidance so they can complete their army service in the best way possible."

Military personnel can only be interviewed in the presence of an escort from the Army Spokesperson's Office, a conscientious and bureaucratic group that both arranges for and supervises every meeting. Johnny Berhanu knew exactly where to draw the line when discussing the state of Israel. He informed us without hesitation that as an officer, he would not say anything critical of the government. Despite what seemed to be a strict boundary, Johnny readily revealed what he believes are the problems of his community and its relationship to Israeli society.

How did you acquire an American name like Johnny?
Everyone asks me that. When you make *aliyah*, they choose a name for you without asking you what you want to be called. I came here when I was ten. My Amharic name was Maledeh, so some clerk said, "Okay, you're Meir." No one asked me what I wanted. A couple of years later, I said, "Okay, I am not going to accept it." A person has to have free choice. So I chose Johnny. Why Johnny? I have no idea.

What was it like for you in school? What prepared you for success in a military career?
I was with my parents for the younger grades and then was sent to boarding school. The most important schooling I received started in high school at Yemin Orde. The principal, Dr. Chaim Peri, is one of the great educators. He was a role model for us. I studied there from tenth through twelfth grade and gained a lot of self-confidence. Then I went to a special preparatory school for the army. My father is a central figure for me. He always said to me, "Your strengths, your ability to connect to people, to give them a helping hand—these things will enable you to integrate into society."

Did your family have to escape? Did other people know that you were leaving?
We had to escape. We left together, six kids and my parents. We lived in a Jewish village where there were fifteen or twenty Jewish families surrounded by a lot of Christian families and some Muslims. It was a center for handicrafts and metal working, like making weapons. That's what the Jews did. Kids were generally not told that they were leaving because they might tell their friends. The parents planned everything. They prepared the food and put it in the storage room. It was totally secret. The government did not allow us to leave, so we left at night. On the night we left, there was gunfire in the village. I remember hiding under my bed, hearing the guns. The surrounding villages must have already heard rumors that we were going. On the one hand, they didn't want us to leave because we were a commercial center. But also they must have wanted to loot our village, to take our stuff.

How long was your journey to Sudan?
About one month. We lived relatively close to the border to Sudan. We would sleep in the day and travel in the night. There were all kinds of difficult encounters, like when people would try to steal from us or take the girls. We call them *shiftas*, people that live in the wilderness and prey on people on their journey by stealing. They would see a girl and take her. They wouldn't kill them. They would just take them, sleep with them, and bring them back.

How did the people endure this?
When I look back, I see their motivation as Zionism, the faith to get to this place at any cost. They witnessed rape, people being killed, and dying in the desert. Someone who dies is buried in that very place. But the faith of the people on the journey was strong, and the faith in Zionism was "to take everything to the bank." As a boy, I didn't understand why we were going, but my parents did.

What happened when they got to Israel?

The moment we got to Israel, everyone kissed the ground. They believed from that moment on they were going to have new and good lives. But later, when they began to understand what it was like here, there was a certain disappointment: the difficulty of living here; difficulty with the language; with integrating into the workplace; with the educational system; with the competitive and progressive culture in Israel. In Ethiopia, the father was the central figure; here, the father isn't worth anything. He is unemployed and cannot speak the language.

What are the other differences between Ethiopian and Israeli culture?

In Ethiopia everything is much more laid back. I'm my own boss. I work until I want to. Everyone is an independent laborer with no bosses. I'm talking about the villages, not the city. Things are calm. A wedding lasts seven days. There is a whole ceremony for making someone coffee. If I invite you for coffee, it could take me two hours, but I invited you, so you'll wait for me. There is no schedule. I breathed clean air, not fumes. I was totally free. In Israel, if I'm late for the train by two minutes, I won't make it. You have a boss who is waiting for you, asking you, "How come you aren't at work on time?" Everything here is stressful. My mind is full of stress. I'm working all the time. That's the culture here. You can also see it on the streets, people on their cell phones asking each other, "Where are you?" It was a total shock, all this technology. In Ethiopia they didn't even have

refrigerators. It was like being born again. I had to understand things anew.

Is there discrimination?

There may be discrimination, but I have to criticize my own community, too. The state of Israel put a decent amount of money and effort into the Ethiopian *aliyah.* They didn't understand everything, and they made some mistakes, but they invested in it—flights, education, mortgage subsidies. So you can't say, if something doesn't go well, that they are screwing us because we're black. I'm not saying there are no difficulties. But some difficulties come from us, not just from the society. If we see the difficulties as the result of discrimination, then we will not succeed. It is not wise to say, "They are messing with us," and then not do anything about it. It's like a car in neutral: you put your

foot on the gas and it makes a lot of noise, but it doesn't move. You have to put it into gear to get somewhere.

What aspects of Ethiopian culture would you like to preserve in your life here as an Ethiopian Israeli?

First of all, I am Jewish, and then an Ethiopian Israeli. That's how I feel. I listen to a lot of Amharic music. It's easier for me to connect to Amharic music, even though I listen to Shlomi Artzi [an Israeli singer] and to pop music. I eat Ethiopian food. I don't wear traditional clothing, maybe because the authentic Ethiopian clothing is more for women. I want to keep the idea of giving respect to those who are older, even if he is even a year older. And in general, we are a culture that listens. These are the things that I will keep.

Gidon Ayech

"Sometimes I think I got my position in the army because I am Ethiopian, and other times I think I got it

even though I am Ethiopian. There are Ethiopians who say they experience racism, and that they are denied positions

because of who they are. I choose to ignore that, even if it might be happening to me.

People in our community who succeed are very strong. If discrimination happens to them, they have to ignore it,

or they have to fight it. My original dream of being a fighter in a combat unit was not realized.

There are times I still want to be in the Golani unit and see action, but what I'm doing now is right for me.

I work hard, and I love what I do."

■

At twenty-nine, Captain Gidon Ayech is one of about 200 Ethiopian officers in the Israel Defense Forces. In past years, Ethiopian soldiers have been promoted to higher rank and admitted to the elite fighting units because of their bravery and combat skills. Gidon, whose academic performance commanded the attention of the army, is pioneering a new path to becoming a career military officer. While most high school graduates complete army service before attending college, Gidon's teachers and the army recruiters took a look at his high school matriculation exam and sent him directly to the university in Ashkelon, where he earned a B.A. and then a master's degree in economics. Gidon joined the IDF as a new recruit in 1999. Five years and several promotions later, Gidon oversees a staff of twenty in the IDF's Budgeting and Economics division. In the interview that follows, Gidon talks about racism, politics, and the attitudes he tries to impart to younger men and women who face military service.

As a captain in the Israel Defense Forces (IDF), Gidon Ayech manages the complexities of budgeting, purchasing, and the economic side of military operations. But he has a more personal assignment too. Through appearances at high schools, he represents the military to graduating students, serving as a powerful role model of achievement for Ethiopian and native Israeli students approaching their military service. His military career is what attracted us to him as an interview subject, but there was an added dimension to his story. He offers an insight into one of the recent big news stories about the Ethiopian community. In April 2005, his mother, Belaynesh, became the first Ethiopian elected to the position of deputy mayor. However, her victory was snagged by a legal battle with the town's mayor, who refused to assign her a portfolio. The case was still in court at the time of this interview.

When did you arrive in Israel?
In 1986 with my little brother. I was nine and he was seven. My parents had good jobs in Addis. My mother worked in a bank and my father worked in the tax department. No one

knew they were Jewish. In fact, I didn't know I was Jewish either. They didn't tell us because they were afraid we would talk about it, and then the neighbors would find out. I had always wondered why we didn't go to church and why my mother told me not to take a shower with the other boys in school. One day, my father told me and my brother that we were going to America, but we were really flying to Israel through Greece. My mother was working outside Addis for several days, so she didn't learn that we left until she came back. When she found out, it was so terrible, she had a breakdown. She was in a hospital for two weeks.

Why didn't your father tell her? Did he think she wouldn't want you to go?
She wanted us all to go to Israel, but only as a family. She didn't want us separated. But my father thought we had to go at that time to get out. It was eight years before I saw my mother and sister again, and it took my father another year after that to leave. So we were not reunited for a long time.

How did you feel when you heard for the first time, at age nine, that you were Jewish and that you were going to Israel?

I thought about the terrible things I had heard about Jews in Ethiopia. There were lots of stories and jokes about Jews—the people who killed Jesus, the people who don't believe in God. It was a caricature. My father explained before we got on the plane that we had a lot of family in Israel. They had stayed with us in Addis before they left, but I had been told they were going to America. Suddenly, I realized my childhood was clothed in a big secret. It was the right thing that they didn't tell us because we would have been frightened by all the things they said about the Jews. I would have had to hide who I am. I understand why the Beta Israel did not want to live in the city. In the village you could be a Jew. It was hard for my parents to be in Addis. It is very hard to hide who you are.

Was there any Jewish observance in your family in Ethiopia that you can recall?
After I began to learn about Judaism, I remembered little things that happened and realized they were observing some laws. For example, on Yom Kippur, they would not eat or work. Of course, I didn't know it was Yom Kippur, but I remember there was a day they would not eat. I also remembered that my father knew the Bible very well. How did he

know so much if he never went to church? When my father came to Kiryat Malachi, he was asked to teach in the synagogue. If we had lived in a village like most of the Beta Israel, he could have been observing all the holidays. Since he could not do that, he would study the Bible instead.

What do you remember about your arrival as a young child?

I was frightened by all the white people. My Israeli friends tell me that when they go to an African country, they are afraid at first because everyone is black. When I saw all the white people, I cried for days. But then I went to my aunt's apartment in Kiryat Gat, and there were hundreds of Ethiopians in her city so I felt more comfortable right away.

Your mother was elected deputy mayor of Kiryat Malachi, but the mayor would not give her any responsibility. What's the story behind that battle?

In Ethiopia, my mother was always the decision-maker and a very strong person. In Ethiopia, we had people cleaning our house and cooking for us, but here in Israel, my mother took a job cleaning houses for other people. In exchange for that, she would get us lessons in Hebrew. She learned Hebrew well and became a leader in our community, helping people at the health clinics and dealing with city hall. The first thing she bought for our house was not a TV; it was a dictionary. It cost a lot of money, but it meant we did not

have to go to the library to look up words. Then she bought an encyclopedia. She taught us that in time we could change our situation. People used to ask my mother what she wanted to do in the future, and she would tell them, "I'm going to be the mayor of Kiryat Malachi." I thought she was crazy, but now she is the deputy mayor. I think it is worth setting high goals, so even if you don't get there, you will get close. But now there is a court case about this. The newspapers present it as a case of racism, but I think it is just politics. My mother says the mayor broke an agreement to provide another Ethiopian synagogue— we have only one for 2,500 people. He also promised to hire an Amharic translator at city hall. The mayor says he had a deal with another Ethiopian to be deputy mayor, but the city council nominated my mother. It's still in court.

When did you decide to make the army your career?

When I was in the absorption center and soldiers came in uniforms to meet us, we Ethiopian boys always thought this was the way we could become better Israelis. Many of the Ethiopians were in the elite fighting units and military police. I wanted to do something for this country, so I felt I could accomplish that through the army. I am not trying to change society; I am trying to change the image of the Ethiopians in society. I graduated with 400 soldiers, and I was chosen by the officers after my exams as the second best

graduating officer. It was the happiest day of my life.

I have heard that the army is not as popular with the Ethiopian youth.

You're right. Eight to ten years ago, the Ethiopians all wanted to be in combat units, the specialty units. But the opinion now is that the community didn't get enough for all the work they did. It was after the Blood Scandal [see introduction to this chapter] that Ethiopians had to wonder what their place was in Israeli society. As Ethiopians, you feel that you have to be the best to get the same treatment as a normal citizen. You have to prove yourself all the time. In the last few years, some Ethiopians are leaving Israel and going to America or other countries. What I tell the students is that we must try not to break down or give up. That will only make things worse. Ethiopians must be part of the history of Israel from now into the future.

What can you say to convince students that it is worthwhile to be in the army?

I tell them that if we don't succeed, it is only because we are not given the chance. I started to believe I could be an army officer when Ethiopian officers came to my school. When you meet people who have done something, it's not just a story, it's real. I also give them my cell phone number and invite them to call me if they have questions about how to get the best assignments in the army. I just try to be a good friend and big brother to them.

Natan Sandaka

"It was a dangerous time. Every day of the week, we worked about twelve hours a day

because there was a lot of tension. This is when the intifada began, after the Al Aksa Mosque incident [on September

28, 2000]. So we got up at four in the morning and by five we were already in the field.

About seven o'clock in the morning, a terrified woman approached us and reported a suspicious man who was

dressed like a *Hareidi* [ultra-Orthodox Jew] with a black coat and a yarmulke, and he carried a backpack.

I asked her what was so suspicious about him. She said she could smell alcohol on his breath.

So I took my partner and we ran in the direction she was pointing to. In about 200 meters, we saw the man.

We asked him to stop, and he started running."

■

While on army patrol in Jerusalem in 2001, Natan Sandaka trapped a suicide bomber who was dressed as an Orthodox Jew. He absorbed the full force of the explosion, remained in a coma for two weeks, but miraculously lived to transform this traumatic event into a heartbreaking avocation. On behalf of the Israeli army, Natan visits the survivors of terrorist bombings and their families to give comfort and hope. He is quoted in the newspapers, interviewed on television, and travels to many countries to speak about the effects of terrorism. At the end of our conversation, he decided to show us the M-16 he had been holding when the terrorist detonated the bomb. Blasted into dozens of tiny pieces, the shattered M-16 is visual confirmation of the power of the explosion. As if it were a sacred object, Natan would not let us photograph it, or the burn scars that are mostly hidden by his long sleeves.

Natan Sandaka was ten years old when he and his family were airlifted to Israel as part of Operation Solomon in 1991. Natan lives with his mother and four siblings in Lod, near Tel Aviv. We met him at their home in a three-bedroom apartment on the fourth floor of a building that shares a parking lot with a rundown community center that serves the Ethiopian community. His mother served grapes, apples, and cold drinks, and, along with a sister and brother, sat patiently during our two-hour meeting, although they understood little of the conversation. They are intensely proud of Natan for his celebrated heroism and his role as a spokesperson on terrorism. Television news programs often interview him after attacks within Israel, and he travels to the United States, Australia, Italy, England, and Canada to speak about his near-fatal experience and his current role in comforting families and survivors.

After the formal interview, his mother and sister brought out his medal, his many official letters of commendation, and newspaper articles about him—none of which he had mentioned. That is when he decided to bring out the shattered M-16 he was holding as he faced down the suicide bomber. As we were leaving, he made a unique request.

Despite the fact that more than 65 percent of Ethiopians live below the poverty line, not one of the sixty or more individuals we interviewed ever asked for payment. Natan, however, did ask for a donation to a soccer club he organized for Ethiopian youth, which he had told us about during the interview.

As a child in Ethiopia, what did you imagine Israel would be like?

I will give you the typical Ethiopian answer, meaning what I thought about Israel was that everybody here keeps the Sabbath and holidays and keeps kosher, and no one drives a car on the Sabbath. We heard that Jerusalem was a city built of gold. Our grandparents told us about the dream to come to Israel. Almost every Saturday, they told us about this dream. It was carried in every generation.

How did you react when you realized Israel was different from your dream?

Of course we were disappointed, but we realized we are here with our brothers. In Ethiopia we were persecuted by people who wanted to destroy us, like Jews everywhere in the world. Here we felt safer because we can protect each other.

Did you experience discrimination after you arrived?

In elementary school all my friends were Israelis. Because of this, I learned to speak the language very quickly and got used to the country. I felt discrimination not in civilian life, but in the army. The life in the army . . . well, I thought that the army is the one place that everybody is equal. I was in a course to become a commander, a sergeant. One of the officers was responsible for promoting me. In some way, he delayed me from graduating and gave the position to someone else. I asked him why, and he said I was too weak. But I was physically fit. My officers trusted me, and when they needed someone to lead a team, to command a team, they chose me. One of the other soldiers had an uncle who was an officer in the border police, so that's what happened. It was *proteksia* [connections]. I was very angry. My commander sent me to the course because he felt I had the ability. He wanted me to continue, but I told him I preferred to stop.

Would you describe how you confronted the terrorist?

I was on patrol in one of the streets of Jerusalem on September 4, 2001, one week before September 11. It was a dangerous time.

Every day of the week, we worked about twelve hours a day because there was a lot of tension. This is when the intifada began, after the Al Aksa Mosque incident [on September 28, 2000]. So we got up at four in the morning and by five we were already in the field. About seven o'clock in the morning, a terrified woman approached us and reported a suspicious man who was dressed like a *Hareidi* [ultra-Orthodox Jew] with a black coat and a *kippah* [yarmulke], and he carried a backpack. I asked her what was so suspicious about him. She said she could smell alcohol on his breath. So I took my partner and we ran in the direction she was pointing to. In about 200 meters, we saw the man. We asked him to stop, and he started running. We ran after him, but we were still not sure he was a terrorist, so therefore we could not shoot at him. We were on a *Hareidi* street in Mea Sharim and there were a lot of *Hareidim*, so it was very difficult to decide.

But at a corner, he turned and we ran after him, and suddenly I saw him standing and waiting for me with a smile. He realized that he didn't have any chance to run away and do what he planned to do. At that time, when he smiled, I realized I had to deal with a suicide bomber. So I raised my gun to shoot him, but it was too late. He had already activated the bomb. As a result of the explosion, I had burns over 50 percent of my body and nails in my leg and in my lung. I lost consciousness. I was in a coma for about two weeks in Hadassah Hospital. My partner was a few meters behind me, and he was only slightly injured, in his hand, because I absorbed most of the explosion.

What were your thoughts in the hospital?
A lot of people came to visit me. When I opened my eyes, the chief of staff was there and gave me some certificate of honor, but I didn't recognize him. I asked someone who was in my room, "What is the reason I'm here?" He said, "You don't know? You are a hero of Israel." Then suddenly I remembered everything. I realized my body was covered with liniment and bandages. Only my nose was showing. Of course, it was very hard for my family. I was worried if I would ever be able to walk again. I had righteous grandparents. Because of their righteousness and the prayers of all of Israel, I am here. I was in the hospital four months.

Do you ever think, "Why me? Did I come to Israel for this?"
I can't say to myself, "Why did it happen to me? Why is it supposed to be me?" But I can tell you that we saved a lot of people by stopping this terrorist. Even though I have the burns on me, for me it's a gift. Why? Because by those burns, I saved a lot of people. If I had the chance to do that again, I would do it, because as a soldier, it is our commitment to save people's lives. The police, as a result of the explosion, found a second terrorist, his guide, before he was able to explode himself. By the way, this guide was an Israeli Arab; he worked in Kupat Holim hospital [in Jerusalem].

Did the incident affect your opinion of Arabs or Palestinians?
In every nation, there are some bad people, but I don't make a generalization because I believe that every one of us is created by one God.

Were you able to find work after the army?
Originally I wanted to study law, but now I am working with children. After what happened to me, I established a soccer team in Lod called Amichai [My People Lives] Lod. I'm the manager of the team. The main purpose is not to play soccer but to help them in their studies. I'm not taking on a child because of his ability to play soccer. I take children who are dropouts, and we help them go back to their schools. We have older students who come twice a week to help them with their studies. The players are mostly Ethiopian children, ages ten to fifteen. Other people are helping, too. We are volunteers. Nobody earns anything from this. The students will be the ones who earn something from it.

[A few days prior to our meeting, there had been a terrorist bombing in which three soldiers had been critically injured. Later in the day, Natan would be visiting them in the hospital.]

What do you plan to say to the soldiers if you are able to talk with them?
First of all, I hope and pray that they will recover and regain consciousness. And then I will tell them that despite what happened to them, they should know that they were not injured for nothing. They were injured because their bodies were protecting other people from the bomb, and they have the merit of saving other people. They should be proud of what they did.

CHAPTER V

IN GOD WE TRUST

In Ethiopia, faithful adherence to the Torah is what gave the Beta Israel their Jewish identity and connection to Israel. The rest of Jewry, however, approached the Beta Israel as a Diaspora community in need of education.

In the sixteenth century, Rabbi David Ben Abi Zimra of Cairo (1479–1573), known as "the Radbaz," issued a *halachic* response (having the force of Jewish law) declaring that "Falahsa" who came from "the land of Cush" (Ethiopia) were from the Tribe of Dan and were Jews. In that *responsa*, he also asserted that they did not follow the Oral Law (the Talmud), not because they rejected it, as did the Karaites, but because they had not been exposed to it. The Radbaz concluded from this that the Ethiopian Jews should be treated "like children who had been captured by Gentiles." That is, they needed to be educated.

In the decades following Jacques Faitlovich's visit to Ethiopia, European and North American Jews spared no effort to do just that. Jews from Europe and America tried to "normalize" Ethiopian Jewish practice, to bring it in line with rabbinic Judaism. Some Beta Israel eagerly embraced the invitation to enter a wider Jewish world, but others felt that the attitude of these well-intentioned Westerners was patronizing and insulting. They felt they were being asked to abandon

a tradition that had kept them together and served as the foundation of their lifestyle for centuries. In their village life, everyone followed these practices and traditions; the concept of a "secular Jew" did not exist. Everyone was religious because there was no other way of life in the Jewish villages. Yet when Ethiopians entered Israel as new immigrants, they were asked to take a ten-month course on how to be Jews, Israeli style.

The large-scale immigration of Ethiopian Jews began in 1984, just over two decades ago, and thus it is no surprise that Ethiopian Jewish practice in Israel is in transition. Their allegiance to their own tradition and a strong desire to integrate with Israeli-style practice has introduced a profound tension, one that resolves into a diffuse spectrum of practices. At present, there are seventeen ordained (Orthodox) Ethiopian rabbis, one ordained Conservative rabbi, and many Ethiopians in *yeshivot* (religious schools) who are studying to become rabbis. At the same time, there are approximately fifty to sixty *kessim* (priests), most trained in Ethiopia, and perhaps a dozen

On Friday afternoon before the Sabbath, in front of an Ethiopian synagogue in Ashkelon, two religious boys study their texts. The book cover of Natan (on right) charmingly expresses the two worlds he inhabits. The Amharic text on the right reads, "These are the Ten Commandments. The Wise Priest, Kess Malke Azariah Melkamu Eyob. What you have studied, you must learn." On the other cover, Natan has written in Hebrew, "Natan Isyassu, the coolest dude in Ashkelon."

young students who are learning the Ge'ez liturgy and customs.

There are thirteen Ethiopian synagogues in Israel. They have a traditional Ethiopian Sabbath service, typically beginning at four in the morning and ending around eight or nine. In many synagogues, an Israeli-style service follows in the same sanctuary, using a standard Hebrew prayer book. The ark usually contains both the Orit (the Ge'ez translation of the Torah bound as a book) and, if the congregation can afford it, a Torah scroll. In addition to observing the Sabbath and biblical holidays, there are a variety of fast days and readings from Ethiopian religious texts that are part of the synagogue ritual. Purim and Hanukkah, which are not mentioned in the Torah, were not observed in Ethiopia, but most Ethiopian Israelis observe them now.

Personal practice, too, reflects the transitional nature of Ethiopian Judaism in Israel, as the interviews in this chapter reveal. Many religious Ethiopians who have kept their own traditions have also adopted Israeli customs and rituals, such as blessing the wine by reciting the *Kiddush* on Friday night and attaching a mezuzah to their doorways. At home, even the *kessim* often mix Hebrew blessings from the rabbinic tradition with Ge'ez blessings so that their children will understand both. While some are solidly in one camp or the other, many religious Ethiopian Israelis create their own highly personal blend of rabbinic and traditional Ethiopian Judaism.

There are two prominent holidays that are unique to the Ethiopian community. Ethiopian Jews continue to observe the annual Sigd, which in Ethiopia was a day-long mountaintop festival that commemorated the receiving of the Torah and the renewing of the centuries-old dream of going to Jerusalem. Based on the book of Nehemia, the annual festival is observed forty-nine days after Yom Kippur and attracts as many as 25,000 people to Ramat Rachel. Ethiopian Israelis also observe Yom Hazkarah, a commemoration they created in 1985 to memorialize the 4,000 to 5,000 Beta Israel who perished while making *aliyah* through Sudan. Ethiopian Jewish practice in Israel merits a book of its own, for the likelihood is high that the expression of rituals and observances during this transitional time will disappear within a few generations.

The core values of Ethiopian Judaism—to summarize what I gleaned from my conversations with the *kessim* and others—are fourfold. First is the belief in one God and that Jerusalem is their true spiritual homeland. Second is the supreme importance of keeping the Sabbath. Third, the laws of purity, which require strict separation from the ritually impure and from the non-Jewish world, are of profound importance. Finally, there is the centrality of the *kessim* as the community's spiritual authorities and leaders. While the first two of these values are entirely consistent with rabbinic Judaism and

have melded easily with Israeli practice, the laws of purity and the status of the *kessim* have been less of a fit.

Village life in rural Ethiopia was conducive to keeping the laws of purity. The villages were usually situated next to a river, making it easy and natural to observe the frequently required ritual cleansing through immersion in water (the *mikveh*). In fact, one of the epithets Christians often used to refer to the Beta Israel was "People Who Smell of Water." Conditions requiring the separation of women were menstruation and childbirth. Each village had its menstrual and childbirth hut (*margam bet,* literally, blood hut) to separate women from men, following the commandments in Leviticus (12:1–8). In contrast, the high-rise apartments of Israel's larger cities, where most Ethiopian Jews live, do not allow for separation of women from men, although many creative accommodations have been made as the interviews in this chapter will show.

The status of the *kess* is perhaps the most difficult of the adjustments for traditional Ethiopian Israelis. Twenty-eight-year-old Sirak Sabahat expressed it well: "I am very angry about the status of the *kessim*. It is because of them that we are here. Without them, we could not have kept Judaism; and they are the ones who told us, 'This is the time to make *aliyah*.' But they have no power and authority in Israel."[1]

Like the Conservative and Reform rabbis of the West, the *kessim* have been disempowered by the rabbinate's attitude that there can only be one "true" Judaism. The *kessim* cannot preside over Jewish marriages or funerals, although they are allowed to participate with the consent of the officiating rabbi. While individual Orthodox rabbis support the Ethiopian religious authorities with heart and soul, the rabbinate as an institution is a rigid gatekeeper of "official" Judaism. By refusing to subsidize newly trained *kessim*, as they do rabbis, the Ministry of Religion has delivered a potentially fatal blow to the future of Ethiopian Judaism.

Despite their lack of endorsement, the *kessim* are revered and in high demand. My interviews with them were frequently rescheduled or cancelled altogether because they were so often called away for weddings, funerals, visits with the sick, and solving various community problems. As we heard from many interview subjects, the overwhelming majority of Ethiopians would choose to be married or buried by a *kess* rather than by a rabbi.

Despite a pessimistic prognosis for the future, Ethiopian Jewish practice in the first decade of the twenty-first century is lively and fascinating. In this time of transition, there is a variety of styles of observance and degrees of interacting with rabbinic Judaism. In the following pages, Ethiopian rabbis and *kessim* talk about their Jewish practices and how they are dealing with the challenges of transition during this critical time.

"When we came to Israel, the rabbinate told us that there are a few things we 'forgot,' that we

didn't have a chance to learn in Ethiopia. We didn't like that way of talking to us. I don't feel that I have to add

anything to my Jewish practice. . . . There is not even one Ethiopian synagogue in Bet Shemesh,

where there are more than a hundred families." —Kess Hadane

Rabbi Hadane and Kess Hadane

"What I believe is that our coming to Israel in Operation Moses and Operation Solomon are miracles.

For us to come out of Sudan [in 1984], which had no formal relationship to Israel, was a miracle.

For us to come out of Ethiopia during the cruel regime of Haile Mariam Mengistu [in 1991], was also a big miracle,

like the parting of the Red Sea. In that operation, Israel brought more than 14,000 people from Ethiopia in only

thirty-six hours. Every single person had food to eat and a place to sleep. There were people here in Israel to help every

one of them. This was our exodus. This is what I teach at our family's Passover.

So I say, after Hashem did such a miracle for us, what is our obligation, how do we thank God for this miracle?

What is our obligation to Israel, after what Israel did for us?" —Rabbi Yosef Hadane

Seated in the rabbinical office of Bet Shemesh, Kess Hadane is seated between two of his sons in a warm family portrait. This iconic moment drew us deeply into a poignant social and religious reality. Kess Hadane, once in charge of twenty-five synagogues in the large Jewish town of Ambover, does not have access to an Ethiopian synagogue for his own Sabbath worship. Instead, he assists the rabbi of a local Israeli synagogue and prays Israeli-style. Yet his children thrive in the Promised Land, distinguishing themselves in pursuits denied to the older generation. Emanuel (on left) is a captain in the army, and Rabbi Yosef, educated in the rabbinical school of Turin, Italy, during the 1970s, is the chief rabbi of the Ethiopian Jewish community in Israel. We had scheduled the interview only with Kess Hadane and Rabbi Yosef. Captain Emanuel was a surprise and welcome visitor, but without permission ahead of time from the Army Spokesperson's Office, we could not interview him.

In the 1960s, Yosef Hadane, the son of a respected religious leader, was a teenager with an aptitude for learning. At the time, some of the most advanced thinkers in the Beta Israel community, such as Yona Bogale and Shmuel Beri, were attempting to connect their own tradition with rabbinic Judaism. Thus the talented Yosef was selected to attend rabbinical school in Turin, Italy. Because his father, Kess Hadane, was open-minded and trusted the people who were taking his son from Ethiopia, he sent Yosef with his blessings. Yosef's mission was to become a rabbi and return to Ethiopia to teach the Beta Israel community how the rest of the Jewish world practices. But by the time he graduated with a rabbinical degree, civil war had broken out in Ethiopia. The Marxists were poised to overthrow Emperor Haile Selassie, and it was unsafe for Yosef to return. He was advised to go to Israel instead, and so he emigrated in 1972, when there were perhaps a few dozen Ethiopian Jews in Israel.

He has been a fortuitous choice to represent rabbinic Judaism to the incoming Beta Israel. He is not only a religious scholar, but also an affable communicator, fluent in five languages, and politically astute. Over the next twenty years, Rabbi Yosef facilitated the

aliyah of thousands of Ethiopian Jews, including his father and their extended family in 1985, and he helped create some of the unifying aspects of Ethiopian Jewish life in Israel, such as the annual Sigd festival in Jerusalem. In 1992, the rabbinate appointed Rabbi Yosef to be chief rabbi of the Ethiopian community. His role is both powerful and subtle. The burden of official work is enormous. For example, he must approve every marriage involving an Ethiopian bride and groom to ensure their Jewish identity and that they are not related. More broadly, Rabbi Yosef needs to help the community transition to the inevitable future while respecting and including the past he shares with them. His original mission as a rabbinical student in Italy is being fulfilled, but in Israel rather than in Ethiopia.

Rabbi Yosef, do you feel now that the relationship between the rabbinate and the kessim *is a healthy one?*
Rabbi Yosef: There is a big gap between the *kessim* and the rabbinate, very little communication. Some *kessim* cooperate with the rabbinate and are willing to learn more about Judaism than they had a chance to learn in Ethiopia. But I cannot say all the *kessim* accept

halacha [rabbinic Jewish law]. My father, though, has always been willing to learn more and to be in touch with everyone.

Kess Hadane, what do you do for religious observance without an Ethiopian synagogue? What do you do on Shabbat?
Kess Hadane: I go to the Israeli synagogue and we pray in Hebrew, not Ge'ez. I was a respected religious leader and in charge of twenty-five synagogues in Ambover. Here I am only allowed to assist a rabbi in one synagogue. There is not even an Ethiopian synagogue in Bet Shemesh, where there are more than a hundred families.

Rabbi Yosef, why is there is no Ethiopian synagogue for your father or the families in Bet Shemesh?
Rabbi Yosef: As the chief rabbi of Ethiopian Jews, I believe there must be synagogues for the Ethiopians, just as there are for the Yemenites, the Ashkenazim, and so on. If they do not have their own synagogues, then not all the people will go to pray. They will not participate because they don't understand Hebrew well enough, and for them to go and sit and not understand for several hours is very disappointing. In Bet Shemesh, I tried to get the mayor to give his full support to the community, but he will not.

In Ashkelon, there are three Ethiopian synagogues. In Ramle, there are also three.

What does the mayor say is the reason he does not approve?
Rabbi Yosef: I don't know exactly why. I spoke with the chief rabbi of Bet Shemesh about this, and we decided to meet the mayor together and listen to his reasons. But still, I really don't know why.

Kess Hadane, what was Fasika *[Passover] like in your village in Ethiopia?*
Kess Hadane: The synagogue was close to my house and all the people would come there to celebrate together. We would eat together, sing, pray, and celebrate. It was something we all did as a community. We had our own Book of Pesach, which explains the Passover story from the Torah, but we did not have the Hagaddah.

Rabbi Yosef: What I recall is that we would pray in the synagogue, and afterwards they would bless and eat the matzah. The family would make matzah, or we would get it from Israel. Before we received matzah from Israel, the Ethiopian Jews practiced animal sacrifice. They would slaughter a sheep. But in Ambover they stopped this in the mid-1900s due to the influence of Dr. Jacques Faitlovich, who taught that we were forbidden to sacrifice outside of the Temple. The Jews of Ambover stopped this practice, but elsewhere in the villages around Ethiopia the sacrifices of sheep continued [into the 1970s in some villages].

Kess Hadane, how do you observe Pesach in your family now that you are in Israel? Are you all together for one seder [Passover meal]?
Kess Hadane: Yes, I have several sons here, and we all prepare Pesach for the extended family, which, if you include everyone, even the little children, is more than 200 people.

Rabbi Yosef: My father and I both lead the seder. We all organize the food and reserve the hall. My father does the Ethiopian prayers in Ge'ez and I use the Hagaddah. We explain to everyone who is there about the Exodus from Egypt. In the next afternoon, we gather again until *ma'ariv* [evening prayers] and we learn. The adults and children ask whatever they want to about the story.

I would like to ask both of you if you are comfortable with the decision of the government to accept the Falas Mura into Israel as Jews.

Kess Hadane: I want them to come, but the people who organized the compound in Addis Ababa have brought in some who are not Jews. They did not always know who was Jewish. That was a problem. We want our people to come, but I think there are some who go through the conversion ceremony and still don't follow Judaism when they finish.

Rabbi Yosef: Those who came from the Jewish tribe, the Beta Israel, should come even if they were living a different lifestyle [as Christians]. Even though most of them are descended from Jewish families, they should do the conversion ceremony because they have been living as Christians. Of course, if there is intermarriage with Christians, then the Christian must do the full conversion. You see, *Yisrael al-fa pisha ka ta yisrael:* "Even if you sin, Jewish people are still Jewish." That's what we decided.

Once they come to Israel, we have to help them no matter who they are. The problem is that the government hears that some people come here who are not Jewish, so they bring only a few hundred a month. If the government was convinced that all of them are from Jewish families, I think they would bring them at a faster rate.

What is the process now for the Falas Mura to be recognized as Jews?

Rabbi Yosef: It is called Return to Judaism. They study Judaism and Hebrew, they go to the *mikveh* [ritual bath], and the men are circumcised if necessary. If they are already circumcised, it was not necessarily done by Jews in a way that is correct, so they have to do it symbolically by taking a drop of blood. The studying and Return to Judaism process takes one year.

What is the process for an Ethiopian couple to get approval for a Jewish marriage?

Rabbi Yosef: I have to confirm that the individuals are Jewish and that they are not related by blood as cousins. To do that, I research their family tree seven generations back. I start with where they were born. From knowing where they were born, I can tell almost 90 percent of what I need to know. Then I ask the parents, uncles, cousins, and the neighbors. Sometimes it's clear, or I already know them because I did the tree for another family member. Other times it takes a long time. I keep my own list. The difficulty with Ethiopian Jews is that it was an oral culture and there were no written documents. There are about 250 to 300 marriages a year that come through my office, but couples can go to their local rabbinical offices too. But these also come to me for approval.

Do you ever refuse a couple?

Rabbi Yosef: Yes, I do. When this happens, they are upset and angry. If I tell them it's because one of them is not Jewish, they have to convert. Whether they do is up to them. Otherwise, I cannot approve it. Then they cannot have a Jewish wedding in Israel.

Kess Hadane, how has the meaning of the Sigd festival changed now that you are in Israel?

Kess Hadane: The meaning that it had in Ethiopia was to make it possible for us to return to Jerusalem. We are still not in the Temple, so we are now praying to rebuild the Temple and also praying for a greater acceptance of our people in Israel. There is an additional purpose now—a competition for status among the Ethiopians who speak at the observance.

Rabbi Yosef, in the future do you think the Ethiopian practice of Judaism will disappear?

Rabbi Yosef: We came to Israel because we are Jews; we believe in one God, the same as all other Jews. Israel is for all of us. We all have to go in the same direction, with the same beliefs. There must be as many rabbis as possible from our own community, and we have to be represented in every field, every kind of job. We must see ourselves as equal to everyone else. This is the only way we will have real integration.

"To become a *kess,* you must remain a virgin until you are married. Being married is a requirement for

becoming a *kess,* but it is not necessary for being a rabbi. The preparation of kosher meat is also different.

Most religious Ethiopian families only eat meat slaughtered by a *kess.*

We accept what Ethiopian rabbis teach because it is based on the Torah, but that does not mean that

they fulfill the requirement of becoming a *kess.*" —Kess Legalem

Kess Legalem and Kess Adissu

"Today, our children are good people, and we hope that they will continue to respect their parents, their tradition,

and their religion. As to the future, only God knows! How would we know? We have about fifteen

students who are preparing to become *kessim*. If we keep teaching them, they will follow our path. But our students are

not getting the support they need in order to replace us when our time is up.

The government will not support them as religious leaders [as they do rabbis]. Looking at the future,

he who wants to keep his religion will keep it, and he who does not want to will lose it.

It is up to the individual to follow his religion and tradition." —Kess Adissu

Kess Legalem and Kess Adissu were spiritual leaders together in Ethiopia and, after they made *aliyah* in 1991, they became co-leaders of an Ethiopian synagogue in Yavneh, a town that is home to 450 Ethiopian families. Trained traditionally in Semien Minata, Ethiopia, they were schooled by monks, holy men who lived monastic lives remote from secular concerns. Before coming to Israel, these *kessim* had an Ethiopian Jewish practice so traditional that it included the sacrifice of animals. Their modern synagogue in Yavneh, which also functions as a community center, was built in 2003. On Shabbat, about 150 worshippers gather in the oval-shaped sanctuary on the second floor. The traditional service begins at four in the morning.

The two *kessim*, surrounded by religious elders and some younger students, lead the chanting of the prayers in Ge'ez. After a four-hour service, the traditional worshippers sit at long tables in a social hall downstairs for an *oneg shabbat* of round, fluffy breads, spicy bean dip, soda, and *tela* (homemade beer). The *kessim* sit at the head table with their families and bless the breads, tearing off pieces for everyone present. During the *oneg*, part of the Torah portion is read in Amharic by one of the men in the congregation. At the same time, an Israeli-style service begins upstairs for a younger generation of teenagers and twenty-year-olds. A few of the twenty-something age group pray in both the Ethiopian traditional and Israeli services.

"Among the Falas Mura, there are devoted Jews who keep their Jewishness, but we also know some people

come here to improve their lives. It is God's responsibility to filter them out. You cannot say to these people, 'Go back.'

Maybe God has brought them to Israel for a reason. If He doesn't want them, He Himself will return them.

We are humans, so we cannot be the judge of others." —Kess Legalem

Rabbi Eliad Senbatu

"In our classes we teach them about the Sabbath, family purity, about faith, the dietary laws,

and about the entire world of Torah. They go through a very comprehensive program for ten or eleven months. The

language problem is difficult, but we are very principled about the fact that they must recite the blessings in Hebrew.

We let them pray in Amharic for about two months, and then we switch to Hebrew.

Of course, some were living as Christians in Ethiopia because their families were affected by anti-Semitism.

There are rumors of some immigrants who return to being Christian after they study,

but I have never come across it myself. It must be very rare."

Seated here in an academic office of the absorption center in Mevaseret Tzion, Rabbi Eliad Senbatu is surrounded by Jewish learning, and it is his job to communicate it to a challenging group of students. Rabbi Eliad is one of four teachers of Jewish studies for 1,500 new immigrants in the largest of the twenty-five absorption centers for Ethiopians. Many of his students know little Hebrew. Some lived as Christians in Ethiopia until they reached the NACOEI-operated schools of Gondar or Addis Ababa, where their reunion with Judaism and initial Hebrew studies began. To be effective, he must strike the right balance between sensitivity to the immigrants' background and the strict standards of the rabbinate. He is the one who accompanies a family to the *Bet Din* (the Court of Jewish Law) where their knowledge is tested. He brings them to the *mikveh* (ritual bath) and supervises the *hatafat dam* (symbolic circumcision), ushering the whole family into their new identity as Jewish citizens of Israel.

After three years living in hiding with his family in Gedarif, Sudan, Eliad Senbatu, then fourteen years old, was secretly brought to Israel with his brother by the Mossad. The rest of the family joined them months later. Eliad was brought to an absorption center near Afula where he and his peers were visited by students from a local yeshiva. It was there that he first thought about becoming a rabbi. After graduating from a religious boarding school, he chose to attend a yeshiva near Ashkelon and was ordained in 1997. He is acutely aware of the transition that awaits the new immigrants he is assigned to teach and their reluctance to give up their lifestyle. Even his parents and siblings remain traditional Ethiopians. Rabbi Eliad is unable to follow many of the traditions he grew up with, such as kissing his sisters on both cheeks, because physical contact with women, even immediate family, is forbidden by his practice. He says his family is proud of what he is doing and has adjusted. Each day he teaches his own practice to new immigrants.

After the immigrants study Judaism, are they tested on their understanding?
There is a summons to the *Bet Din* [the religious court]. I go with them. The rabbis on the court ask questions, and not simple ones, about matters of faith, blessings, prayers, family purity, and proper preparation of the kitchen and food. After that is the *mikveh* [ritual immersion in water], and then there is circumcision for those who need it. If he doesn't need it, there is a *hatafat dam* [literally, a drop of blood, a symbolic circumcision when there is doubt about the religious correctness of the original circumcision].

Are there people who fail the test of the Bet Din?
Of course. They must then study a number of months longer and then go back. Here in Mevaseret Tzion we receive a very high mark for our classes because rarely do they have to come back.

What is the most important thing the rabbinate or Israeli society can do to improve the well-being of the Ethiopian community here in Israel?
Education. Without education there won't be religious people. Our youth will return to religion if they have the knowledge. I would really prefer the state to emphasize the education of the children.

What about the need to educate Israeli society about the Ethiopian community?

I believe that this will come with time. The *aliyah* is part of history. The Ministry of Education can't escape from the issue of the *aliyah* of the Ethiopian Jews. This can enter into the education system and create an awareness and ability to see the Ethiopian Jews in a different way then they are seen today.

From your rabbinic point of view, how do you feel about the 15,000 or so Falas Mura waiting to be taken to Israel? Should they be brought? Are they Jews in your opinion?
Anyone who wants to be Jewish and is connected to the seed of Israel [by family relationship with the Beta Israel], we can't close the gate on those people. Our goal here is to let them in if they are Jewish. In Ethiopia most of us didn't know what we had inside of us [our ancestry]. We certainly have to check. That's what the Ministry of Interior does. If they are coming to improve their living conditions, then that is not relevant. I came as a child on foot through Sudan, and we did not know anything about the conditions in Israel. But the Falas Mura know everything now. Still, you cannot determine if they are coming to improve their lives or because they are Jews and their families are here. You cannot measure their intentions.

As a rabbi, do you participate in Ethiopian religious events such as the annual Sigd festival?
Of course, but the Sigd is not an Ethiopian invention; its origins are in the books of Ezra and Nehemiah. Its meaning is to strengthen the religion, to renew the covenant, to prevent mixed marriages, and to maintain the religious law that we had there. Of course I am at the Sigd every year. It is not something that is against the *halacha* [rabbinic Jewish law]; it's a tradition. [Other meanings have been attributed to Sigd beyond those Rabbi Eliad mentions here. These are noted in the introduction to this chapter.]

How is Yom Hazkarah observed in the Ethiopian community? Is it accepted as a holiday by the rabbinate, or is it only for the Ethiopian community?
It is for the Ethiopian community. I don't think there is a day of remembrance for those who died on the way in Sudan for the general Israeli public. It's not a national holiday. But when we march, some Israelis come on their own accord. About 10,000 to 15,000 people attend, maybe 200 [native] Israelis. Some leading rabbis attend and give a talk. It has been in Ramat Rachel [a kibbutz outside of Jerusalem] but I would like it to be on Mount Herzl, like an official national holiday.

In Ramat Rachel, we say the memorial prayer, *el maleh rahamim la-neshamoy she-nispu baderech,* and it gives us the feeling that we didn't forget those who perished on the way. They are with us.

Why doesn't the rabbinate give the kessim *some official authority?*
Because we will have a problem of *halacha*. To permit a *kess* to sanctify a marriage or a divorce or to allow him to certify what is kosher, according to *halachic* parameters—they would lack the knowledge of the world of the oral Torah, of the things that have been changed [through the influence of the Talmud]. But not all the *kessim* have the attitude "We don't want to change." I know of one *kess* who studied and became a rabbi.

In the future, will the Ethiopian community practice Judaism according to halacha, *or will some Ethiopian Jews continue to maintain their own traditions?*
Twenty years ago we didn't think there were going to be any changes. There was a lot of anger about the lack of status for the *kessim*, and the entire community was angry and resisting. Today, they are not angry. Today, if you have *halachic* issues or questions, you go to the rabbis. Today, in practice, I think most of the community follows *halacha*.

Kess Shimon Meherat Elias

"In the synagogue, we recite a *Kiddush* [a sanctifying blessing] on bread, not on the wine like the Israelis.

It emphasizes the blessing of the Sabbath and the Ten Commandments. There are younger Ethiopians who do the

blessing on lighting the candles and the *Kiddush* over wine at home. What I do is a *Kiddush* in Hebrew over the wine,

but then I do a *Kiddush* on the bread in Ge'ez from our tradition.

I combine these traditions for the children, to integrate them, so they know both."

Among the roughly sixty *kessim* (priests) in the Ethiopian community, only a few were trained in Israel. One of them, Kess Shimon Meherat Elias, age thirty-four, leads a synagogue in Rishon Letzion, home to 900 Ethiopian families. A simple two-room community center serves as a synagogue where seventy to eighty worshippers gather each week for Sabbath services. When we met, it had only been six months since this modest building was first used for worship. Weather permitting, they pray outside because the room isn't large enough to hold the congregation. The ark contains the Orit (the Bible in Ge'ez) and the Chumash (five books of Moses in Hebrew), but this congregation cannot afford a Torah scroll. As in most Ethiopian synagogues, the first service is traditional Ethiopian, in Amharic and Ge'ez; the second is from the Hebrew prayer book. Israel's policy toward *kessim* presents Kess Shimon with a personal challenge. The Ministry of Religion pays a base salary, as it does to congregational rabbis, to *kessim* who were trained before 1992, but Kess Shimon became a *kess* after that and thus does not receive any financial support. More than any other policy, this one undermines the future continuity of Ethiopian Jewish practice. Kess Shimon supports himself in part by working with Ethiopian families on behalf of the Joint Distribution Committee.

In 1984, Shimon Meherat Elias, still in his early teens, left his village on foot with his family for Israel, but it took them more than three years to get there. Their journey was circuitous and eventful. Soon after starting out, they paused along the way in Wolkiet to mourn the death of his aunt. During the thirty-day mourning period, they met Ethiopian Jews fleeing from the refugee camps in Sudan who told of deaths from disease and frightening stories that some Jews had been kidnapped and sold into slavery. While they deliberated about continuing, the religious leader in a nearby village died. Shimon's father, Kess Meherat, was asked to lead the mourning for him; afterwards, the village asked him to stay and fill the vacancy of leadership. Shimon's family remained there for more than two years, until Kess Meherat decided they should resume their original journey. But by that time the route to Israel via Sudan had been closed. Still, as Kess Shimon recalls it, "We decided to go and whatever happens, happens." In our conversation, Kess Shimon spoke in detail about how Ethiopian Jewish practice differs from rabbinic practice.

Do you remember how your father reacted when you first arrived in Israel and realized that your people might not be able to keep their own religious traditions?

After all the stories we heard about Jerusalem, our dream was to get to Israel, to be more righteous, to be more holy. This was what kept us going on our journey. The gap between the expectation and the reality was very difficult. The dream was shattered. For my parents' generation, and for a lot of adults to this day, they can't understand what is happening here in Israel—the idea of secular and religious, that there is such a thing as a Jew who doesn't keep Shabbat and holidays! And the issue of purity, that there isn't *nida* [a time of ritual impurity], that there is no separation of the ritually impure from the synagogue—all that is very difficult for them.

When do you read Te'ezaza Sanbat [Commandments of the Sabbath, written centuries ago by Ethiopian Jews]?

In principle, you should read it every Shabbat, but it is very long, so we can't. We have both the Hebrew and the Amharic services, so we can't add more text. *Te'ezaza Sanbat* has in it the laws of the Sabbath. *Te'ezaza* means "law," the same as *halacha*. In my congregation, I read it on holidays when there are a lot of people there. Each *kess* decides when he needs to transmit its message, to preach from it to the public.

How is the Ethiopian brit milah [circumcision] different from the ceremony in rabbinic Judaism?

In Ethiopia, women would do the circumcision because the mother still had to be in *nida* [seclusion for reasons of ritual purity]. Israelis do the *brit* in a hall as a more festive event and invite guests, and there are some Ethiopians who follow this. But in synagogues where there are traditional Ethiopians, you don't do a *brit* there, and the *kessim* cannot participate. Only after forty days seclusion of the mother is there is a celebration.

How is the separation of the new mother practiced on a daily basis by Ethiopians in Israel?

Those who keep these traditions usually have a special room inside the house, and they give the room to the woman who has given birth [the *yoledet*]. She stays there. If you have a circumcision, you do it in that room with a limited number of people. When the wife of a *kess* gives birth, the *kess* sometimes has a ground-floor apartment with a separate entrance to the room from an external door. So they have a kind of

bet nida [house of separation] as we did in Ethiopia. If they have no separate room for her, they have her stay with a different family where there is room. The women who maintain the tradition stay in that one room. They don't cook; they don't do any work. They recruit relatives or the husband to do everything in the kitchen and the home.

After the fortieth day, or after the eightieth day if it's a girl, there is what we call *erdet* [sacred water]. There are verses that are taken from the Torah and from Ge'ez scriptures. You bless the water and spray or splash it in the entire house. It is taken from the book of *Vayikra* [Leviticus] plus a few other sections of the Torah. What is written is that after the time of purification, the woman must offer two sacrifices. Since she can't offer sacrifices today, we use the water, the *erdet*, to purify the house and the woman.

Why did the other Jewish communities not maintain the commandments in the Torah as strictly as Ethiopians did?

I can't be pretentious and say what the reasons are. I think maybe modernization won.

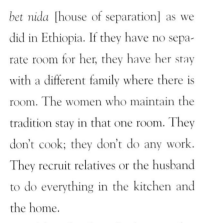

Maybe the more advanced you are, the more you try to adapt religion to the technology, to the advancement of life. Some Ethiopian Jews come to me and say, "You are in Israel, you need to adapt yourself to Israel, to the customs, to the religion, to the culture, to the mentality." I say to them that the religion has been, is true now, and will also be in the future. It doesn't change. The Torah has been, is true now, and will be in the future. The Torah doesn't change just because you change where you live.

What is the attitude of the kessim *toward Ethiopians who have become ordained rabbis?*

The attitude toward them is a sense of betrayal, not because they learn from the rabbis, and not because they learn the Gemara or the Mishna and become rabbis. That's not the problem. The problem is that they actually aren't willing to accept the guidance from the *kessim*. They don't even want to eat what the *kessim* butcher [i.e., do not consider the meat kosher], and this infuriates us a lot.

Are there any Ethiopians who believe that if God enabled the Ethiopians to come to Israel, his intention was for them to adapt to Israeli custom?

No, absolutely not. And I'll tell you why. As I said earlier, the issue of religion, of Torah, it doesn't have borders and it reaches every aspect of life and is eternal. You can't take what you preserved—keeping the Sabbath, the laws of purity—and go backwards instead of trying to be more righteous. Of course, you must integrate yourself with technology—study and get an education, be involved in society, and so forth—but without giving up on the issue of your religion. Religion is a personal matter, a matter of faith, a faith you can't erase.

Rabbi Yefet Alemu

"In 1985, I was leading a demonstration against the government because they were not bringing our families here like they do for every other Jewish immigrant group. Students from the Solomon Schechter Institute of Jewish Studies arrived to show support for us. I asked them, 'Who are you? What do you do?' They said, 'We are learning.'

So I asked, 'What are you learning?' They said, 'We are learning to become rabbis.' I said, 'You don't have black clothing, how can you be a rabbi?' I was joking with them, of course. They explained, 'No, we are a different kind of rabbi,' and they invited me to the Schechter Institute. At the Institute, when I told them what I did in my Jewish practice in Ethiopia, they showed me these things in the *Tanach* [Jewish scriptures: Torah, Prophets, and Writings].

I talked about Shabbat, when we did not work or light fires, and when a woman was menstruating, she was outside the home in a special hut for seven days. All this, they showed me, was in the *Tanach*. They said, 'You are showing us what our ancestors were doing in the time of the First Temple.' This was very affirming, very supportive."

▪

As a young boy in Ethiopia, Yafet Alemu spent his childhood in training to become a *kess*, like his father and grandfather. However, at fourteen he did something almost unheard of for an Ethiopian Jewish child—he rebelled and asked to leave religious school. Many years later in Israel, his independent nature asserted itself again, and in 2000 he became Israel's first Ethiopian Conservative rabbi. Rabbi Yafet is full of passion, energy, and idealistic visions for the future of his community. He is without a congregation, not surprisingly since Conservative Ethiopian Jews are very rare. Trained in medicine in Ethiopia, Yafet works as a nurse at Hadassah Hospital to support his wife and two daughters. He fulfills his role as rabbi by counseling Ethiopian families on education and raising funds for community centers, which he feels are necessary to keep Ethiopian youth out of trouble. This photo of Yafet was taken on the rooftop of the Mandel Leadership Institute in Jerusalem from which he graduated.

As a teenager, Yafet Alemu challenged parental expectations and abandoned his religious training for a secular education. A talented student, his academic record earned him the opportunity to enroll in medical school in Addis Ababa at age twenty. It was a time when many Ethiopians were fleeing the repressive Mengistu regime, and after two years, Yafet left school to make *aliyah*. Carrying a strategic "student visa" to study in the United States, Yafet planned to use America as a passageway to Israel, but he aroused suspicion and was stopped at the airport. Instructed to report to the authorities the next day, Yafet assumed he would have to surrender his passport and visa. Instead, he left by bus for the Sudanese border, risking a jail term or worse if he had been caught. Eventually he crossed into Sudan and met an Israeli operative who found him a flight to Israel.

After five years of study at the Solomon Schechter Institute for Jewish Studies in Jerusalem, Yafet was ordained the first conservative Ethiopian rabbi in the year 2000. Yafet faces a difficult challenge. The religious Ethiopians are either Orthodox or practice their own traditional Judaism.

Given his unorthodox perspective, leading a congregation is going to be nearly impossible. Yafet tries to accomplish his goals in his own unique way, as he explains during our conversation.

How did things change for you in Israel religiously?
When I first came to Israel I was religious. But after I was here for a while, I left religion because of the fighting. Also, the rabbinate asked us to have a "conversion." When I was in Ethiopia, people used to look down on us and say, "You're Falasha, you're Jewish." After praying to come to Jerusalem, I arrived here and people were telling me I'm not a Jew, I'm not a full Jew. I said to myself, "I have to stop being religious." It was very painful. But I couldn't succeed as a nonbeliever. I realized I was unhappy not being religious.

The rabbinate has a problem accepting someone who is different. Most of our older people are still religious, even though they have a big problem with the [Orthodox] rabbis. But the younger people have left religion. Not only did they leave religion, most of the time they hate religion. For example, Ethiopian students go to religious boarding schools. They teach them rabbinic Judaism. They tell the students, "What you know about Judaism from Ethiopia is meaningless." When a child hears that, he is just praying to finish that school and throw his *kippah* away. We have a problem here.

You've told us how supportive the Conservative rabbinical school was toward your background. What does the Ethiopian community, and your family, think about your becoming a Conservative rabbi?
I think the majority of the Ethiopian community doesn't know the difference between these movements in Judaism. When I studied at the Schechter Institute, I learned about Conservative, Orthodox, Reform, and many other groups. I never knew there was such hatred between different Jewish groups. An Orthodox rabbi once said to me, "I prefer to talk to Palestinians rather than with Conservative rabbis!" There is not any logic to that. It's terrible.

Without a congregation, how are you making use of your rabbinic training?
I feel I have a mission in this world. When I traveled from Ethiopia up to Sudan, it was a time of examination. The problem was not only physical, it was also inside. God was with me, helping me. Five thousand people died on that journey, and I survived. It means that

there's a reason I'm here. He [God] drives me. I have a lot of things inside me. I have a lot of motivation. I have set up a nonprofit organization, the National Movement for Equal Opportunities for Ethiopian Jewry. This organization was formed to create multidimensional community centers. It will work mostly to improve educational opportunities, but the focus will be on the family, not directed only at children. Israelis see the [Ethiopian] parents as the generation of the desert, and they forget about them and concentrate on the child. This has caused the breaking up of the family unit. My community centers will have a goal of decreasing the number of children who drop out of school, helping children improve their performance in the school, and teaching children the importance of helping others. Children should develop a sense of contributing to society. The centers will also be a place to perform music and theater and invite the surrounding community. Then the Israelis will learn about Ethiopian culture, too.

Kess Mekonen Yeheyes Yetayew

"In Ethiopia, the Beta Israel from Tigray and Gondar were friendly. We were a strong community in Tigray.

In Israel there started to be a division between the two communities because we [Tigrayans] decided to 'convert'

[undergo the symbolic circumcision, *hatafat dam*] and the Gondari Jews did not. That is why the division happened.

Our decision was made because it was written in the Torah. The Lord said to Joshua that he should circumcise

the men before he brought them into the Promised Land (Joshua 5:2). So we did it; the Gondari did not.

But now we are as one community. In my synagogue, I have Jews from Gondar praying, and also five or six

ferenjim [white Israelis] who know the Hebrew texts very well."

▪

Kess Mekonen Yeheyes Yetayew of Kiryat Gat is one of only a few *kessim* from the province of Tigray. From 1977 to 1983, Tigrayans were the first to come in large numbers to Israel through Sudan, but the Jews from the neighboring Gondar province now represent 85 to 90 percent of the Ethiopian Israeli population. There has been talk of bad feelings between the two communities, but Kess Mekonen says that is no longer the case. He lives in a tiny fifth-floor apartment in a poorly maintained building with boarded-up windows and no lighting in the stairwells. In his living room, well-cushioned couches form a small semicircle. Kess Mekonen's circumstances are meager, but he radiates an abundance of warmth and joy, especially when he talks about his faith and religious practices. As the photos demonstrate, he never missed an opportunity to show us textual sources for his opinions.

In this photo, Kess Mekonen holds a picture from 1998, when he and his wife were waiting for a flight back to Israel from the Addis Ababa airport. Kess Mekonen has returned to Ethiopia four times to bring his wife to the Shera waterfall, which is believed to have healing powers. The oversized hundred dollar bill was given to him by a family member as a playful tribute to how much money he has spent on these trips. His wife is still not well.

Kess Avihu and Kess Malke

"We strictly follow the Torah that has been given to Moses. What we are saying is that we cannot accept a new Torah that has lost its original meaning. Our fathers did a very good job of preserving the original scripture and passing it on to us. We want to pass this scripture to the next generation without any alteration." —Kess Malke

▥

"At first, some neighbors were opposed to our building because it was going to be an Ethiopian synagogue. They even dismantled signs we posted. There was a legal battle. Since we had permission from the municipality of Ashkelon, we won the case. There were three people who left this area when we won. Now some of them throw their dirt on our lot. These people who are acting in such a way have no respect for Shabbat or Torah." —Kess Avihu

In 1993, Kess Malke Azariah and his son, Kess Avihu, brought together a small congregation for worship in an abandoned bomb shelter in Ashkelon. Through hard work and skillful fundraising in Canada, they built a handsomely appointed synagogue that attracts more than 100 worshippers every Shabbat. It is one of three synagogues serving the 6,000 Ethiopian Israelis in Ashkelon. Behind their modern sanctuary is a *tukul*-shaped hut reminiscent of the Ethiopian structure where Sabbath prayers and other community gatherings were held. Kess Malke was an esteemed religious authority in Gondar and established some twenty synagogues. His son, Kess Avihu, is adamantly traditional but also well versed in *halacha* (rabbinic Jewish law). To help support his community, he has been trained and authorized by the rabbinate to be a *shochet* (ritual slaughterer) and he supplies kosher meat to his community. Although the synagogue is filled to capacity on Shabbat, they worry about the future. Kess Avihu has several students who attend his religious classes, but so far he is far from achieving the goal of funding an institute for training new *kessim* to carry the Ethiopian Jewish tradition forward.

The synagogue of Kess Avihu and Kess Malke in Ashkelon

Because he was a well-known *kess* in Gondar, Kess Malke was offered an apartment in Ashkelon upon his arrival in Israel. Instead, he chose to move with his family to a caravan site in Nehora, which had no religious leadership. Along with his son, Kess Avihu, he established a synagogue and built a *margam bet* (blood hut) to observe the laws of purity (separation of women during menstruation and after childbirth). He remained in Nehora until the site was closed in 1993. After moving to Ashkelon, Kess Avihu and Kess Malke obtained permission to use the bomb shelter of a neighborhood apartment building for Sabbath and holiday worship. With donations from American and Canadian Jews as well as from their own community, they built a synagogue that compares well with the architecture and amenities of much wealthier communities. Most importantly to them, the seats are usually filled on Shabbat. They are also trying to achieve a more challenging goal: establishing and funding an institute for the training of new *kessim*. While most of their community is beginning to embrace rabbinic Judaism or a secular lifestyle, they are doing their best to keep Ethiopian Israelis close to their religious roots.

When you were in Ethiopia did you understand that Jewish practice was different in Israel?
Kess Malke: The language [Hebrew, rather than Ge'ez] might be different, but the Torah is the same. Yona Bogale opened a school in Ethiopia and taught us all for twelve years. We were educated to understand Judaism in Israel. And then Israeli and American Jews used to come to our synagogue, so we knew there were differences in Shabbat rituals.

Kess Avihu, what did you know about Israeli Jewish practice and Jewish life here?
Kess Avihu: There were people from Israel who came to teach in Ethiopia, but they didn't reach all of us. I was aware only that Jews in Israel pray in Hebrew and that their practices are different. Even then, we were praying to be in Jerusalem. It was our dream to come to this holy place. I always thought that this place is holy and so are the people who live in it. I used to think that people in Israel would not practice any wrongdoings.

How did you react to the realization that not everybody in Israel behaves as you expected?
Kess Malke: We pray to God that everybody will become religious and will build His Temple again.

Kess Avihu: First of all, we were very happy to

be here, but we were very sad to see all the divisions between Jews. Despite our difficulties while in Ethiopia, we strictly practiced and protected our religion. In Ethiopia, many were forced to change their religion by the government. Some people were killed for being Jewish. We lived outside cities to keep our religion away from distractions. We suffered so much to preserve the religion. Then we came here, and our Judaism was not even accepted. We [*kessim*] are still struggling to get the official status that a rabbi has.

Do you feel that there is any part of rabbinic Judaism that is valuable and helpful to the Ethiopian laws and customs?
Kess Avihu: I don't think there is anything it can add to our religious practice. We only accept what is written in the Torah. We are strongly opposed to accepting rabbinic Judaism because the rules are greatly modified by many individuals. Some people say we did not have electricity in the past, but we have it now. Similarly, there are certain things that were not part of our religion in the past, but we have them now. We shall adjust our religion so that it suits the modern ways of living. We say no. They say, "We are very suspicious of the way you lived in Ethiopia. We don't have trust that you have

practiced Judaism fully. So we urge you to convert into our form of Judaism." But the fact is we have never lived a non-Jewish lifestyle during our time in Ethiopia. Had our sons not been circumcised at the age of eight days, we would have agreed to conversion. We are determined Jewish people. We won't give up our true Jewish identity. We tell them, "You are the ones who dishonored the rules. How could you say that we are not good enough to consider ourselves Jews when you actually pray with a revised Torah [i.e., the Talmud]?"

How does your religious community feel about those Ethiopians who have become rabbis? I have heard that seventeen have been ordained.
Kess Avihu: We think of it as their profession. Individuals can pursue any kind of profession to support their families and themselves. We do not have a problem with individuals who decide to follow that path.

How well attended is this synagogue on Shabbat and holidays?
Kess Avihu: During Shabbat, both Friday night and Saturday morning, the synagogue is full. We strongly encourage young people to come. A main purpose of this synagogue is to teach the young people Ge'ez and the important practices

of our religion. We also provide for a bar mitzvah. We try to teach the boys to read the Torah in Ge'ez, but it doesn't always work. We cannot teach every boy how to read Ge'ez because of financial obstacles. All of the money we spend on this building comes out of our own pockets. We cover the everyday expenditures, including teaching materials for youngsters. For example, we have purchased a computer program that teaches children Amharic. We receive our salaries from the contributions made by our community to the synagogue.

Are you optimistic about preserving the Ethiopian style of Jewish practice?
Kess Avihu: Yes, we are very optimistic. We also want to make sure that our kids will be able to learn every aspect of our culture, language, religion, and customs and pass it on to the next

generation. But the rabbinate does not give us a role. I know ten men who have completed all the requirements to become a *kess*, but they cannot find jobs as a *kess*. They are working in construction sites to feed their families. In Israel, there are around sixty *kessim*, I think.

If the Ethiopian community could send a message to Israel or Israelis, what would you tell them?
Kess Avihu: Israelis are very nice people. When we first arrived, they welcomed us warmheartedly. They were all waving at us from their cars. After we settled, they brought food, clothing, and other good things that we do not forget. They came and visited us year after year. They encouraged us by telling us that we are among the chosen people. Although we strongly oppose the way the government treats us, we are very thankful to the people of Israel.

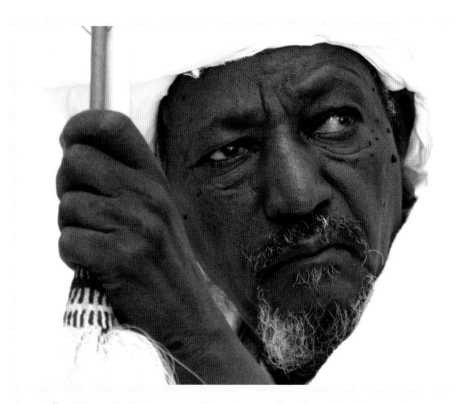

Kess Malke: We would like them to follow the original messages from the Torah. We do not want them to change the Torah in order to fulfill their individual wishes. They must follow the Torah as it was stated originally, not the new revisions.

In Ethiopia, women were separated from the community during menstruation and after childbirth. How has the community adapted this practice in Israel?

Kess Avihu: We do not keep the woman at home after childbirth. We send her to her parents or to other relatives. If people do not have a choice and cannot do this, they sometimes have a special place in their own home. It is very difficult to keep the laws of purity as they are written in the Torah, like we were able to do in Ethiopia. But we live here now.

What about the placing of a mezuzah in the doorway? Do you have one in your house?

Kess Avihu: I have one, yes, but it was already there when I moved in. We did not know about the mezuzah in Ethiopia. God's word should always be with you, and you should study it. It is not for decoration [on the door jambs]. It is not a mitzvah [commandment] to have a mezuzah.

The mezuzah derives from the Pesach story, when the children of Israel identified themselves by putting the blood of the sacrificial lamb on the doorpost. So isn't it from the Torah indirectly?

Kess Avihu: The mezuzah is from the Oral Law, Torah *ba'al peh*. There is not even one rabbi who has the same Torah *ba'al peh* as another rabbi. I took a class in this, and I have not found one rabbi who will approve another rabbi's Torah *ba'al peh*. There are no instructions for the

mezuzah in the Torah. That is why we only follow what is written in the Torah—because there is no confusion about it.

As an American, I have to ask about the American Jewish community?

Kess Avihu: The American Jewish communities are like Moses for us. They helped us with their power and money to bring us out of Ethiopia and to reach our Promised Land, just the way Moses helped the Jews in Egypt. Although the Israeli government took the initiative to give us a home, Americans were the ones who worked hard for the success of the Ethiopian Jewish community. They are still helping us. We are very grateful.

CHAPTER VI

SINGING A NEW SONG IN A NEW LAND

"Hallelujah. Sing to the Lord a new song," begins Psalm 149.

For Ethiopian Israelis, these words resonate with deep meaning. In their new home, Ethiopian Jews have an opportunity for the first time in their long history to express their individuality and originality through the arts. In the context of village life in Ethiopia, the Beta Israel were governed by the needs of their families for food, shelter, clothing, and sometimes self-defense. Artistic pursuits would have been an inconceivable luxury. As Batia Eyob expressed it, "No one woke up in the morning saying, 'I think I'll spend the day practicing singing'."[1] Among the few Ethiopian Jews in Addis Ababa, there were a handful of musicians and actors. The music was primarily functional, for example, traditional songs played at weddings and official state events. Music with artistic goals was reserved for the wealthy, and it usually came from the West. The Beta Israel were greatly admired for their pottery and weaving, but they made primarily traditional and utilitarian household artifacts.

During the 1990s, embroidery was exported by the Ethiopian Jews under the guidance of the National Conference of Ethiopian Jewry (NACOEJ). NACOEJ employed as many as 800 men and women to make colorful embroidered challah covers, *tallit* bags, and pillow cases with biblical motifs that the organization then sold to raise funds for their programs. Similar embroidery projects have been set up in Israel, for example at the Neveh Yosef Community Center in Haifa and in Beersheva. Institutions like Bahalachin also have an interest in collecting and exhibiting traditional crafts as a way to teach Israelis about Ethiopian Jewish society and to preserve cultural identity.[2]

Beyond the traditional crafts, Ethiopian artists are branching out and blossoming. Acting has become a natural outlet for many talented Ethiopian Israelis. In fact, their dramatic *aliyah* and the challenges of integration provide many opportunities for them to play themselves. A prominent example is the feature-length French film *Live and Become,* which tells the story of the *aliyah* of the 1980s and the painful feelings of rejection experienced by an Ethiopian boy, played by Sirak Sabahat. Another powerful and engaging film, *Caravan 841,* documents the *aliyah* of 1991 through the story of a young boy hiding out in an abandoned "caravan" site in the vain hope that his mother will be able to find him. An Ethiopian Israeli filmmaker, Destau Damto, focuses on the community's crises in Israel. He has made several powerful and controversial films about the loss of identity among Ethiopian youth and their desperate emulation of African Americans.

Ethiopian culture has made inroads into Israeli music through the widely popular band of Eidan Raichel, who incorporates Ethiopian singers and traditional rhythms to give his music ethnic overtones. Ethiopian musicians are also finding their own voices in the Israeli environment. One example is Abate Berihun, a jazz saxophonist who

was limited to playing weddings in Addis Ababa but now plays jazz clubs and concert halls in Israel. Another innovative musician, Yehye Shimon, expresses his personal history in music. In his home studio in Tel Aviv, he created an intriguing CD of computer-generated music, but he also returned to Ethiopia to record children singing traditional songs in the more remote villages. Traditional Ethiopian dance, known for its unique shoulder movements, has been transformed by Eskesta, a troupe created by six University of Haifa graduates. Its director, choreographer Ruth Eshel, encourages her dancers to use traditional Ethiopian movements as a starting point for creating interpretive Ethiopian Israeli dance. The results have won the Eskesta Dance Theater tours of Europe, South America, and the United States.

The Ethiopian Israeli community has a unique and powerful story to tell, and we can expect that, using the studios and stages of Israel, they will be expressing much of it through the arts.

Embroiderers

■

The women showing their handiwork in this photo—*(from left)* Molo Ketema, Tazzu D'meto, Ketma W'ndo, and Amlumal Avra—are part of an embroidery project run by the Neveh Yosef Community Center in Haifa. Created and supported by the Women's Fund of the Boston Jewish community, the embroidery project enables twenty-two women who practiced this traditional art form in Ethiopia to transplant it to Israeli soil. The funding supplies workspace, materials, and a coordinator who markets and sells their work in Israel and abroad. In four years, the project has taken root and blossomed. The colorful designs reflect a

mix of traditional themes and Jewish artifacts that were unknown to the Ethiopian Jews before they immigrated, such as *kippot* (yarmulkes) and mezuzahs.

The embroidery project is thriving to a greater extent than are the women themselves. After six years in Israel, they still find the adjustment difficult. They miss their villages and the sights and smells of the land where they grew up. With no formal schooling in their background, learning Hebrew has been a struggle. Finding employment beyond sweeping floors or cleaning hotel rooms is a challenge. But embroidering Jewish

artifacts makes them feel they are preserving their culture. The project pays them for the pieces they produce, even before they are sold, but it is not enough to offset their poverty. One of the women arrived in Haifa as a single mother with seven sons. The husbands of the other three have only occasional work in menial jobs. Of all the burdens they carry, the heaviest is that they are "sad and hurt" by the feeling that many Israelis do not see them as equals and some do not even consider them to be Jews. It was not what they expected. Nevertheless, the easy conversation and frequent laughter among the group make it clear that working together brightens their lives.

Meskie Shivru

"I got my start by writing a show for myself called *Song of the Humble People* which ran from 1994 to 1996.

I like dramatic acting and get a lot of TV series work, but what I would really like is a talk show . . . I am married to a

native Israeli whose family came from Poland. We have two children, and we live outside of Tel Aviv in a suburb.

Our families accept each other, and we have our Passover seder together every year. We are very close."

One of the first Ethiopian Israeli actors, Meskie Shivru made *aliyah* in 1985 at age seventeen, a high school graduate who had already begun an acting career in Addis Ababa. Meskie's family was openly Jewish, although she hid it from her dance and theater groups. "I fit in pretty easily," she said. "I just never ate meat." Her mother was an activist in the Beta Israel community and spent two years in jail after being caught with false passports. She came to Israel after one of her sons came back to Ethiopia to buy her release. Meskie's six brothers and sisters arrived at various times between 1981 and 1991.

Meskie is doing her best to break down the inevitable typecasting that threatens to confine her as a dramatic artist. Her recent solo show, *About Women*, played at the Beit Tami Theater in Tel Aviv to a full house. Elaborately costumed, Meskie plays ten female lead characters from famous plays. Of course, her dramatic power is undeniably enhanced when she draws on her Ethiopian identity. In a recent award-winning French film, *Live and Become*, she delivers the title line in the intense opening scene.

As Shlomo's mother, in Live and Become

Destau Damto

"A lot of people ask me if I am always going to make movies about the Ethiopian community.

My response is that I have to do what my heart tells me. What it tells me is that I see problems, like the image

on the news of the cop running after the Ethiopian teenager with no shirt on.

When I see something in the community that needs to be exposed, should I ignore it and make

an action movie or a love story?"

Destau Damto is a filmmaker driven by the social issues of his community. While still in high school, he decided to make films and began writing letters to every one of Israel's movie and television studios until he found a producer willing to take him on. Destau became a producer's assistant and worked on a talk show before being called up for the army. While serving in the IDF, he began work on his script for the critically successful and controversial docudrama *Outcry* (2003), which depicts the racial tensions between Ethiopian youth and the police. The violent conclusion leaves both groups grieving. Many Ethiopian Israelis decried the negative portrayal of their community, and the government ministries and the Jewish Agency bristled at the criticism.

For Destau, that meant success. "That is what I wanted," he says, "to wake people up."

Destau followed his debut film with *Black Music* (2005), which explores the fascination of young Ethiopian musicians with rap music and culture, revealing their illusions about their African American role models. His current projects are "Open Wound," a documentary that focuses on what really happened in the infamous Blood Scandal of 1996[3] and a new film about the struggle of the *kessim* to retain their revered status in Israel. In this photo, taken in one of the bedrooms of his mother's apartment, Destau demonstrates post-production editing of the Blood Scandal project.

Tagist Yosef

"When I was younger, I was fascinated by Israeli culture and made an effort to become as Israeli

as possible as quickly as possible. I was first in my class all the time because I was trying so hard. When I was thirteen

at boarding school, I had to make a presentation about my culture. I went to my father and started asking him some

questions and read some books about our history. I realized we have a rich culture and inspiring values,

so as an Ethiopian, I have much to be proud of."

■

When Tagist Yosef took time off from work and came by bus from Tel Aviv to meet us in Netanya, she carried with her a large portfolio of her personal work. We were moved by the many sensitive and emotional drawings. Tagist helped us understand how the Israeli environment has enabled Ethiopian Jews to explore the creative arts, originality, and self-expression. Tagist credits her father and mother with giving her the background to succeed. "When we came to this country, my father was always encouraging us to study. Education was the most important thing to him, and his own knowledge of things is very wide." Tagist's mother, who died in 1994, was a source of strength for her. "When I would come home and look into her eyes, I would see how beautiful she is and I would feel confident just because I was her daughter."

As a staff designer for *Eretz,* a bimonthly, glossy feature magazine produced in both Hebrew and English for Israeli and North American readers, Tagist is a pioneer for Ethiopian Israelis in the publishing industry. At the same time, she continues to explore her heritage as a creative artist and pursues a graduate degree in art history at Tel Aviv University. Tagist created the map for the historical chapter of this book, "From King Solomon to Operation Solomon." This photo with her husband, Golan, the marketing director of *Eretz,* was shot in the conference room of the Eretz Group office in Tel Aviv. Tagist and Golan are a hard-working and courageous couple. Just how courageous became apparent when they showed me the very small motor scooter on which they ride to work together through terrifying Tel Aviv traffic.

Yossi Wassa

"People try to compare the relationship between blacks and whites in the United States to Israel.

It's very different. In Israel the basic thing is that we are Jews, we feel like Jews together, so there is something that

connects us. In the United States, blacks and white people won't curse each other, but they sit separately.

In Israel, blacks and white people curse each other, but then they will sit next to each other.

So I think it's easier to solve the race problem in Israel."

■

Like the two shapes of the Yin and Yang, humor and seriousness fit together to complete Yossi Wassa. A name recognized by virtually every Ethiopian Israeli, his one-man show *It Sounds Better In Amharic,* which he performs in Hebrew, English, or Amharic, portrays the Ethiopian *aliyah* though the lens of his personal story. Yossi also played a charming supporting role in the wonderful film *Caravan 841* about the makeshift absorption centers of the 1990s. Most influentially, Yossi is also the playwright of a one-hour drama about the Ethiopian experience, *Our Journey,* which has been staged for thousands of Israeli children. It turns a bright spotlight on dark memories, on the absorption, its insults, misunderstandings, and oddly funny cultural conflicts. We saw one performance in a Tel Aviv theater along with 800 schoolchildren, and it had a magical effect on the audience. When the Ethiopian family in the play finally entered Jerusalem, the children erupted in deafening cheers. If anger is part of Yossi's repertoire, it is hard to detect it on stage or off. He believes that making people laugh is the only way to accomplish his mission—to enable native Israelis "to see themselves through our eyes."

Born Andargee Vassa in 1974 in the Beta Israel village of Wuzaba, Yossi Wassa immigrated with his family during Operation Moses in 1984. After ten months in an absorption center, the family moved to Netanya, but Yossi spent most of his youth separated from them at a boarding school. In the army, he entertained soldiers in the field as part of a theater group that included an aspiring writer, Shai Ben Attar. With the support of the army, the two began working on a piece that would dramatize Yossi's immigrant experiences. Their collaboration evolved into his dramatic and comedic show about the Ethiopian Israeli experience, *It Sounds Better in Amharic*. At the University of Haifa, Yossi met Shmuel Beru, with whom he co-wrote a series of skits in Amharic exposing the frustrations, indignities, and ironic humor of Ethiopian life in Israel. Entitled *Addis Zemen [New Times]*, their show played on Israeli television and subsequently sold widely on video cassettes, elevating Yossi to celebrity status in the Ethiopian community.

Yossi describes his exodus and surviving the Sudanese refugee camps as a life-changing experience that continues to echo and reverberate internally. His family traversed more than 400 miles from Gondar to Sudan in a perilous three-month trek on foot and on donkeys. They spent nine months in a tent shared with another family in a Sudanese refugee camp, an experience Yossi speaks of as European Jews might recall the concentration camps. Two of his brothers died there.

It Sounds Better in Amharic has become the centerpiece of Yossi's career, and he gives nearly 100 performances of it a year at schools and theaters in Israel, the United States, and Canada. Usually billed as a standup comic, Yossi describes himself as a storyteller. His objective is to provoke Israelis and Ethiopians through humor to look at themselves through the lens of his immigrant experience. As he told one interviewer, "It is important for the Israelis to know about the Ethiopians—not just the facts, but the feelings."

How would you summarize the point of It Sounds Better in Amharic?

First, I'm not trying to criticize. I'm trying to interest the audience in my life as an Ethiopian immigrant to Israel. The story is about my personal life, about my family life and my loss along the way to Israel. Many children died, and we dug the graves with our hands. I lost my two little brothers and my grandmother in Sudan. I remember we were sitting around the table one morning, and my grandmother couldn't get out of her bed. She had a rope and was screaming at us, begging us to help her hang herself. She died two weeks later. When people talk about Ethiopians, I want them to know a personal story. I want them to know me. I've had people come up to me and say, "I've read the literature, I heard about the Ethiopian Jews, but I never had the experience of someone telling me from his own life, his own material."

Your parents' generation had no tradition of formal schooling, and it is said that Ethiopian parents are out of touch with their children's schooling. Was that true for you?

Parents of kids in my generation don't understand what is going on at school. When my parents first sent me to school, they wanted me to be excellent. But excellent at what? They knew that I was going to a school building, but they didn't understand what was going on there. They just assumed that at four o'clock, I had to be smart. When I finished fourth grade, my father expected me to start fixing things in the house like the TV, electrical stuff. Ethiopians are very practical. They say, "He studied, he knows something, so he has to fix things." You don't sit down and study philosophy, talking about the meaning of life and the relationship between you and God. It's absurd to them. "Do something useful," they say. "Bring me some food, for example."

The organization Fidel is training mediators to help the communication between the parents and the teachers at elementary schools.[4] Doesn't that help the communication?

We wrote something about that for a show. A parent is invited to a parent-teacher meeting. The son had to translate for the mother [from Hebrew to Amharic] what the teacher said about him. So what did he say? He translates what he wants her to hear. The teacher was screaming about him and he knows his mother is going to be mad, so he has to try and fix things. He translates for both of them what they each want to hear. The teacher is yelling, and he says, "She is so excited, they want to send me to another boarding school, but first they want to send me home to rest from my hard studies." At the end, everyone is happy, and the boy becomes a great translator.

Are your parents still isolated? Do they speak Hebrew now?

Not much. Most of the adult Ethiopians are isolated in neighborhoods. That will also be one of the problems for the next generation. People my parents' age want to be close to their families, to live next to them. They have celebrations; they have a lot of family events, things to do. It's easier when they are together. So what happens is one Ethiopian buys an apartment next to another Ethiopian, and soon there is a group of them living in one place. Then there are a lot of Ethiopian kids that go to the same school, so the Israelis who live in that neighborhood leave. Ethiopians have to take some responsibility. They can try not to live in a place where there are a lot of other

Ethiopians. But parents don't choose a place to live for the school or because of the children; they choose because of their relationships, because their family is there. I can understand that.

Before you made aliyah, what did you imagine it would be like to live in Israel?

My grandma used to tell me that in Jerusalem there are rivers flowing with milk, stones are loaves of bread, and from the trees dripped sweet honey. That's what the Ethiopians thought when they were in the villages. Imagine you are isolated in a village without connection to the outside world. That's how we were. When I first saw a white guy I thought it was a medical miracle. Spiritually, I can say it is still like heaven in Israel. I'm sitting here talking about myself, about my life. That could only happen in Israel.

Beyond your personal story, what would you want to tell Israelis about your experience as an immigrant?

As a newcomer, there are four stages that you have to step through. The first is when you are shocked. Some people stay at that level, like my parents. The second step is when you are in shock but you want to be like them [other people] so you leave your culture. And then the third step is when you try to come back to your culture, and you criticize their culture. So we're at this point and I'm trying to give them a look at themselves. I'm trying to say, "You are not as developed as I thought. I wanted to be like you, but actually you are like me more than I am like you." In Israel I see people who go around with earrings and rings through their noses. At the Tel Aviv central bus station, I see people with tattoos all over, and I'm saying to myself, "I'm from Africa; this has been done for ages. I thought this was a developed country! What is going on?" The fourth step is when people are just people. There are differences, and if we understand those differences, we will enrich each other.

Tehitina as the grandmother in a scene from Yossi Wassa's play Our Journey

Tehitina Assefa

"Every Friday night, I felt something was missing—the Sabbath, the feeling of togetherness. There was no togetherness in the United States. In Israel, you feel the Sabbath even if you're not religious, even if you're not Jewish. I realized how attached I am to this country. I missed the food, the people. I started listening to Israeli music. I said to myself, 'Okay, something is happening to me.' I knew when I got back, I would study Judaism to see if I wanted to convert."

■

With a B.A. in linguistics from Hebrew University, Tehitina Assefa was introduced to us as a capable trilingual interpreter. After traveling and working together for a month, it became clear to us that she would be a unique subject as well. Born and raised as an Orthodox Christian in Addis Ababa, she came to Israel at twenty in 1987, not to fulfill her Jewish destiny, but to study linguistics. She had learned about Israel from an uncle who had immigrated to become a tour guide for visiting Christian groups. Uncomfortable after several years of trying to explain her presence in Israel as a black Christian, Tehitina moved to live with her sister in California, where she tried to find a job. Unexpectedly, she began to miss Israel, the land, its people, and Judaism.

She returned to Israel and soon began the conversion process. Then she confronted an ironic obstacle. At the time we met her, Tehitina was an aspiring actress who was just finding her niche in a theater group. Although she had completed her Jewish studies, the Ethiopian rabbi who was supervising her refused to accept her conversion when she mentioned in passing that she was an actress. "I was shocked," she said. "The rabbi told me I can't be an actress and also be religious, so he wouldn't convert me. He was telling me that the only way I can be a Jew is to be religious like him. In his mind, he felt he was doing the right thing because he is supposed to protect Judaism. That is his job. For me, though, I already feel like I am Jewish and that I belong in Israel."

Abate Berihun

"For my next project, I will make a CD with the *kessim*. It will be a synthesis of their

traditional chanting in Ge'ez and jazz. I want it to be a bridge between cultures, and I want to show

Israelis that we can contribute to the culture here."

Abate Berihun came to our attention through an ad for his perform-ance in the courtyard of the Rubin Museum in Tel Aviv. As the sun set on Shabbat, we sat in the audience of fifty as Abate came to the band-stand accompanied by native Israeli keyboardist Yitzhak Yadid. Rather than put his tenor saxophone to his lips, Abate stepped up to the microphone and began to sing "Kadeus Kadeus" to a rhythmic and exotic keyboard background. The lyric was a Ge'ez language prayer, a distant cousin of the standard Hebrew prayer known as the *Kedusha*, proclaiming God's holiness. Abate sang in the style of the *kessim* chanting but with a blues flavor. After the vocal statement of the theme, he improvised on saxophone, creating melodies that com-bined Ethiopian scales with jazz phrasing. The audience was stunned by the originality and intensity of this hybrid music.

After the concert, we talked with Abate and his wife, Rachel, at their apartment in Bat Yam. A full-time musician in Ethiopia, Abate was introduced to American music by his father, who listened to Frank Sinatra and big band recordings. His attention turned to jazz when another musician told him he sounded like John Coltrane. "Who's that?" he recalls asking. Before long, he was also listening to Duke Ellington and saxophonists King Curtis and Charlie Parker. Working as a musician under the communist regime in Ethiopia meant he could not play jazz in public. Abate made *aliyah* in 1999. In Israel, he found both religious and artistic freedom.

In an amusing coda to our meeting, we learned later that Abate returned to Ethiopia in 2006 to perform with his Israeli band at the Addis Ababa Hilton in honor of Israel's Independence Day.

Sirak Sabahat

"How can Israel deny the *kessim* the authority to perform marriages and to have some role in our society?

We came to Israel because of the *kessim*. They kept our people together and helped us keep our faith.

They were the ones who told us we should make *aliyah*. So if Israel doesn't give respect to the *kessim*, they are rejecting

me, too. When I was growing up in Ramle, I saw my *kess* sweeping a floor. This was his job.

I cried when I saw that, and I went to help him clean."

▪

Sirak Sabahat, an actor from Ramle, plays the lead role in the award-winning dramatic film *Live and Become*. In 2005, Sirak became the first Ethiopian actor to be nominated by the 500-member Israeli Film Academy for an Oscar in the Best Actor category. *Live and Become* is an epic story about the Ethiopian *aliyah* of 1984, about motherhood, about the painful ambivalence of Israeli society, and, ultimately, about color-blind love. Sirak's high school teacher urged him to think about acting. "The idea that people would pay to listen to me stand on stage and talk didn't make any sense," he recalls. Nevertheless, he studied theater at the University of Haifa. He was also an activist and was elected head of the Ethiopian National Students' Organization. He has played a variety of roles on Israeli television and in stage productions of Shakespeare, Strindberg, and several Israeli playwrights. In *Live and Become,* he was able to draw directly from his own heritage for the first time. "This is the story of my people, so I suddenly understood the power you have inside you as an actor to bring something to a part."

Sirak Sabahat's insights reveal wisdom beyond his years, and in a way that is not surprising because, he says matter-of-factly, "I didn't have a childhood." Sirak's biography reads like the storyline of a historical novel. His early years were dominated by poverty and wandering. In the southern village of Wallita, Sirak's grandfather was killed in mysterious circumstances, probably by the Mengistu government. The family had to flee to Awassa. Realizing that they could reach Israel only from Addis Ababa, they traveled on foot for one year, hiding on the outskirts of villages along the way. In 1991, at age eleven, Sirak was swept up on a moment's notice into a seatless jumbo jet bound for Israel as part of Operation Solomon. After several years in absorption centers, Sirak was enrolled in a boarding school for gifted children. One of his teachers introduced him to the idea of acting, an almost inconceivable concept. "Acting was not respected in Ethiopia," Sirak recalls. However, in Israel he seems to be thriving on it. At the same time, he is disturbed by the current state of the Ethiopian Israeli community. Introspective and humanistic, his acting goes deeper than entertainment; it is driven by sensitivity, painful memories, and the belief that we need to recognize each other's humanity.

What were your early years like in Israel?
It was just like you saw in the movie; we kissed the ground. They took us on a bus to the north of Israel, Kiryat Shimona. We stayed in a hotel for months. After the hotel, they put us in a caravan site [temporary housing in mobile homes]. We studied Hebrew with other Ethiopians. We didn't have any contact with Israelis. But it was a very important time because we had to decide for ourselves if we were going to accept a new life here or not. Some people could not adjust, and there were a few who committed suicide. Not every human mind can adapt.

After three years in this absorption center, we took a test, and because of the results, I was allowed to go to school with the Israelis, to a secular boarding school. The education was excellent, and I will always be grateful to my father because he understood that education was the most important thing. I was the first Ethiopian they [the kids at school] knew. This was the most difficult time of my life. My Hebrew was not good. My clothing was different. My behavior was different. They used to call me old-fashioned, which I was. I did not have a lot of friends. But I didn't call home to tell everyone I was having a hard time, because men don't cry in our culture. Our culture says you have to face everything. My parents would

have thought I was a disappointment if I did not handle it myself. So I had a lot of time to read books.

Why do you think you were strong enough psychologically to handle it?
Psychology is not the thing that defines you in our culture. When we face a challenge, we have to survive. We don't discuss how we feel about it. What happened in high school was that I learned I was able to survive children laughing at me. I had to adapt, adapt, adapt. It was in perspective for me—I have food, I have clothes, and no one is trying to kill me.

Did your parents make the transition to Israel successfully?
Not completely. At first, I was upset with Israel. Why did they put us in the city? We are farmers. Why didn't they put us on the kibbutz or the *moshav* [a cooperative village, usually agricultural]? But I assumed they had their reasons and that they were doing what is best for us. That was how I thought at that time. My mom cleaned in places she never thought she would work. She was still a young woman; I was born when she was fifteen years old. So she started to study at school in Israel. It took my mom eight years to finish her academic studies, and when I

saw her do that, I knew that anything was possible. In a way, she is my role model. That she had the strength to have a job cleaning and at the same time to study and raise children made me believe that we could cross any bridge. She works now with children who have trouble in school and with their parents, trying to explain the importance of education. My father also went to school, and I am proud of him, too, because he gave my mother the freedom to be educated and to work. This is not usual in our community.

How did you become an actor?

In boarding school, there was a teacher who told me I should be on the stage. I thought it was crazy. You mean, I will talk and people will listen to me? He said, "If you have talent, people will pay you." I will talk, and people will pay me? That didn't make any sense. But I decided to go to the acting class, and there I found my destiny.

What can you contribute to the Israeli film industry as an Ethiopian?

I can bring my own perspective. You have to bring your own experience to a part, not so people will like you, but so you will educate them to a different point of view. You have to connect what you are saying to something inside of you. If you don't feel the emotions, the audience will not understand you. An actor who just says the lines, who is not inside the character and doesn't feel the character, doesn't have anything to add. *Live and Become* was the first time I could use my experiences. This is the story of my people, so I suddenly understood the power you have inside you as an actor to bring something to a part.

What do you want the Israelis or Jews in the Diaspora to learn from Live and Become?

It's very simple. I want them to understand that human life is valuable, no matter where it is. In black Africa, children are dying every two or three seconds. People don't see beyond where they are living. I want them to understand that they are very lucky, that they should not take things for granted. You have advantages. When you wake up in the morning, you don't have to wonder how you will find food to eat, how you will survive to the next day. You don't have to worry that people are trying to kill you. You will see that the complaints you have in life are not that much compared to other people.

Do you feel your integration into Israeli society is complete? Is it still a struggle?

It will be many generations before we can say we are integrated. We are working on it, and when 60 percent of the Ethiopians are part of Israeli society, then we can talk about integration. When Ethiopian students can study in schools without barriers, when the mayor of a town cannot say you can have only twenty-five Ethiopian students in your school, then there is integration. When they accept us as Jewish completely, then we have integration. Until all these things happen, I will not use the word "integration."

In the movie, Shlomo [the hero] marries a white Israeli. Is the film trying to say that this is the road to integration?
For me, the film is saying, "There is no color to love."

The character says that in the movie. She says to Shlomo, "I don't care what color you are."
Yes. People also ask me, "Why is the hero Christian in this film?" When people ask me that, I remind them about the gentiles who hid the Jews in the basements and in the attic [during the Holocaust]. We are talking about humanity. When we talk about mothers, they don't see the religion. In this film, there is a white mother, a Jewish mother, and a Christian mother. They don't see color or religion. They see a child who needs to be saved.

But Sarah's father could never make the change to seeing Shlomo as a person. That is part of the reality.
Yes, we are not trying to avoid that. There are people who do not accept Ethiopian Jews. They are fanatics. But I don't care. We know what we

have sacrificed to be here. We make the effort with the people who do understand. They accept us not because they have to, but because they are human and they understand. This is what I tell Ethiopian kids whose self-esteem is very low because they live in bad neighborhoods. Many of them are using drugs or alcohol. They are trying to escape the reality because they are not finding their place in the society. The question of identity is becoming very scary. Now that I have studied life—not books at the university, but life—I understand that you must be the master of your destiny. If you define yourself, you will be much more able to preserve your culture. Don't wait for an organization or the government to tell you what your destiny is, what your identity is. If you do that, you will never find your way and your past will be forgotten.

Are Ethiopians trying to deny their Ethiopian heritage when they lose themselves in rap music?
I don't think so. They are not escaping; they are just trying to find their place and they think hip-hop might be a way to express their feelings because other black people find it meaningful. What is rap music? It is a comment on how we feel about our society. Before they find themselves, they need to get lost. I am happy that they are exploring new places. I think they have to discover themselves. No one can come and say, "You are like this, or you are like that." They need to find out for themselves who they are.

What do you think will contribute to the goal of integration with Israeli society?
I want to do it in an artistic way. People in the arts need to be in touch with their roots and also know how to live in Israel. We need to work on our own projects and be at peace with our culture. Then integration will come, slowly. Building self-esteem and self-identity will lead to integration. As one who looks at us from the outside, don't you think this is true?

I do. But not everybody has the resources and talent to develop in the way you have.
I believe everyone has the talent to grow. I am not an exception. There are a thousand people like me. If there are people who do not bring out their own talent and express themselves, it means they were not given the emotional resources. Nobody made them feel they are worth something in this world. That's why we have to give the kids the confidence that they can be something. Then they will be something.

CHAPTER VII

GETTING ORGANIZED

An American psychiatrist from Boston told me this story about his visit to an absorption center in Beersheva in 1985:"I witnessed something that I will never forget.

It was lunch time and a group of Ethiopian kids, maybe a dozen or more, not more than five years old, was sitting at tables with their trays of food in front of them. We were observing them, but there were no other adults supervising at the time. They had begun eating when one of the children pushed his tray away and started to cry, very quietly, sobbing more than crying. As if it had been rehearsed, all the other children got up from their places and came over to this child and began touching him, talking to him, comforting him. Whatever was upsetting him eventually subsided, and he took his food again. Only then did the other children go back to their places and continue to eat."

After conducting more than sixty in-depth interviews with Ethiopian Israelis, my own predominant impression of the community is consistent with the psychiatrist's observation: these are people who care about each other. Everyone I spoke with, regardless of personal circumstances, was quick to bring the conversation around to what the community has experienced, how it is being treated, and what it needs.

The community's needs are oceanic—deep and vast. Roughly 65 to 70 percent of Ethiopian Israelis live below the poverty line, unemployment is at about 60 percent, and most of those who are employed, even university graduates, are in unskilled service work (e.g., as hotel cleaners, supermarket stock boys, and the ubiquitous security guards). According to statistics for 2004, Ethiopian Israelis— only 1.5 percent of the population—accounted for more than 4 percent

of crimes. These statistics could grow still more dismal because the Ethiopian population is growing faster than any other single group. The Ethiopian family averages four to five children, and, adding to the population increase, Israel is committed to absorbing another 15,000 Falas Mura (depending on whose data you accept) who wait homeless and impoverished in Addis Ababa and Gondar. The greatest fear of the Ethiopian Jewish leaders is that their community will be seen as "a permanent underclass of Israeli society," a phrase that has become a rallying cry for them and their American Jewish supporters.

Caring about each other comes naturally to the Ethiopian Jews, but political organization is a new and uneasy fit. In Ethiopia the Beta Israel lived as a decentralized scattering of Jewish villages. In many cases, daily survival was an all-consuming task. Because it was a challenge to travel and communicate between villages, organizing politically was beyond reach. The Beta Israel lived under a monarchy until it was overthrown by the communist dictatorship in 1974. Until 1974, they could not legally own land. Thus, they had few rights to protect. Although the Communist Derge (Committee) nominally offered the right to own land to Ethiopia's minority groups, the discriminatory measures against Jews were soon worse than they had been under the monarchy of Haile Selassie.

Nevertheless, the Ethiopian Israelis have learned quickly that even in a democratic Jewish state, achieving civil rights and equality for ethnic minorities requires advocacy. They have excelled in the

creation of *amutot* (non-profit organizations), and they are beginning to gather momentum in the political arena. While Diaspora communities are raising money to help with immigration and absorption, the Ethiopian Jews' instinct for caring about each other has spawned about eighty nonprofit advocacy and social service organizations. These are largely local and aimed at specific challenges, such as overcoming educational deficits, reducing crime and unemployment, and preserving Ethiopian Jewish culture. There are nationally focused organizations that have buoyed the hopes for progress. They include many discussed in this chapter, such as the Ethiopian National Project, the Israel Association for Ethiopian Jewry, and Bahalachin (the Ethiopian Jewish Cultural Center). Determination, ideas, and people to implement them are abundant, but government aid is in short supply largely because of Israel's demanding security requirements.

As the Ethiopian Israeli community evolves in its capacity to organize for advocacy and social services, it is beginning to acquire political clout. Undaunted by their mere 75,000 voters, two Ethiopian Israelis vied for Knesset seats in Israel's general election of March 28, 2006, and there is one former Ethiopian Knesset member. (See the interviews with these three activists in this chapter.) One of these long-time political activists, Avraham Neguise, co-founded and headed Israel's first Ethiopian-led political party, Atid Echad (One Future), which fielded ten candidates, including both Ethiopians and native Israelis. Two developments became clear in the run-up to the general election of 2006: first, Ethiopian Israelis know that they need more than self-help NGOs, they also need a national platform for advocacy; second, they are no longer the political property of the Likud party, to which they had been loyal because it was Likud prime minister Menachem Begin who made the political decision to bring them to Israel.

Like the Boston psychiatrist who visited the absorption center, I was also struck by the profound instinct for helping. One of my interpreters, a twenty-eight-year-old university graduate who was expecting her first child, turned out to be a perfect example. I asked Yuvi what her professional plans were after the baby arrived. Her answer was immediate and well-thought out. She and her husband, Yoni, a mechanical engineer, plan to move from their middle-class neighborhood in Yavne, along with eight other young families, to the poorer city of Gedera, where there are high percentages of street crime and high school dropouts among Ethiopian youth. They have created a nonprofit group called Friends in Nature dedicated to keeping Ethiopian teenagers in school and out of trouble.

It is a sad irony that the Ethiopian Israeli community is most often perceived and reported on by the press as a burden to Israeli society, because they are in fact an asset to Israel capable of unique contributions. While this may be known, it needs to be acknowledged more readily in publications, fundraising efforts, and conversations.

Adissu Mesele

"The Ethiopian Jews always thought that their fate was in the hands of the Israeli government.

On the day of the Blood Scandal of 1996, they learned that the fate of the Ethiopian Jews is in our own hands.

Ethiopians thought that if the Israelis could pull off Operation Moses and Operation Solomon, they could take care of

the future of the Ethiopian Jews. But I have always said that the responsibility is ours. Right now, the

Ethiopian community is taking more responsibility for its own future than it ever has."

One of the heroes of his community, Adissu Mesele was the only Ethiopian to become a member of the Knesset (1996–1999). He proudly asserts that he did not earn that seat by being a "yes man." Seemingly born to resist, by age sixteen he was a machine-gun-carrying member of the Ethiopian People's Revolutionary Party, fighting the communist regime. Hearing rumors about his imminent arrest, he fled on foot to Sudan, a thirty-two day journey, and spent one year there as a hotel waiter, secretly working with the Mossad to rescue other Ethiopian Jews. In 1980, at nineteen, he made *aliyah*. Very quickly, Adissu concluded that Israel's plan for absorbing the new immigrants was inadequate. Blasting virtually every Israeli institution and ministry, he became a self-appointed gadfly. He led mass protests against policies he considered unfair, and he helped create a national holiday, Yom Hazkarah, to memorialize the thousands who died en route to Israel between 1979 and 1985. Adissu lost his Knesset seat during Ehud Barak's administration, but his activism has not waned. Still a member of the Labor party, Adissu works full-time for his community through his Tel Aviv-based United Ethiopian Jewish Organization.

Adissu Mesele, born in Wazawa, a small Jewish village outside of Ambover, was the only one of his nine siblings to receive a formal education in Ethiopia. He attended a Jewish elementary school in Ambover and was sent to Gondar for high school. In Israeli politics, he has positioned himself as the loyal opposition, monitoring the Israeli government and its official agencies, explaining to anyone who will listen that they are not doing enough. His knowledge of the community's history in Israel is encyclopedic and, because of his three years in the Knesset, he is no doubt the most widely known Ethiopian Israeli.

Can you explain why you began to protest the treatment of Ethiopian Jews so soon after you arrived?

I was in the Shaul Melech (King Saul) absorption center in Beersheva. When I met with rabbis and people from the Ministry of Absorption, they wanted to change my name. They didn't understand when I said my name is Adissu. They wanted to call me David, and they gave me a piece of paper with my new name. After two weeks, I tore it up. They said, "Do you know who David was? He was a king." I told them I'm not a king, I'm Adissu.

They wanted to pull down my trousers and take a drop of blood [*hatafat dam*, symbolic circumcision] in a "second circumcision." Every Jewish boy in Ethiopia is circumcised on the eighth day. Should we do this again? It is primitive. I said, "No, I won't do it." I am not a "yes man." Another man, Abebe, came next. They asked his name. He said, "Abebe." They looked in their catalogue of names and gave him a Hebrew name. He was asked, "How old are you?" He told them forty. They said he looks younger, he is thirty-two. That's the kind of reception that made me want to become a community leader. They even gave Ethiopian women the name Levana, which means "White." They were trying to take away our identity.

Were the Israeli people more receptive than the rabbinate?

Yes, Israeli society accepts us as Jews without a doubt. The problem is that the Ethiopian community has a big gap to close, educationally, culturally, and economically. The younger Ethiopians who were born here speak Hebrew fluently and have had an academic education, so they are more or less Israelis. Even for them, I would say the integration is difficult. In my case, I have been here for twenty-five years and I still do not feel Israeli in every way.

At the time the Ethiopians came during Operation Moses and Operation Solomon, the Israelis almost cried [for joy]. But when the Ethiopian Jews left the absorption center and moved to their neighborhoods, then the Israelis began saying, "My property will be worth less, the school will not be as good." I think the integration will take generations. I want more patience and tolerance from Israeli society. There are Israelis who have done a lot for our integration, but these are exceptions.

Is there any good news?

Some things are going well. The generation in military service now is very capable. There are about 200 Ethiopian officers in the military. There are 3,000 university students. There is a big motivation to integrate, but after these 3,000 students graduate, they won't find jobs. Go to the shopping mall and you will find the security guards are 90 percent Ethiopians and Russians, and the Ethiopians, almost all of them, have B.A. degrees. I don't want to see a graduate of the Technion sweeping floors in the mall. He worked very hard for his degree and had a lot of financial problems just to attend the university. So I want him to work in his profession or work for the Ministry of Education. High school students come to me and I tell them to go to school. Then they tell me, "My older brother went to the university and worked very hard for a degree, and now he is a security guard at a store. Why should I go to school?"

Many people have mentioned to me that the Blood Scandal in 1996 was a turning point for the Ethiopians and changed their attitude toward Israeli society.[1] Do you agree?
It was also a turning point for the Israelis. Until January 1996, the Israelis thought the Ethiopian Jews were shy, quiet, and would never raise their voices. But on that day, which I organized, we had 20,000 Ethiopian Jews demonstrating, and it was very violent. Israelis were shocked. That was the message for the Israeli society. Our culture tells us to be very quiet and respectful. For us, being quiet is a strength, not a weakness. But now the Israelis know that we can produce a very strong reaction. They learned. The next time we had a demonstration, the number of police was greater than the number of demonstrators.

Will the Ethiopian National Project [ENP] help the community's attempt to integrate more fully?
The Ethiopian National Project [see the interview with Nigist Mengesha in this chapter] is the initiative of the Jewish Agency and other groups, like the Federations of America. It's not

independent enough, even though the director, Nigist, is Ethiopian. It is like they are cooking food for me, but they don't ask what I like. They cook what they like, bring it to me, and then tell me, "Eat this." Well, they are cooking with a spice they like, not one I like.

Is that true? I have heard that the whole point of the ENP is to provide consultation from the

Ethiopian community itself?
That is what they say.

Do you feel that the kessim *[priests] should be given more of an official role to play?*
The rabbinate does not give the *kessim* any authority; but the community does. Every year at Sigd, 35,000 Ethiopians come together and they are led by the *kessim*. My organization plans

171

this festival every year. The *kessim* cannot marry couples because the Ministry of Interior will not recognize anything but an Orthodox marriage. If they don't recognize your marriage, you cannot get a mortgage. If a rabbi immigrates from Russia or England, the rabbinate recognizes him. But not the *kessim*. Why? Because they say we were separated from the Jewish community for thousands of years, so we did not know *halacha* [Jewish law]. If religion and the state were separated in Israel, there is no doubt that 90 percent of the Ethiopian Jews would get married by the *kessim*. The government does recognize *kessim* as spiritual leaders of the Ethiopian community and they give them a salary, but only those who were *kessim* before coming to Israel. I am trying to convince the government to accept the *kess* who is trained here. But right now, they do not.

What is the most effective way to unify the community and help them politically?

I would like to see Ethiopian youngsters in politics. I am very happy to see some of them becoming rabbis. When we see Ethiopian Jews in every field, we will know that integration has happened. I am proud to be the first Ethiopian Jew who was a Knesset member. I broke the stereotype. There was a low ceiling for Ethiopians, but we broke through it. When I entered the absorption center in Beersheva in 1980, I was talking with the manager and I told him, "I want to study in the university." He laughed—"You, study at the university?" Well, I got my

degree from Bar Ilan University.

To have an Ethiopian as a member of the Knesset is difficult because we are a very small community of 100,000. That is one reason why our issues were ignored for many years; we have very few votes. Look at the Russians—they have twenty-two seats. The parties run after them because they have a lot of votes. They also know how to play the game. They are a swing vote, and they go to the party that will improve their own circumstances. Ethiopians didn't know about this. They did not try to influence a party. We would just vote Likud, Likud, Likud. Why? Because in 1977, Menachem Begin [prime minister from the Likud party] made the decision to bring us here. Labor, Mapai, and many parties refused to commit to bringing the Ethiopian Jews to Israel. Another reason we have voted Likud is that the Ethiopians, because of their love of the Holy Land, thought Likud was stronger on defense. Likud said, "Peace for peace," while Labor said, "Land for peace." So the Ethiopians voted for Likud. Even when I was running on the Labor ticket, the majority of Ethiopians still voted Likud. I was criticized for being a member of the Labor party. But I told them, "You forgot that we were born as Jews. That's why we're here, not because of Likud." We immigrated to Israel according to the Law of Return, which applies to every Jew in the Diaspora. It's Labor or Meretz that are good parties for the Ethiopians, because they speak about human rights and social issues. Things have changed. Many Ethiopians are running for

seats in the next Knesset and in different parties. Likud hit us financially during the last [Sharon] government, so Ethiopians will not be voting one party any more.

No party is running after the Ethiopian candidates because they want to appeal to us. They are asking us to join them so they can say, "Even the Ethiopians are with us." We are political decoration. The political involvement is not the solution for the Ethiopian immigrants. The solution is a combination of the political, education, social integration, and economic improvements. The solution will not come from having one Knesset seat. We also need to have good role models for the Ethiopians in every sector of society.

What is the image of American Jews in the Ethiopian Israeli community?

If I said I am here because of the American Jews, I would not be exaggerating. They put pressure on the Israeli government to accept us. They put pressure on the Israeli government to integrate us. When Israel said there were not any problems for the Ethiopian Jews in Ethiopia, the American Jews organized to help us. Before Operation Solomon [1991], the American and Canadian Jews brought people to the compound in Addis Ababa. It was their initiative to concentrate the Ethiopian Jews in Addis to put pressure on Israel to bring us in. Operation Solomon would not have happened without the involvement of America. Every school child knows this.

"*The solution will not come from having one Knesset seat.*
We also need to have good role models for the Ethiopians
in every sector of society."

—Adissu Mesele

Avraham Neguise

"I think the problem now is that the community is not united. Like all Israelis, everybody has his own opinion.

Some right wing, some left wing, some in the center, so Ethiopians are distributed in all the political parties.

There are people in Labor, in Shas, in Likud. So it is really a problem for us that we don't have a political party that will

represent the community. I hope and I believe we will create some kind of leadership and come together."

—Avraham Neguise, prior to the creation of the Atid Echad party

Trained as a social worker in Ethiopia and India, Avraham Neguise remembers the day he made *aliyah*. It was March 28, 1985. On the same day in 2006, Israel's national election day, Avraham was running for a Knesset seat as the leader of the new social justice party Atid Echad (One Future). After Operation Solomon in 1991, Avraham understood something that Israeli officials did not fully appreciate: the massive airlift, which brought more than 14,000 people to Israel, still left thousands stranded in Ethiopia. In response, he founded South Wing to Zion, which advocates for the rescue of the remaining Jews from the hazardous limbo in which they linger. "They will eventually come," Avraham asserts. "The only question is what kind of shape they will be in when they arrive." Although Atid Echad did not get enough votes to win a seat, observers of Israeli politics should not count him out. If there is anything Avraham exemplifies, it is hard work and perseverance. His signature British racing cap is a fitting symbol for his breakneck schedule. Avraham chose the location for this photo, on Mt. Scopus overlooking Jerusalem. "Let's make it historic," he said.

Avraham Neguise typically works twelve-hour days, driving around Jerusalem and between cities, from one meeting to the next, with only minutes to spare. His expression flickers readily between intensity and boyish charm. Aggressively lobbying for the speedy "ingathering of the exiles" (the thousands of Falas Mura who remain in Ethiopia), he cites the deplorable conditions in which some of them linger for years: the painful separation of family members, the prolonged poverty, malnutrition, and exposure to HIV, among other hazards.

Avraham was raised in a small Jewish village, but when he was a teenager he left for Gondar, where he could get a better secular education. After high school, he found work in a multicultural orphanage, home to Jewish, Christian, and Muslim children. In 1981 he won a scholarship to get advanced training in residential childcare in India. En route, he visited Israel, where some of his relatives were already living. In 1985, Avraham, his wife Leah, and their daughters made *aliyah*. Avraham attended Hebrew University's School of Social Work and earned a B.A. and master's degree. Leah went to nursing school and is currently on the staff of Hadassah Hospital.

Avraham was a prominent organizer of many of the community's political actions, such as the protest against the conversion requirement for the Beta Israel in 1985 and the demonstrations against the Blood Scandal of 1996. From 2002 to 2004 he served as president of the seventeen Ethiopian-led nonprofits that guide the Ethiopian National Project. Life in Israel has changed Avraham religiously, too. He describes his life in Ethiopia as "nonobservant, not practicing at all," but in Israel, he has enthusiastically embraced Orthodoxy.

As someone educated in the childcare field, how do you feel about the fact that so many Ethiopian teenagers were sent to boarding schools? Was taking them out of their homes the right decision?

Of course, it is better if they stay with their parents, but there were reasons for it. When we see the reality, most of the Ethiopian families can't provide all the necessary things for their children. Most families have many children, and there is a shortage of rooms in the houses. If they are in an absorption center, you only get a few rooms for everyone. That's very difficult to take for adolescents. The children are in a small room with many brothers and sisters. It is very difficult to study. So the boarding school has

been a good answer for that. About 90 percent of the Ethiopian children ages fourteen to sixteen go to boarding schools. Also, the families usually cannot afford to buy all the books and school supplies the child needs. The boarding schools provide that. Another advantage of the boarding school is that Ethiopian kids will mingle with Israelis of the same age. If they went to school in their neighborhood, they would only see Ethiopians.

Another problem at home is adolescence. The behavior of the adolescent in Ethiopia is completely different than it is in Israel. The parents expect their children to behave as they did in Ethiopia, whether it is in how they dress or the haircuts, the styles, the attitudes, the respect they show. So the parents are angry with them and there is conflict.

What do you think will happen to the Ethiopian synagogues? In twenty or thirty years will Ethiopian synagogues exist?

Ethiopian synagogues will exist, but they probably will be conducting prayers [only] in Hebrew, like the Moroccan and Yemenite synagogues. You have to understand that for the adults, the *kessim* [priests] are meaningful and very important. It's the only spiritual leader they know. But for the younger ones who are now studying in Israel, they are praying and studying in Hebrew. So going to the Ethiopian synagogue where the *kess* prays in Ge'ez and someone translates into Amharic does not make sense to the young people.

It's good that the tradition is kept right now; it is good that the *kess* is here now. But you see what status the *kessim* have here. They don't have any authority here in Israel. Only our community respects them, not the Israeli religious establishment. I'm not a prophet, but when I look into the future of the community, I think it will be a full integration, even in religious practice. I think that's the best way.

Is the Falas Mura immigration being conducted properly?
At the rate we are bringing them, it will be six to seven years to complete the *aliyah*. That is too long. Everyone who is coming from Ethiopia now has family members in Israel—parents, children, brothers and sisters, uncles and aunts. They are reunited with family. At the same time, when they come here, they leave family in Ethiopia. When they are given the chance to make *aliyah*, it is not the whole family, the extended family, who comes. The families are always divided. This is stressful. Conditions in Ethiopia are unhealthy, so the immigrants are arriving sicker and needing more help.

Do you believe they, or their ancestors, were forced to convert to Christianity, or did they become Christian to improve their lives?
In some cases they had no choice; it was a life or death situation. There was also the problem of land—they could not build houses. They had no place to settle in the villages [except as tenant farmers], and so if there was a famine, they had to leave and find more land to cultivate. They could starve to death. There were so many reasons. But the important reality now is that the people we see today are completely committed to Judaism.

Do you believe all the Falas Mura to have been converted—or reconverted—back to Judaism?
In Addis and Gondar, they practice with a *siddur*, a prayer book in Hebrew and Amharic that is sent from Israel. When they come to Israel to the absorption centers, they study Hebrew in the morning, and in the afternoon they study Judaism. After a year, they complete a process that is called Return to Judaism—a symbolic conversion. They do it willingly, and no one is forcing them.

At first, the rabbinate demanded that all Ethiopians Jews undergo symbolic conversions. That led to the demonstrations of 1985. So then the rabbis said, "Okay, anyone who wants to can go through this; anyone who doesn't want to does not have to. No one can tell him you cannot become a citizen." If they are Jewish on the mother's side, then it's not a big issue [Jewish identity is matrilineal, according to Orthodox interpretation]. However, if they are not Jewish on the mother's side [that is, the Falas Mura, who previously lived as Christians in Ethiopia], and they don't go through the symbolic conversion, the government will not write "Jewish" on their identity cards. This will affect their ability to be employed, to go into the army, and so on.

According to our experience in the absorption centers, at least 95 percent are going through the Return to Judaism ceremony.

Are you optimistic about the Ethiopian National Project [ENP] providing national leadership?
The ENP is very important for the Ethiopian Jews in Israel because we need to have national leadership and a role model for the new generation. We have to give them optimism, the belief that they can succeed. There must be an "address" for the Israeli government for dealing with our issues. This one organization is a partnership with the Israeli government, the Jewish Agency, the Joint Distribution Committee, and the United Jewish Communities. The ENP is the address for the establishment to deal with and advance projects to benefit our community.

Is there a push to get an Ethiopian elected to the Knesset?
I think the problem now is that the community is not united. Like all Israelis, everyone has their own opinions. Some right wing, some left wing, some in the center, so Ethiopians are distributed in all the political parties. It is really a problem for us that we don't have a political party that will represent the community. I hope and believe that we will create some kind of leadership and come together.

Note: In the March 2006 national elections, Avraham led the new Atid Echad party. They received 26,000 of the 70,000 votes they needed to win one Knesset seat.

Shlomo Molla

"When Ariel Sharon created the Kadima party, he called me personally to ask me to join.

I was very happy about that because I agreed with their political philosophy. Sharon was very popular

in our community, but I told him that I could never deliver 100 percent of the Ethiopian vote.

He understood that. But I am happy about that, though, because it means Ethiopians understand democracy.

It means we have different opinions, and we know we can make choices."

■

After walking 300 miles from his village to Sudan, Shlomo Molla, at age seventeen, made *aliyah* in 1984 as part of Operation Moses. A talented student, he graduated from Bar Ilan University, became a lawyer, and worked for the Ministry of Absorption. In 2005, Prime Minister Ariel Sharon invited Shlomo to run for a Knesset seat with the newly formed Kadima party. Although Kadima won the national election of 2006, the party did not get enough votes for Shlomo to win a Knesset seat, so he remained in his critically important role as the director of Ethiopian Immigration and Absorption at the Jewish Agency for Israel. In June 2006 Shlomo was the first Ethiopian to be elected to an executive position in the World Zionist Organization; he is in charge of education and the struggle against anti-Semitism. Shlomo is photographed here in front of a sculpture across the street from the Jewish Agency headquarters in Jerusalem.

Shlomo Molla has not always taken popular positions, but his political instincts have enabled him to operate in the corridors of power. His escape from Ethiopia is a story of drama and personal loss. After walking 300 miles with teenage friends to reach Sudan, one of his friends was killed by Sudanese soldiers. Shlomo was thrown in jail. He was released to a refugee camp where he remained until he was brought to Israel with Operation Moses. Shlomo was one of the first Ethiopian army officers, among the first graduates of law school, and the first Ethiopian elected to the executive body of the World Zionist congress. Most importantly for his community, he is the Director of Ethiopian Immigration and Absorption at the Jewish Agency for Israel.

What did you know about Israel as a teenager and what motivated you to make this journey?
We grew up in a village close to Ambover where we did not know there were such things as white Jews. But we were Zionists, dreaming of coming to Israel one day. A dream is a dream. Jerusalem was a holy place, and Israel was the Land of Milk and Honey, the land promised to Abraham, Isaac, and Jacob. When you grow up with this kind of ideology, it is easy to try to

leave, even if it's dangerous. Through Sudan was the only way. It was dangerous. There were robbers, soldiers. We had no shoes, no food. The other part of the story is what happened in the refugee camps. The Israelis worked in the camps in great danger to rescue Jews from Gehenna. There was dysentery, many serious diseases, lack of food and water. Thousands of people were dying. But the Israelis went in to find the Jews and bring them to a safe place. I was rescued along with 400 others by Israeli commandos who landed helicopters in the desert. I was seventeen at the time, and I was alone. My father and mother were very frightened that I would be killed by the Sudanese or die of illness. Later, my parents came through Sudan, too, with my younger brother, who died there. He was only eight years old. We are now nine brothers and two sisters. My parents are still alive, so we thank God that we are all in Israel.

What is your role in the Jewish Agency, and what is the Agency's role in managing the absorption centers?
I am in charge of the *aliyah* and absorption of the Ethiopians, and the Jewish Agency operates the absorption centers. We have forty absorption centers and there are about 8,000 Ethiopians in twenty-three of them all over

Israel. Our job is to prepare the immigrants for life in Israel. We have to teach them everything from how to use electricity and plumbing to how to get a mortgage from a bank. We have both Israeli teachers and Ethiopians who are educated in Israel. We try to work with all immigrants sensitively. After one year or, at the most, one year and a half, they have to go to their own housing.

Many people have told me that the housing subsidies enable Ethiopians to live in the same neighborhood as other Ethiopians, and that this leads to a kind of ghetto. Is that a problem?
Yes, I am sorry to say. We don't want them to create ghettos. There are subsidized mortgages only for certain cities, which helps distribute people to places where there are not big economic problems already. But there is not any way you can obligate people to distribute themselves to different parts of a city. If you go to Ashdod and Netanya, you will find Russian neighborhoods, too. In America, you will find Spanish neighborhoods and black neighborhoods. It's normal to want to live around family and your own ethnic group. I chose to live in Modiin just because there are very few Ethiopians there. Of course, I would like to live in Rishon Letzion with my own

family in an Ethiopian neighborhood, but I feel it's a responsibility to be an example, to show that Ethiopians can live elsewhere. If we don't live among the Israelis, we cannot be completely integrated. The other way to help integration move ahead is to become educated. Education is the key to employment. We have to do this ourselves as much as possible. No one will help you if you are not helping yourself.

Do you think the Ministry of Education can do

more to educate Israelis about the Ethiopian community?

The Ministry of Education can't do much nationally because education is locally controlled. The bureau in Haifa, for example, has its own ideas and its own population. So there really is no national policy that applies to everyone. It's not like the military, where everyone follows the same orders. The military does an excellent job of integrating the Ethiopians, and we often advise ministries to learn from what the military does. But the military has control

over all its locations. Their policies are good, and all the officers have to learn them and follow them everywhere.

What will happen in the next few years if the Falas Mura arrive at an increased rate, which is the plan? Can the absorption centers handle it?

We are planning to bring another 12,000 to 15,000 in the next few years. Operation Promise is a fundraising campaign in the U.S. trying to support that goal, and Keren Hayesod [a fundraising arm of the Agency that works outside of the U.S.] is trying to raise the money for it in Europe. We expect that as new people arrive over this time, another 5,000 Ethiopians will leave the centers and that will help ease the strain on facilities. Of course, we would love to have more absorption centers.

Will the new Falas Mura immigrants divide the community? I know some Ethiopians want them to come, and others are opposed because their families lived as Christians in Ethiopia. In fact, you yourself were opposed to their aliyah *originally.*

The whole story is very complicated and problematic. But in the end, we all understand that the Falas Mura are coming. Many are already here, about 20,000. About 8,000 of them are still in absorption centers. We both [Beta Israel, who lived as Jews in Ethiopia, and Falas Mura, who lived as Christians] come from the same place, and we have common problems in Israel. We have to be united; it's the only way. I think that from the perspective of fifteen or twenty years down the road, we will see that the community is not divided. Look at this country's history. The Ashkenazi and Sephardic division was a big issue in the 1950s and 1960s, but no more. So with us, for the first few years it will be a big deal, but after twenty years no one will know who came when, or whose ancestors are Falas Mura and whose are Beta Israel.

What happens when the Jewish Agency makes a decision that you think is unfavorable to the Ethiopian community? Can you do anything about

it, or do you have to support it as an employee? It has happened, and I will give you an example. There was a decision to cut millions of dollars out of the budget of our KEDMA program. [KEDMA, a Hebrew acronym for "Promoting Personal Readiness," offers new immigrants ages seventeen to twenty-seven an intensive 1,000 hours of language and academic study over ten months.] I was very afraid of the consequences, so I called the chairperson of the Board of Governors [Carole Solomon] and explained that this cut would mean hundreds of Ethiopian teenagers would be out on the streets instead of in classrooms. I asked her, "Do you want that?" "Of course not," she said. So she arranged for me to speak to the board and make my argument. I presented my argument and millions of dollars were returned to the budget for this program. In fact, I got an increase in the budget.

Speaking of politics, I know you are running on the Kadima platform. How will the Ethiopian community vote in the upcoming election [March 2006]?

I think the Ethiopians want to see an Ethiopian in the Knesset. I hope they will want me enough to vote Kadima. The Ethiopian community used to vote Likud as a rule. But there are two reasons not all of them will vote for Likud this time. First, the Likud finance minister recently made some decisions that were very hard on the Ethiopians, so they are angry about that. And something else I will tell you: although the Ethiopians have voted Likud for many years,

never did Likud put an Ethiopian on the ticket. But there are many political opinions in the Ethiopian community, so I don't think all will vote Kadima.

How would you describe the agenda of the Kadima party, and how will it help the Ethiopian community?

First of all, we have to solve the situation with the Palestinians. There are two things Kadima has to accomplish in this area. We need to establish the final border of Israel in the next four years, even without the Palestinians' participation. We will not be able to establish the borders ten years from now. Time is against us. Also, I believe Israel cannot be responsible for millions of Palestinians. We need three or four of our largest settlements to be included in Israel's borders, and that's it. If we have a clear border and we invest our resources within our own borders, we will then have much more to give to the Ethiopian immigrants and the low-income parts of our society in Israel. I am not running on an Ethiopian platform, but on a national platform. Yes, I am going to work for the Ethiopians, but our community is affected by these national issues.

"The Ashkenazi and Sephardic division was a big issue in the 1950s and 1960s, but no more. So with us … after twenty years no one will know who came when, or whose ancestors are Falas Mura and whose are Beta Israel." — Shlomo Molla

Batia Eyob

"The thing that really struck me the most was seeing new immigrants who were

living in caravan sites on the outskirts of the cities, seeing the elderly trying to find the right bus, walking hours, not

able to speak Hebrew. This was right after Operation Solomon.

I felt that I was lucky, that I was privileged not to have to go through this. Maybe it was a sense of responsibility;

I said to myself, 'What can I do?' Every parent, every grandparent makes sure that you feel

a responsibility for your family, for the collective. Even though most of us really don't do much with it,

the sense of belonging and the sense of wanting to do something are pretty much ingrained in all of us."

In her elementary school in Addis Ababa, Batia Eyob was intrigued by the fanciful myths she was taught as fact about the Falashas, never suspecting she was one of those "weird hyena people who worship the evil eye." Meanwhile, her parents were secretly orchestrating the escape of Ethiopian Jews through Addis Ababa to Israel. When she turned nine, Batia learned of her Jewish identity as she and her sister were flying to Israel. After following her family to Canada where she lived for eleven years, she returned to Israel. From 2003 to 2006, Batia served as director of the Israel Association for Ethiopian Jews (IAEJ). Her fluency in four languages positions her as a capable liaison between communities and cultures. With a full-time staff of ten and dozens of volunteers, the IAEJ advocates for the Ethiopian community in the areas of education, employment, and community empowerment.

When she was only nine, Batia Eyob and her sister were told they were on their way to Rome for a vacation. En route, her father revealed that they were Jews and that Israel was to be their new home. The plan was for her parents and the remaining siblings to join them in a few months, but the government was closing in on her mother and father, who were deeply involved in helping Jews escape Ethiopia. Fearing arrest, the family was forced to flee to Canada. After three lonely years in Israeli boarding schools, Batia rejoined her family in Canada. There she attended a Jewish high school and Concordia University, graduating with a degree in Applied Social Work. A brief visit to Israel drew her back to stay and help the community there.

Spending three years of her childhood without her family left an indelible imprint on Batia, and it remains one of the central themes of her personal immigrant experience. Professionally, her energy is devoted outward, to her community. After returning to Israel in 1997, she enrolled in Hebrew University and earned a master's degree in Israeli Society and Politics. She worked for two years as a consultant to Ethiopian nonprofits through Shatil, a division of the New Israel Fund that supports social change. In 2003 she began an ongoing relationship with Israel at Heart, a program which sends a diverse set of young Israelis on speaking tours to many countries to talk about everyday life in Israel. However, she made her professional home in the Israel Association for Ethiopian Jews (IAEJ), a lobbying and advocacy group started in 1994 by Micha Odenheimer, an American rabbi. (The IAEJ was originally an American organization, the AAEJ.) With a staff of ten and dozens of volunteers, Batia directed the IAEJ's major programs: lobbying for policy reform in education and employment, fostering community empowerment programs, and publicizing the contributions Ethiopians are making to Israeli society.

As a child in Ethiopia, you didn't know you were Jewish. But did you know about the existence of Falashas, as other Ethiopians called them?
In elementary school we learned about different ethnic minorities. The description of the Falashas included all of the negative stereotypes. I came home all excited, and I remember my mom was in the kitchen washing dishes. "Oh Mom, Dad, I learned about the most fascinating people in Ethiopia, and they're called Falashas. And they worship the evil eye, and they are hyena people. Falashas eat other people, they look weird, and they basically live their lives at night." I remember my mom dropped the plates she was holding, and my dad just stared at me. I didn't make any associations to myself, though. It was just a fascinating story.

The Ethiopian schools taught that as factual, even in the 1970s?
That is what I was taught.

Do you remember how you felt when you learned you were Jewish?
My dad told us when we were flying to Israel. He explained what Israel was, what being Jewish was, and that his uncle, who was once a spiritual leader of his community, had been living in Israel since the late seventies. It made no sense. All I knew is that I had been told a lie. I was angry, not because he told me I was Jewish, but because I had been lied to. My dad stayed with us in Israel for a month, and then he left for Ethiopia and promised to come back in six months with my mom and my other two sisters. But that did not work out. There were many complications. He had not told the authorities that he was going to Israel. He told them he was going to take his daughters to Italy for a vacation, so when he

came back, they asked him what happened to the children. He said he left them to study in Italy. Things were very tight in terms of his safety. The situation was very shaky in 1983; people were already being pointed out and put in prison for their involvement with Israel. Since my mom had a brother in Canada, they were able to get exit papers, but only to Canada. My dad had non-Jewish friends who helped him out. One of them was caught and imprisoned after my dad left. Some people died in prison, but his friend was released a few years later.

Were you afraid, angry, or unhappy?

All my anger started to surface when my dad did not come back as he said, and on top of that I learned that my mom left for Canada with my sisters. I was eleven, and I did not see my parents for three years. I was a very angry child basically. The only person I could depend on was my sister, who was with me. She acted like a mother, but she was too young for that role. The fact that I was not with my family during those years had a huge impact.

We were sent to a girls' religious boarding school in Rishon Letzion. We were taught how to be Jewish in that boarding school. People are really nice to you because you are just a child. They tried to make us feel comfortable so we wouldn't miss our parents. It compensated a little for that mother figure we were missing. But at the same time, we had to learn Hebrew and how to be Jewish in Israel.

Most Ethiopian children were sent to boarding schools, even those who came with their parents. Do you think that was a good idea?

It was right for the early 1980s when so many children came without their parents. You needed an environment where they were protected, where they could get an education, and a place where they could get all their needs met. The logic behind it was good, but the quality of some of the boarding schools was poor. They taught Torah and Gemara [Talmud], and that was it. They had inadequate funding. There were other religious boarding schools that were great. In my school, I studied all the subjects, so it was well balanced, and afterwards the students had choices. But many children were sent to weak schools and came out with no choices.

But children were still sent to religious schools when they arrived in the 1990s, a decade later.
The assumption was made that since the Ethiopian community is religious, they need to be sent to religious schools. This was a misconception. Ethiopian Jews are traditional, but they really did not define themselves as religious or secular. This was a modern distinction, but it didn't apply to us then. In Ethiopia, you had your priest [*kess*] who teaches you the dos and don'ts. It was a lifestyle. You practiced. If you lived in an Ethiopian Jewish village, you practiced Judaism—the dietary laws, the purification laws. There was no choice.

Today, parents are able to choose if they want to send their children to a boarding school or a community school. Most choose boarding schools, especially for high school. If a couple has five or six children and lives in a

small apartment, it is very difficult to have everyone at home.

I have heard that many Ethiopian parents are not sufficiently involved in their children's schooling. Do you think that is true?
In Israel parents have a larger role to play in the education of their children than they did back home. In Ethiopia, the majority did not send their children to school, but if you did send them, the responsibility for the child belonged to the school. The school taught them not just academics, but also values to make them a better human being. In Israel you have PTAs where the parents are on the board. The parents can influence the school curriculum to include Ethiopian Jewish traditions and so forth. Also, as a child you want to know your parents care about you, and that they are curious about what you are doing. When you see other children's parents coming in and talking to the teachers, or when there is a performance, all the Ethiopian parents should be there.

I have heard it said that the Ethiopian homes do not typically have enough books or games and toys that native Israelis consider educationally stimulating.
That's true for some people. In the minds of the Ethiopians from the villages who did not go through the Israeli system, they believe the child needs love, food, shelter, and clothing. If the parents provide these basic needs, there should be no reason the child cannot

be whoever or whatever he wants to be. Among the ones who had what you would call Israeli socialization, they know what additional curriculum is needed in order to expand the child's mind. And in those houses you would find books, children's videos, games.

I suppose there was no need for those other things in the Ethiopian village. Culture, education, and technology must be luxuries in that environment.
That's right. It made sense to study mathematics, engineering, medicine, and so on. But the arts? In their mind, the arts are not thought of as something that requires study. If you are an artist, you are someone who just paints. You have a talent. There is no need to go to school to get talent. Creative arts is not even a concept, it doesn't even exist there. To be a singer, a musician, or an actor—these are talents you have or you don't have. It is not something that you seek or develop. Also, it is not seen in a very prestigious light. It has a very low status. No one woke up in the morning saying, "I think I'll spend the day practicing singing."

All the Ethiopian Israelis I've met are deeply concerned about their community, sometimes more than their own personal circumstances. It seems almost a universal feeling. It's very inspiring.
You are right. They are very concerned. Part of it has to do with our forefathers. It had to take them a lot of energy, creativity, and wisdom to sustain the Jewish lifestyle of our community.

"We need political and economic leadership, but we need something more—a person who is going to be able to give everyone hope for the future, a vision." — Batia Eyob

They instilled in every generation that came after them a faith that they will be coming to Jerusalem. The sense of belonging to a community is something that has been transferred to each generation. Every parent, every grandparent makes sure that you feel a responsibility for your family, for the collective. Even though most of us really don't do much with it, the sense of belonging and the sense of wanting to do something are pretty much ingrained in all of us.

Can you identify the major thing that the Ethiopian community is in conflict about? Is there a major difference of opinion that divides the community?

There is a conflict about the norms we conform to socially. There is something we call in Amharic *suminyela*—what do other people say about me? That is a literal translation, but the concept is a responsibility to think of yourself not as an individual, but as a collective. What this meant back home is that people had a responsibility to come together in times of need and times of happiness. So if there is a wedding, for example, everybody is there to help you make this wedding a success. They would prepare food and bring it to you. People come to be part of the happiness. But it wasn't a *must*.

Today in Israel, everything has turned into a *must*. A person cannot have a small wedding; funerals are the same thing. It is your responsibility to invite everybody in the family and the extended family, and it does not matter where they live. And we have large families. With extended family, it can involve hundreds of people.

Why do people keep that up? It's so expensive.
If you don't invite everyone, or if you don't attend a celebration, you are looked upon negatively. There is a social consequence. They ostracize you, they talk badly about you, they curse you. They would boycott anything that you do. The financial consequence of this norm is that you spend too much money on celebrations instead of things you need, or what your children need. There is an employment consequence too, because the celebration lasts days and you must be away from your job. There are so many things that are impacted by this one behavior.

How serious is the need for national political leadership for the Ethiopian community?
We need political and economic leadership, but we need something more—a person who is going to be able to give everyone hope for the future, a vision. Where do we want to go? Where will be going ten years from now, twenty years from now? How do we see ourselves? How do we make our day-to-day reality better? There is really no single voice that speaks on behalf of the community or who can carry the voice of the people. So we are not understood. That kind of leadership is extremely important.

What is your own vision of the future, or the future you want for the community?
I want to see the community integrated into all aspects of Israeli society. I want to see a community that is proud of who they are, that is not seen as something to be ashamed of, but a community to be embraced and to be proud of. To be comfortable with who we are—Ethiopians, and Israelis, secure in our identity.

Shlomo Akale

"We are trying to preserve Ethiopian Jewish culture and heritage and to pass it on to our children in order to

give them self-identity, to teach them to be proud of themselves. . . .

The other objective for Bahalachin is to teach Israeli society who we really are."

Through a combination of cleverness and chutzpah, seventeen-year-old Shlomo Akale managed to escape Ethiopia in 1977, during the early years of the communist regime. It is a story he clearly enjoys telling in his interview in this chapter. Well-educated in Ethiopia, Shlomo worked hard on his language skills in Israel and was soon able to enroll in Bar Ilan University. After graduation, he went to work for the Ministry of Absorption until 1993. In 1996, he raised sufficient funds to found Bahalachin (Amharic for "Our Culture") with the mission of promoting an understanding of Ethiopian Jewish tradition for Israelis. From its five room Tel Aviv office, Bahalachin (known in English as "the Ethiopian Jewish Cultural Center") sends musical groups, dance troupes in traditional clothing, and crafts to schools and other public venues. Bahalachin also provides Ethiopian-style family mediation of domestic conflicts, employing the community's elders to resolve hundreds of cases annually. Also on the staff is a genealogist, Eneyew Yosef, who plays a vital role in tracking family relationships. As a new generation of Ethiopian Israelis comes of age, Bahalachin finds it must also teach them about their own roots. In this photo, Shlomo displays a stringed instrument (krar) and a basket with a removable top that serves as a portable table (mesob).

Shlomo Akale is the founder and director of Bahalachin (the Ethiopian Jewish Cultural Center), which was created to promote an understanding of Ethiopian Jewish culture among both Israelis and the Ethiopians themselves, many of whom never experienced Jewish life in their country of origin. Shlomo grew up in a small village outside of Gondar and attended a school of mixed population. He and his seven siblings were among the first to realize the Beta Israel dream of making *aliyah*. His father was self-educated and organized his own school for Jewish children. Many of his father's pupils, including his older sister, were among the Ethiopian teenagers who studied in Kfar Batya in the mid-1950s. She made *aliyah* in 1956, and an older brother found his way to Israel in 1970 and fought in the Yom Kippur War of 1973. Shlomo's escape from Ethiopia was imaginative and even slightly comical.

How did you manage to get out of Ethiopia in 1977, when the Mengistu regime had already closed the borders?

I'll give you the background. After the revolution of 1974, there was a program of the Derge [the Marxist committee that ruled Ethiopia] called Development through Cooperation for students from eleventh grade and older. We went out to the rural areas to teach the inhabitants there. We were supposed to teach them how to read and write, how to organize, whatever the government wanted us to teach. I did that for two years. I was lucky; I went some place about forty kilometers from Gondar. Some people had to go far away to dangerous places. After two years, I didn't want to do that anymore. Also, going to Israel was our dream, what we thought about. We were educated by our parents to believe that Ethiopia is not a permanent home for Jews. It was always "Next year in Jerusalem." I was a good student, but after we decided to leave, I no longer had the desire to sit in classes. I went to see one of my father's friends who was in ORT (the Organization for Rehabilitation and Training) and worked in Jewish villages trying to help the people. He connected me with people who could help me get to Israel, but I needed a passport to get out of Ethiopia.

So I went to the passport office in Addis Ababa, which was hundreds of kilometers from home, and told them I have a chance to go abroad and study. The clerk yelled at me, "Go away." I said, "Why won't you help me. I have no parents." That was a lie. "I came from Gondar, and I am here two days. I can't go home with nothing." I was despaired. He was annoyed. Then I saw a manager in another office. He was a big man, a huge man. "Excuse me," I knocked on the door. "Sir, I have nobody. I have no parents. I have a chance to go abroad. Please help me." He said, "I can't do that because no one is allowed to leave." I told him, "But my case is special because I have this chance to learn abroad and I can come back and help Ethiopia." And he said, "I would like to help you, but I can't." He said he was afraid of his colleagues and what they would say. It happens the man who I talked to first was walking by that office, and so he saw me talking to his manager. When I went downstairs past his office again, this clerk asked me, "What did the manager tell you?" I said, "He told me you should give me my passport." I don't know why, but it just came to me to say that. "Just go in and fill out the papers," he told me. I didn't plan to do that; it just happened. I had to pay twenty dollars and come back in a week. I was scared. I thought they would figure out what happened and put me in jail, but I went back the next week and got the passport. Then I flew to Kenya and from Kenya I got a plane to Israel.

You have been here thirty years. Is Israeli culture difficult for your family?

Our children are fifteen, nine, and five years old.

They are Israelis, but we are teaching them Amharic. They understand it, but they don't want to use it much because their friends are Israelis. They feel comfortable, and I feel comfortable with how they are. The problem will be when the children graduate and try to get jobs. If they [employers] put them in a category—if they label them "Ethiopian"—it will be hard for them. Employers must accept people according to their ability; not because they are Ethiopians, but because they can do the work. To tell you the truth, I hate the term "affirmative action." We all have rights. The government and business people need to see all people equally and be ready to accept Ethiopian Jews because of their ability, not because they're doing us a favor.

Can you explain what are you trying to accomplish with Bahalachin?

There are a few different programs. We are trying to preserve Ethiopian Jewish culture and heritage and to pass it on to our children to give them self-identity, to teach them to be proud of themselves. We do not want them to imitate African Americans, as we see many young people doing. We teach them about their historical, cultural, and social background, how we came to Ethiopia, how our forefathers lived as Jews. We teach about our culture and how everybody was treated in his own family system. We are also doing a genealogy project here. People didn't know how to write, so there were no family records. But we developed the ability to remember our family history, and Eneyew Yosef is putting it all on computer.

The other objective for Bahalachin is to teach Israeli society who we are. We didn't come here because we were starving. We came because we are Jews, and we found a way to escape Ethiopia as our forefathers tried to do. We have many good things to teach Israeli society. We can teach respect for people, especially to honor the elders, which is what we always taught our children, to help each other in the community. I was shocked to see that people in Israel do not give their seat to elders on a bus. We respect the elderly; even if someone is not much older, we show him respect. We have nicknames for people older than us. It is a way to honor them.

Another important part of our work is counseling. Unfortunately, many couples are getting divorced in our community because of the stress. The main problem is that the cultural system is so different. In Ethiopia, it was a patriarchal system. The father made all the decisions, but here we have a democratic system and everyone has rights. In Ethiopia, Jewish women did not go out to work; they worked at home. Now they work outside the home and they go out dressed up. People sometimes think other things [i.e., infidelity]. The cash used to be in the man's hand; now a woman can go and get money from the bank by herself. These changes are difficult for the husband. So the elders [*shemagleoch,* Amharic] in the community are respected by the people, and often they can help the couple through the conflicts. But now the budget for our counseling work has been cut. We used to have nineteen centers, but now we have four. This is tragic because if people do not have happiness in

their families, they will not be able to succeed in other areas. Everyone thinks that only employment and education are crucial, but the family is central. The elders are able to help people by speaking to them in their own language with their own cultural understanding. Israeli social workers cannot do that.

I see all these beautiful crafts here in the office. Are these for display or do you have a program to develop these artistic skills in Israel?

We bring them with us to show what our life was like. Everything in Ethiopian Jewish life was individually made. The tools that the farmers used, the furniture in their houses, their weaving—they made everything. They were craftsmen and made what they were taught by their parents. There was not a tradition of individual expression. They did not question or express themselves in art. To express something individual is new for us here.

Is it true that there is a conflict with the Russian immigrants who came at about the same time as the Ethiopian immigrants?

There is a lot of tension between some Russian children, who say, "We don't like these black kids, we don't want to be related to these children." We see it reported in the media and on television. But at one school, after two days of our educational program, I saw a Russian child with his blond hair embracing an Ethiopian child at that school. I felt like we accomplished something. This is what we need to do. If we are integrated well, we can give so much to this country and to this society.

Eneyew Yosef

"These days, we are extremely concerned about the young people—the way they dress,

the way they behave, and the way they follow fashions. Young boys have their hair dreaded and their ears pierced.

This is not a part of our culture. I would like to preserve a culture of respect. Sons and daughters must know how

to respect their parents and anyone who is older. . . . We do want to adopt some aspects of Israeli culture.

When we were in Ethiopia, there were things that we forgot, that we didn't practice, like the

wearing of *tefillin* [ritual leather binding for prayer]. The Israelis helped us to remember these things now.

Our goal is to preserve our culture, but also to be absorbed and integrated into the Israeli society."

Through his work at Bahalachin, the Ethiopian Jewish Cultural Center, Eneyew Yosef is the unofficial chief genealogist of the Ethiopian Israelis. A serious and studious man, his work is significant to Ethiopian Israeli society in two respects. First, the perilous and ongoing exodus from Ethiopia and immigration to Israel between the late 1970s and the present divided many families. Parents, brothers, sisters, uncles, cousins, and even husbands and wives were forced to escape at different times. Family members reached Israel years apart. Eneyew's genealogical research helps people locate lost family members and clarify ambiguities in lineage. Second, Ethiopian Jewry is a relatively small population of very large families, and therefore they are vulnerable to same-family marriages between cousins. In Israel, Eneyew's database of 30,000 individuals and counting helps ensure healthy marriages.

Simcha Getahune

"In the other social services departments, they wait for them to come in,

but Ethiopian kids won't come to them. The Ethiopian youth don't know what a social worker is.

In Ethiopia, there wasn't such a thing as a social worker. So we go out to look for them . . . .

I'm not afraid of these kids. I really, really love them a lot. So they probably sense that in me.

Also, in the Ethiopian culture if you are educated as I am, your status as a woman is above even the men,

so I get respect for that. I am on television a lot. The teenagers see me and they say,

'Wow, I saw you on TV, and here you are!' It's like a gimmick."

With a social work degree from Bar Ilan University and years in the front lines of poor neighborhoods in Bat Yam, Simcha Getahune is well prepared for her role of preventing youth who drift close to the brink from falling over the edge. She is an Israeli "catcher in the rye," one of six directors of ELEM, an acronym in Hebrew that translates as "Youth in Distress." ELEM is a sprawling nonprofit organization, founded in 1981 to rescue young people in need of intervention. The staff, assisted by 1,800 volunteers, delivers programs all over Israel to thousands of young people, ages twelve to twenty-one. Simcha supervises a workforce of sixty and is responsible for Russian, Arab, Druze, and native Israeli youth, as well as 3,000 at-risk Ethiopian Israeli kids. Her management position in ELEM's Tel Aviv headquarters, the setting for this photograph, does not stop her from taking a hands-on approach. She still befriends troubled teens in nightclubs, parks, and abandoned bomb shelters. She wins their confidence and then entices them with professional help and hope for the future.

If anyone is in a position to take the pulse of Ethiopian youth in Israel, it is Simcha Getahune. One of six ELEM (Youth at Risk) directors, she supervises the outreach to troubled young people all over Israel. This interview was conducted while she was on a U.S. State Department tour billed as "Civil Society and Emerging Leaders of Israel." Simcha, along with Russian, Arab, and Bedouin community workers, presented the work of Israeli NGOs. Although her portfolio includes children from many ethnic groups, this conversation focused on her personal background and how she manages to connect with Ethiopian teenagers who reject the kind of social institution she represents.

Tell us about your family in Ethiopia.

I was born in Sermaleh, near Gondar, and my father taught Hebrew. I was the oldest of nine children in a religious family. My father was the son of a famous *kess* [priest] from the Baruch family. My grandfather and his brothers taught the Torah, how to live as Jews and observe holidays, but it was not formal education. When my father was young, he learned that Israelis had opened a school for teachers in Asmara. The teacher was the well-known scholar Yona Bogale. But my father's parents would not allow

him to go there, so he ran away. This was in the 1950s. He went with my cousin, and they learned there for about a year. Some of the students there went to Israel, to Kfar Batya, but my father came back to the village and started to teach in Gondar and other villages where there were Jews. He was promoted to teach at a school in Ambover. My father taught for twenty-one years, until Mengistu came to power [in 1974], when teaching Hebrew was prohibited. The communist regime decided to destroy anything related to Hebrew or Israel. So what happened was that my father and all the teachers were suspected of being involved with Israel. So they arrested them, and my father was in jail for a year. After a year, he and five others like him were freed and returned to the village.

The new government was looking for a leader in our community, and they appointed my father to be a magistrate to overseeing several villages. It was a paradox because he was just in jail, but he was respected in our community. He was more lenient with Jews and helped them legally with property disputes.

Was your Jewish practice at home traditional Ethiopian or was it influenced by your father's education in rabbinic Judaism in Asmara?

It was a mixture of both traditions. For example

the *siddur* [Hebrew prayer book] was brought to us from Israel for prayer. My father would pray from the *siddur*, and he would also read the Orit [the Bible in Ge'ez]. On the other hand, my grandfather kept the Ethiopian traditions.

What would you say are the fundamental difficulties facing Ethiopian youth, if you had to choose three or four?

The first is the problem of personal identity and cultural identity. The second is the misunderstandings between the parents and kids. The parents are physically in Israel, but their mentality is as if they were still in Ethiopia. But the kids are in the Israeli world. There is a deep conflict between these worlds. We provide help to bridge the gap between them. Many times the parents say, "Thank you very much for returning my child to me." You have to work with the whole family, not just the kids. The third problem is the environment they are in, which is very dangerous. Because of it, they can get involved in alcohol, drugs, and prostitution.

On the topic of cultural identity, is it true that a lot of the Ethiopian kids are taking the African American rap artists as models?

I'd say that the researchers are exaggerating this phenomenon. Yes, some kids listen to rap music and take American blacks as their role models. They are like all adolescents, but I don't think that most of them understand the meaning of the songs. It's really a small group that wants to identify with the African Americans.

When I spoke with Yafet Alemu [see Chapter Five], he said that if the youth had somewhere to go, like a community center, they wouldn't get into so much trouble. Do you think that's true?
He is right. Instead of being busy with after-school programs, they get involved with crime and antisocial behavior because there are no appropriate programs. Another thing, even if there is a place like that, there has to be an Ethiopian professional involved to bring them there. Even some older kids working with them can motivate them. It doesn't have to be a professional social worker.

How do you get the Ethiopian kids involved in ELEM? Why do they come to you?
They don't come to me. I don't wait for them to come to my clinic; I go to where they are. They'll push me away many times, but I chase after them. That's the way. They'll say, "Nudnikit! Why are you chasing after me?" And I smile. I connect with them. First of all, I speak to them in Amharic. It makes them feel as if they are doing me a favor, so then they come to me—it's a game. They are everywhere—clubs, bomb shelters under the apartment buildings, the parks. They go there and smoke and hang out. The teenage girls

sometimes sell their bodies where people are waiting to hitchhike. So I go there. It's hard. But we succeed sometimes. There is violence. They use knives and guns. They injure each other and take revenge on each other.

If you go into a bomb shelter and there are five kids there, what do you say? How do you begin?
I say, "Hello." They say, "What are you doing here?" I smile. I sit in a corner and talk with the one that seems the most friendly. I get into their issues. After, they start to ask me some questions. I tell them who I am, at their level. You are not allowed to lie to them. I flow with them. It takes time. I ask them, "Do you want to speak now? It's okay if you want to speak another day." I give them all the options.

Do you feel it's safe for you? In Ethiopia the role of women is very restricted. Is it unusual for young Ethiopians to see you seeking them out?
My big concern comes when they are involved in organized crime, because then I am threatening their "mafia." The mafia doesn't want me to take the youth from them. But the young people, no, I'm not afraid of these kids.

Do you see any signs of hope?
What is nice is that when they are doing drugs, or when they are doing their vandalism, and they see a little kid, even if they don't know him, as soon as they see him they'll do everything they can to get the kid out of there. They say, "What's that little kid doing here? Get him out of here." It really bothers them. They protect the young kids like that. This shows that they care about them and have not forgotten their tradition, and this makes me happy.

Nigist Mengesha

"I have been in Israel for twenty years and there have been many different programs for

Ethiopians, but there were no Ethiopians involved in the decision-making process, in the planning process, and

even the problem assessment. But this program [the ENP]

is from the bottom up; the Ethiopian immigrants are the ones who are setting priorities and

they are making the assessments."

Nigist Mengesha first tried to get to Israel at age fifteen by attempting to board a merchant ship sailing from the Eritrean coast. Lack of an entrance visa from Israel thwarted her plan. Thirteen years later, in 1984, she qualified for leaving Ethiopia by showing officials an offer to study at Ben Gurion University. But there was a catch: married and the mother of four, Nigist had to leave her family in Ethiopia as collateral. She took the leap of faith, and, after several anxious months, the family managed to escape and join her. In Israel, Nigist earned two advanced degrees in education. In 1996, she founded Fidel ("Alphabet" in Amharic), a successful program that supports Ethiopian elementary school children by providing mediators in the schools to work with parents and teachers. In June 2003 Nigist was selected to become director general of the Ethiopian National Project (ENP), the first program of national scope addressing the needs of the Ethiopian community. The Jewish Agency, the United Jewish Communities of America, and her own community are pinning their hopes on the ENP to help create a better life for the Ethiopian Israelis.

In an expansive conference room adjacent to her office in one of the Jewish Agency buildings, Nigist Mengesha sits at the head of a long, highly polished table and speaks of the task confronting her community. Descended from a family with many models for a life in public service, she is not afraid to take on responsibility. Her grandfather was a spiritual leader, Kess Akale, who founded the Jewish village of Woyniyeh near the large city of Ambover, which had a Jewish population of nearly 10,000. During her childhood, her father moved the family to Gondar, where he became active politically, the only Jew to govern a city district.

Nigist's background in Ethiopia prepared her for an activist role in Israel. As early as 1975, she volunteered to operate an Oxfam feeding station in Wollo. Soon after, she moved to the capital and attended the University of Addis Ababa's School of Social Work. Her first job was in the Department of Prison Administration, where she met many Jewish prisoners of the Mengistu regime who had been accused of working with Israel and the Mossad. It was during those years that she orchestrated her move to Israel in the guise of an invitation to study at Ben Gurion University.

In Israel, Nigist earned several degrees: a B.A. from Bar Ilan University, a master's degree in social work from Hebrew University, and a post-graduate fellowship at the Mandel School for Educational Leadership in Jerusalem. Based on the research for her master's thesis, Nigist created Fidel, a program to improve early education by training mediators to bridge the gap between Ethiopian parents and teachers. (See interview with Takele Mekonen, Nigist's successor at Fidel, in Chapter One).

Can you tell us the story behind your escape from Ethiopia?
In the 1980s, you were not allowed to leave Ethiopia. There were two ways to escape. One was to run away to Sudan during the night. The other way was to work through all the bureaucracy, as I did for two or three years. You have to have someone guarantee some amount of money, have rich people to guarantee you. I got a scholarship offer from Israel—first for a master's in social work. The government refused to approve it. "You are already a social worker," they told me. "We don't need extra education for you." So I wrote back to my sponsor in Israel and got another scholarship, this time from Ben Gurion University for computer science. This time the government said I could go but I had

to sign an agreement promising to come back. They said, "Many Ethiopians are not coming back. How can we guarantee it? So you have to leave your family here." I had to bring two guarantors to sign for me: If I remain in Israel, they have to pay money—thousands and thousands of birr. Two people signed for me, and I left my children and my husband and my family and made *aliyah.*

Weren't you afraid that your family was not going to get out?
We were all crying. It was a painful separation. But I believed that they were going to join me soon. I arrived in Israel and was given a dormitory room that I shared. One small room, two beds. After two months of pain and worry, my husband and children joined me.

Men were like lords in the Ethiopian family. How has the role of men and women changed with the move to Israel?
The bottom line is that Ethiopian women are now the heads of the family. They are more integrated than the men, generally speaking. For women, status is nothing, so they are willing to work anywhere. They are cleaners. They go to the school to arrange things for the children. They can go to the social security office. All of

the outside connections for the family are through women. That is a big change from the way it was in Ethiopia.

Because the women are taking the role of the head of the family, and because of unemployment, and because of the economic problems, there is a high divorce rate. The skills that we brought from Ethiopia cannot fit here. That is, our traditional agriculture, traditional handicrafts. We can't go into the work force to compete. You need skills in high-tech and modern things. Even to work as a blue collar worker you need the basic skills. So there is high unemployment. Women are more independent than they were in Ethiopia. If they divorce now, they have an income, they work, they have government support.

What was the main rationale for the Ethiopian National Project?
This program was conceived by the Jewish Agency for Israel and Stephen Hoffman [then president of the United Jewish Communities]. Having a national program is the right concept because the Ethiopian problem is an Israeli social problem. There is low educational achievement; there is a high rate of unemployment; there is a high rate of school drop-outs; there is a high rate of crime among

the Ethiopian children. It was not like that in Ethiopia. There were no drugs. Children were not acquainted with such a life, such a terrible life. Most of the children were not going to school, but they were educated by their own families to be good citizens, to be good people, to contribute to their family, to contribute to their society. Now that we are here, we should not be the Israeli underclass. If we do not find a solution for these problems, it will be a very big problem for Israeli society.

Where do you think the solution lies? There are so many different issues that need attention.
There are some problems affecting only the Ethiopian community because of the gap we have between ourselves and Israeli society. The gap in education, the gap in language, the gap in skills, the trauma of the exodus to Israel, the

role reversal between the parents and the children [in which the parents depend on the children to help them navigate society]. These problems need patient treatment in this community. People are talking about integration. For me, integration into Israeli society means equal opportunity, less discrimination, opportunity for employment, and a good future here in Israel. Integration is not bringing an Ethiopian kid together with ten non-Ethiopians and teaching them the same way. The Ethiopian child has a very big gap to overcome and sometimes he is ashamed of himself and thus ashamed of his background.

What is the ENP doing specifically for children?
The ENP is focusing on a specific age group, from twelve to eighteen years old. There are about 14,000 children in that age group.

We help them prepare for the *bagrut* [matriculation examination]. Our strategy is working individually or with small groups with children in need. We use a push-and-pull process. We are taking the lowest one-third of underachievers or weak students and working with them. We also have a program for the upper one-third of students who are talented and have high potential. We give them intensive work to bring them into excellence. The Youth at Risk program is supporting and rehabilitating those who are involved with drugs and alcohol. At the same time, we also have a community empowerment program. So our challenge is both in education and social welfare and on the community level. This program is called SPACE [Schooling Priorities and Community Empowerment].

How do you reach out to all these kids?
Originally we worked in six pilot cities. The reason we started working in those cities was because PACT [Parents and Children Together, a JDC-sponsored initiative] was working in those cities, and the infrastructure that PACT created was very helpful. We form steering committees whose members are 50 percent from the Ethiopian community. At this point we have seventeen Ethiopian-run nonprofits who advise the ENP. But the ENP is our own, run by Ethiopians. It is our culture, and we are the experts on our problems.

Should there be some type of affirmative action program, as there is in the United States, to address employment discrimination against African Americans?
We don't have the same situation or history. We were not brought here to be slaves. We are here because we are Jews. We belong to the Jewish state the same as any other group of Jews. But Israel should provide incentives to put qualified Ethiopian workers in mainstream Israeli jobs. I don't know about making affirmative action a legal requirement. I think it would be a stigma to the community.

Do you think bringing to Israel the many thousands of Falas Mura in Ethiopia will worsen the social problems of the Ethiopian community already here?
First of all, there are emotional problems for those who are in Israel because part of the family is still in Ethiopia. There is hunger there, anti-Semitism, communicable diseases. They are in danger. Some of the families here are working day and night to send money to Ethiopia, and so there is starvation here in Israel. Nobody speaks about it. The Falas Mura must be here, not because they are starving, but because they are Jews. They are recognized by the rabbinate. The Jewish Agency and other organizations are working hard to bring Jews from all over the world, trying to convince them to come to Israel. But the Falas Mura are just sitting in Ethiopia. Really, what a pity!

How are you going to change the perception Israelis have about the Ethiopian community?
I believe that my culture has something to contribute to Israeli society. The melting pot concept didn't work. What we are doing now is retraining the school staff about the Ethiopian culture. There is support from the Ethiopian organizations and the Ministry of Education. They are trying to give some tools to the schools so they can teach children about the Ethiopian culture.

CHAPTER VIII

PROFESSIONALLY SPEAKING

Employment is a revealing lens for measuring the degree to which Ethiopian Jews have become Ethiopian Israelis.

The employment problem presents a perfect opportunity to apply the proverb "Little by little, even the egg can stand on its legs and walk." While integration is clearly a work in progress, progress may be more gradual here than in any other area because it is dependent to a great extent on Israeli attitudes. Statistically, Ethiopian Israeli unemployment tops any other ethnic group in Israel, at about 60 percent. This is what prompted Israeli, Ethiopian, and American Jewish community leaders to reiterate the phrase "permanent underclass of Israeli society" to express what they fear may happen to the community.

Ethiopian Israelis experience not just unemployment, but under-employment—the need to take jobs that are below their level of education and competence. In 2005, there were about 3,000 Ethiopian Israeli university students, most of whom were well aware that even with a diploma, finding work in a mainstream sector of the economy would be unlikely. University graduates often find themselves in low-level service industry jobs, such as security guards or hotel room cleaners, and no better off in the short term than high-school graduates. Thus under-employment compounds the problem for the next generation, because it discourages younger students from pursuing higher education.

The Israeli work environment is one of many areas that required a radical reorientation for Ethiopian Jews. In the villages from which they came, a man was his own boss. He worked when necessary and was responsible primarily for himself, his family, and the land he worked. When there was no work required, there was no need to "show up at the office." Work went hand in hand with nature or with wood, clay, and metal. The product of one's labor was tangible. Furthermore, it was understood in Ethiopia that family celebrations and funerals were commitments that superceded work. Even in Israel, Ethiopian weddings and funerals can last two or three days, and Ethiopian employees feel obligated to attend to avoid insulting the family. When such unplanned absences occur, they stretch the flexibility and tolerance of Israeli employers.

About 65 to 70 percent of the community lives below the poverty line, according to most estimates, but lack of work has an impact that goes beyond poverty itself. In Ethiopia, the men were always the breadwinners, controlled the family finances, and distributed money to their wives and children. In Israel, the roles have, in many cases, been reversed: women are more likely to be employed than men. As Nigist Mengesha explains, "Generally speaking, for women status is nothing, so they are willing to work anywhere."[1] Now, the women earn the money, and because of it, they are experiencing increased independence. For the older and middle-aged generation, the men are not accustomed to women leaving the home every day, while they stay behind with nothing to do. The greater success women have had in the Israeli work environment—combined with the failure of their husbands to adjust to it—is considered one of the causes of depression and alcoholism among men and a contributing factor to a relatively high incidence of domestic violence. At the same time, however, women have gained the financial independence to initiate divorce.

Finally, for those who have broken into the professional ranks, there is another, more subtle barrier. As Shlomo Berihun explains, "Today when Ethiopians finish academic studies or professional training, they are asked immediately to work with Ethiopians. Unfortunately, they are not being hired to work in the general Israeli community."[2] Sometimes, as in Shlomo's case, Ethiopians are hired to work with several minority communities, but not usually in the mainstream economy. The message they read into this restriction is: "You are qualified, but not good enough to do the job for us." It is axiomatic that Ethiopians have to outperform native Israelis to prove that they are equals. Thus, lawyer Itzik Dessie, (see his interview in this chapter), who has won cases before Israel's Supreme Court, says he still has trouble attracting native Israeli clients.

The role that discrimination plays in hiring invites scrutiny. While there are certainly employers who discriminate against those of a different skin color, some Ethiopians doubt that being black is the essence of the problem. The discrimination is multifaceted, of course, but based in large part on two dubious assumptions: first, because most Ethiopian Jews arrived uneducated, it is widely believed that they cannot become adequately educated in Israel or acquire relevant professional skills; and second, there is a common fear that the cultural divide cannot be bridged. There are thousands of Ethiopian Israelis—and dozens in this book—who present a convincing challenge to these assumptions. Additionally, the demographics are changing in a way that makes these damaging beliefs increasingly irrelevant. In 2006, about 28 percent of Ethiopian Israelis were born in Israel, and that percentage will increase every year. While some cultural differences remain, the academic and professional gap will continue to shrink as the number of *sabras* (those born in Israel) grows

Gidon Ayech,[3] who has a master's degree in economics, whimsically remarked, "Sometimes I think I got my position . . . because I am Ethiopian, and other times I think I got it even though I am Ethiopian." Ethiopian Israelis do not like either of these options. Therefore, they reject the strategy of affirmative action—addressing employment discrimination by requiring the government and businesses to hire minorities. There have been voluntary "affirmative action" practices among some enlightened organizations. The University of Haifa, for example, has made it easier for Ethiopian Israeli students to qualify for admission by reducing the importance of their scores on the psychometric exam (a kind of aptitude test), because that test is clearly culturally dependent. Some government ministries have voluntarily decided to hire more Ethiopian Jews, especially after they realized that doing so increased their own competency. Nevertheless, the individuals interviewed for this book generally disapprove of affirmative action on the grounds that "it creates a stigma." They want to be hired based on their qualifications, not their ethnicity. It is no secret that it will take a change in the attitude of the Israeli business environment to make significant progress against employment discrimination. That is why in 2006 the Jewish Agency initiated a campaign of publicizing success stories, highlighting the accomplishments of Ethiopian Israelis in print and in television spots.

One of the reasons for optimism, as you will discover in this chapter, is that those who do succeed in crossing the boundary into the mainstream are aware of the need to bring others along with them. The concern for their own community is one of the most inspiring assets of the Ethiopian Israeli community. Little by little, the egg will indeed walk, although it will take time.

Abebe Molatu

"Since I became a citizen, I have done all kinds of work to support my family. Cleaning jobs, security guard,

anything I could find. I went to the Technion to study mechanical engineering. I was one of three Ethiopians in my

class, and the only one who has graduated so far. Every employer is looking for someone with experience.

So you can't get anywhere. I don't think the discrimination is based on color.

Some people think that because Ethiopians come from a small village and are not educated the way Israelis are, that

they cannot learn or work professionally. If I have a boss like that, it's going to be difficult for me."

■

This photograph of Abebe Molatu, taken on the rooftop of the Neveh Yosef Community Center in Haifa, reveals his strength and his burdened state of mind. At the time, he was unemployed, his wife was ill and in the hospital, and he was doing his best to care for their children, visit his wife daily, and work at whatever low-paying, part-time jobs he could find. Abebe is an educated man who had been an officer in the Ethiopian Air Force. When Mengistu's regime was toppled in 1991, he spent six months in jail as a political prisoner. When we met Abebe, he had recently graduated from an engineering program at the prestigious Technion in Haifa, but he could only find menial day jobs in Israel.

When we next spoke with Abebe, his life had changed markedly for the better. His wife regained her health. Then, the Neveh Yosef Community Center helped Abebe get an interview with the same pharmaceutical company where his friend Eshetu, interviewed in this chapter, also works. He was assigned to the chemical division, where the active ingredients of the medications are made. Abebe recommended an improvement in the production line that reduced an eight-hour process to four hours. In February 2006 he received an award for Outstanding Employee of the Year for 2005 in his division. We wanted to shoot another portrait of Abebe in a happier frame of mind, but on the day we arranged to be in Haifa, he had to work.

Eshetu Kebede

"I consider myself a very lucky person. Generally, Israelis don't believe that Ethiopians are professional

enough, but this is not true. They do excellent work. However, even the Ethiopians who are educated

and get positions in good companies have to use personal connections. I got my job because there was a fellow in my

company who I studied with at the Technion [the Israel Institute of Technology] in the Ph.D. program.

He brought me in."

■

Eshetu Kebede, a Ph.D. in chemistry, is responsible for guaranteeing the shelf life of medicines produced by the Israeli division of a multi-national pharmaceutical company. Though raised a Christian, Eshetu was taught by his mother that he was one of the "children of Israel," so he made the transition to life in Israel and Judaism smoothly, as he explains in his interview. Like so many Ethiopian Israelis, Eshetu identifies his own well-being in part with the community's success. As a scientist, his analytical and organized approach to complex problems enables him to take a leadership role in Haifa's sister-city relationship with the Boston Jewish community. Eshetu is also co-chair of a committee that works with the mayor's office to improve the quality of life for the 5,000 Ethiopian Jews in Haifa. Eshetu's daughter, Aklile, a university student with a lot to say about life in Israel, appears in Chapter Three.

Eshetu Kebede's academic talent was the force that propelled him from life as a Christian in Ethiopia to Israeli citizenship. After his mother moved to southern Ethiopia, he was raised by an uncle who lived near Gondar, and Eshetu attended a religiously mixed high school. As a result of his high school performance, he received a scholarship from the United States Agency for International Development (USAID) to attend the University of Southern California, where he completed his B.A. and master's in chemistry in four years.

After graduation, he returned to Ethiopia and taught science at the high school where he had been a student. Subsequently, he worked as a technology specialist in the food industry during the Mengistu regime. In 1992, after the communist government was overthrown, he was surprised to find that many of his personal friends were moving to Israel. He had not known they were Jews, but he decided to follow them. He applied successfully for a scholarship to study chemistry at the Technion (the Israel Institute of Technology). Eshetu decided to stay in Israel for further study and in 1997 was awarded a Ph.D. in chemistry from the Technion. In 1999 he converted to Judaism and became a citizen.

As a Christian in Ethiopia, what do you recall about the Christians' attitude toward Israel?
I remember that during the 1967 war, Muslims and Christians were separated into pro-Israel and pro-Egypt. The Christians were dominant and pro-Israel. Our teachers in Ethiopia happened to be Russian, but we were opposed to Russia because they were supplying the Egyptians with armaments. When Israel won the war, everyone was happy and celebrated. At our school, the Christian students had a real emotional involvement with the state of Israel.

Did you speak English well before you left for school in the United States? You seem to have no difficulty speaking in English.
When I grew up in Ethiopia, English was the instructional language beginning in sixth grade. In my case, I began studying English in the first grade. Of course, at home we spoke Amharic, but all my textbooks were in English. These days in Ethiopia, nearly everything is in Amharic. Only in college do they use English as the language of instruction.

You were able to get a professional-level job because of your education. What are the problems preventing Ethiopian youth from following an educational path to employment?

Many immigrants come here when they are over eighteen, and if you are over the age of eighteen, you cannot go to the public school. We need a way to make sure they get training, vocational or academic. I know there are some programs now. [The Jewish Agency's KEDMA program provides education and training for this age group.][4] But this type of program has to be expanded to include more people. There is another kind of problem for the younger children. If a child comes here at age nine or ten, they put him in a class with his age group, but that is not his academic level. He should be in a lower grade because he has a language problem. So this student is going to fail in school.

What kind of academic assistance were the Technion students getting?
The University of Haifa opened a preparatory course for Ethiopians, that is, pre-university and after high school. There was an Israeli teacher at the university who really tried to help Ethiopians. He knew I was at the Technion and that I spoke English, so he called me to be one of the teachers. He said, "I don't care how much English you teach them. I want you to be an example of an Ethiopian who can complete university study, who can earn a Ph.D."

There have been many complaints about how Ethiopian children were placed in schools. Some were labeled as learning disabled, when the real problem was cultural. Is this still going on?

This categorization of children as learning disabled was very common. How did this tendency come about? I don't know if it was lack of patience on the part of the teachers or lack of understanding about Ethiopian families by the schools and government. Was it racism, discrimination? Personally, I think it was a lack of understanding. Most Ethiopian children come from families where the parents cannot read or write. They cannot assist their children with homework. They do not know how to check their schoolwork; and if they have many children, there is no space for them to study. Now the tendency to categorize children as learning disabled is reduced because of Fidel, which started training mediators as a bridge between the family and the school.[5]

People talk about the "breakdown" of the Ethiopian family. Do you think that is what's going on?

I don't know if it's a breakdown, but it is a big problem. The man was earning the bread for the family [in Ethiopia], and he comes to Israel and all of a sudden he earns nothing. If he tries to discipline his child, the social worker comes and tells him, "You have no right to shout at your child, let alone beat him." [Hitting a disobedient or disrespectful child was an accepted practice in Ethiopia.] At the same time, he has nothing to do, so he sits and gossips. This is

definitely a cause of depression. There are conflicts when the woman works and the husband does not. All this is a stress on the family.

What about your own family? Has your family adjusted to Israel?

Personally, I am lucky to have a good job. Someone I studied with helped bring me in. But my wife, who is also in the technical field, has had an employment problem. She was doing very well and advancing quickly, but suddenly there was a problem with an individual, I think because of cultural differences. But I don't feel comfortable going into the specific situation. My daughter has always been the only Ethiopian in her class. Of course, she has experienced discrimination, but it is on an individual basis from certain types of people. The first few weeks she was going to school in Haifa, some children started calling her *kushi* [equivalent to "nigger"]. Both of our children came home and cried, "They called us *kushi*." My wife and I sat down together and said, "Look children. What are we? Look at our skin. Are we white? No, we are black. So they call you black. Don't react, don't get angry. Tell them that you are black. So what?" So both our children responded to these kids by saying, "So what? You are white cheese; you are like

the rear end of an ape," or something like that! That stopped the other children.

Not many families have parents who are role models of success like you and your wife. Where will these children get the encouragement to be educated?

I want to tell you one small story. When my daughter was in elementary school, her second-grade teacher called me in and said, "Eshetu, I am very sorry, Aklile is not doing very well." I asked, "Where does she stand in the class?" She told me, "I don't care where she stands in the class; she is not working according to her ability. She can do a lot more than what she is doing." That was an Israeli teacher. We need these kinds of teachers in every school.

Dan Berkolin

"Twice a month, I do presentations for kids between ten and fourteen years old. I should do it more often, but this is

how much I am doing it now. I tell them to believe in themselves, that they should be proud to be here in Israel and

that they can reach their goals, not just in sports—in anything. But you have to believe in order to make it happen.

Everything is in the mind. If you believe it, you can touch the sky."

Dan Berkolin leads a charmed life, doing what he loves and making a lot of money at it. One of a handful of Ethiopian Israeli professional athletes, Dan plays soccer for Tel Aviv's B'nei Akiva club. When the great Diego Maradona led Argentina to the World Cup in 1986, Dan was only six years old, but he recalls watching the match on Israeli television and deciding then to get serious about soccer.

The youngest of nine children, Dan made *aliyah* through Sudan with his father as part of Operation Moses. The rest of his family immigrated a month later. They lived in an absorption center in Kiryat Gat, then moved to Arad for several years, and in a bold move left their predominantly Ethiopian neighborhood for a home in Yehud, just west of Tel Aviv. In Yehud, Dan went to school with native Israelis, and since that time only one or two of his close friends have been Ethiopian. The family is religious and strictly observes the Sabbath, except for Dan, whose games are sometimes on Saturday. His parents were opposed to his career for religious reasons. "They couldn't break me," he says, "so they decided to be supportive." They go to his games, but not when they are on Saturdays. The only scheduled part of Dan's life that is not devoted to soccer is working with Ethiopian youth at the school where his sister teaches. There he gives the children pep talks on self-esteem.

Dr. Seffefe Aycheh

"By origin, the Ethiopian Jewish community has been a rural one, and the patterns of diseases that existed in Ethiopia were mostly infectious and simple communicable diseases that were caused by uncontrolled environmental factors like water quality, mosquitoes, and lack of good sanitation. Of course, in the short term those diseases killed a lot of people, but they could be controlled easily when the environment was proper. When they came to Israel and the environment changed, the rate of these diseases dropped very drastically. On the other hand, the community is now challenged by another health situation. Their lifestyle changed to a modern one—different food systems, lack of physical exercise, and psychological stress—so chronic acquired diseases, which are very difficult to control, are rising to a high level. For example, diabetes, hypertension, obesity, and mental illnesses."

Dr. Seffefe Aycheh is the director of a community center in Netanya, home to 10,000 Ethiopian Jews, and is a classic example of underemployment. What he should be doing is monitoring and addressing the health issues of his community nationally. With years of public health experience in Ethiopia and a Ph.D. in epidemiology from Tel Aviv University (in 2000), his doctoral thesis "Epidemiological Study of Disease Patterns in the Ethiopian Jewish Immigrants in Israel" is timely and relevant. The Ethiopian Israelis have endured a radical change of diet and lifestyle, stress imposed by poverty, and exposure of many young men to HIV in the slums of Addis Ababa while they waited to immigrate. Despite a perfect match between the need for public health professionals and his qualifications, Dr. Seffefe cannot find work in his field. "I was turned down three times due to lack of a budget," he says with evident astonishment. "How could there be not one single salary for the health of the Ethiopian community?" He does have one outlet for his knowledge of and passion about public health issues: every week, he volunteers as a guest on the Amharic broadcast on Israel Radio, where he provides advice about HIV and other prominent health issues. Dr. Seffefe and his wife have put their four children through college, and two of them are now studying for advanced degrees. Perhaps in Dr. Seffefe's children's generation, the waste and frustration of under-employment will be less common.

Dereje Reta

"After I graduated from Jimma University in Ethiopia, I was already twenty-five years old. NACOEJ was able to get me a

'scholarship' that enabled me to leave Ethiopia as a student, and then get to Israel. This was in 1984. I went to Hebrew

University and a very generous American couple helped pay my expenses. Without them, I could not have completed my

degree because I couldn't afford textbooks or any of the materials I needed. I met my wife while I was in school;

she was in nursing school. I was very lucky again, because after I got a degree in biochemistry, I saw an ad for a job at T'nuva,

and I applied and got it! That is very unusual. We got help originally from Israel, NACOEJ, and many American Jews,

but right now, the Ethiopian community is trying to solve its own problems with its own organizations and leaders."

■

With a degree in biochemistry from Hebrew University, Dereje Reta manages a quality-control department for T'nuva, the Israeli company that supplies more than 70 percent of the milk products in the Land of Milk and Honey. As a teenager, Dereje was among several lucky students who benefited from the Adopt-a-Student program, a creation of the North American Conference on Ethiopian Jewry (NACOEJ). Although the government pays the tuition of Ethiopian university students, it does not cover living expenses, which often forces students to take jobs and abandon their studies. A Jewish American couple from Los Angeles "adopted" Dereje and helped to set the stage for his academic success. With funding for program administration from the Vidal Sassoon Foundation, Adopt-a-Student matches 300 Ethiopian Israeli students with donors who reduce their need to work while studying. The investment in Dereje's education changed his life, and his success may have a ripple effect on others because it has helped him become more effective. He has served on the advisory council to the Ethiopian National Project in Rehovot, and in March 2006 he ran for the Knesset as a member of the new Ethiopian-led political party, Atid Echad (One Future). In this photo, Dereje and his wife, Edna, offer some freshly made *injerra*, the traditional Ethiopian flat bread that was a staple of their diet growing up. Their two sons probably won't be preserving that element of Ethiopian culture. "We forgot to teach them to eat *injerra* when they were young," says Dereje. "Now all they want is white bread."

Tsega Melaku

"Amharic radio is very important for our community because we don't have any other way to communicate

as a group. There are not enough of us for an Amharic newspaper. We broadcast two hours daily,

of course the news, but also practical advice, such as banking and how to use the health care system.

Originally, to explain these things to the community, we had to interview native Israelis in Hebrew and translate

into Amharic. Now I am very happy to say we have Ethiopian experts we can interview.

These are Ethiopian Israeli professionals—doctors, lawyers, social workers, and rabbis. It's been a short time that our

community is here, twenty years or so for most, and we have closed the gap a lot."

∎

From her perch behind the microphone of Radio Amharic, Tsega Melaku is well positioned to hear her community's concerns. The two hours of daily airtime is a mix of news, interviews, and talk radio. With her listeners numbering about 90 percent of Ethiopian Israeli adults, her programs are a magnet for diverse opinions on virtually every topic from religion to health care to the economy. Radio Amharic is part of Reshet Klitah Aliyah (The Immigrants' Network), which is operated by the Ministry of Communications and allots time to fourteen different language groups in Israel. In 1988, Tsega started out as an occasional fill-in for the Amharic spot, which was then only ten minutes daily. In 2003, she became the director of programming for Radio Amharic and for several other ethnic language broadcasts. We interviewed and photographed Tsega in the only available broadcast booth, belonging to another station, Reshet Gimel, whose logo appears in the background. Every day, Tsega hears and speaks about what's on people's minds. In the midst of her own success, she is saddened by the community's lack of opportunity and its struggles on so many fronts. She is afraid that the religious devotion of her generation is being replaced by secular youth who identify primarily with being black. "The community," she says, "is confused."

Tsega Melaku was born in the city of Gondar into a religious and Zionist family. During the 1950s, her father learned Hebrew in the celebrated school in Asmara run by Yona Bogale. In 1984, Tsega graduated high school and her parents sent her with a group of seventeen teenagers on a flight to Egypt under the pretext of heading for a tour of Canada. Egyptian officials did not accept the story and they put the teenagers in a Cairo jail for several days. "We were all crying and very frightened," she recalls, until the group was ransomed by unknown rescuers, probably the Jewish Agency or Mossad. Tsega's parents were expected to follow her within a few months, but they were not able to leave Ethiopia. She did not see them again for eight years. In Israel, Tsega was ambitious about her education and earned a B.A. in political science from Bar Ilan University and a master's degree in business administration from Touro College in Jerusalem. She worked briefly as a medical lab technician, but she soon recognized that her work at the radio station, despite its infrequency and meager salary, was her calling. In fifteen years, she progressed from an entry-level, part-time job to the director of programming for the broadcasts of several ethnic groups. Under her direction, Amharic radio for the Ethiopian Israeli community has become an essential resource for education and social awareness.

Hearing all the points of view that you do on your shows, are you optimistic about the future?
I think the next generation will have a good life. But our generation has to work very hard, and we need a good education. Family planning is something we have started doing here. In Ethiopia, we had children until we could not have any more. Our generation has fewer children, especially educated couples. I'm thirty-eight and I have two kids, ages eight and eleven. If a woman has four children now, we joke with her and ask, "What are you, *Haredi* [ultra-Orthodox]?" So this is a big change. I tell my kids, "You have to believe you can succeed, and you have to work very hard." I remember when I was at the university, I worked three or four times longer than the Israelis.

When you let listeners call in to talk about any topic, what do people want to discuss?
There are a few main topics. The first subject is the children failing to succeed at school. According to Israeli law, the government says there is free education through high school. But it's not really free. There are after-school programs that cost money, which the Ethiopian kids cannot afford. There are also books you need to buy, and trips, and visits to museums. They tell the kids who can't pay that they have to stay home. So they drop out of school; they don't keep up. It's a terrible problem. Everyone talks about it. The Ministry of Education knows the problem well. Still you hear the mayors of certain towns say, "We cannot accept any more Ethiopian children in our schools." But to integrate this society, the main path is education. Our immigrant community is very young. The average family size is six children, and most of them are under eighteen years old. The problem starts very early. The Israeli children go to preschool and learn a lot about shapes and colors, the words for the voices of the different animals, and how to listen to stories, while the Ethiopian child stays home. So when they come to the school, they are already behind the Israeli children.

You said there were other topics that listeners want to talk about.
The second topic is the middle-aged population, forty to forty-five years old. In Ethiopia that was old, but here it is middle-aged. Because most are unemployed, there are

some who become alcoholic and then the family problems start. Another thing that has come up is the problem of HIV infection. You heard about the Blood Scandal in 1996, right? (See introduction to Chapter Four.) The blood banks said, "Okay, you are from Africa, and you might be infected with HIV, so it's not good for Israeli society for you to donate blood." They had been throwing it out. We organized a big demonstration, Adissu Mesele organized it (see Chapter Seven), and I got the permission from the police station in Jerusalem. At the demonstration we were saying, "You need to talk with the Ethiopian community and not decide yourselves what is good for us." So Shlomo Molla and I began to talk with many professors and doctors. Every month we met in Tel Ha-Shomer Hospital. It was decided that we needed to inform the community when there is a crisis, especially the *kessim*, who are the leaders of the community.

What is the station doing to educate people about HIV prevention?
First of all, we had to convince people that the problem really exists. In the beginning, many Ethiopians were saying, "It's because we're black that they say this about us." But now they are starting to understand that the higher rate of HIV in our community is a reality. Last week, I interviewed two Ethiopian men who are HIV positive. They talked about how they must take their medicine every day, about how their lives have changed.

Are people still concerned about being accepted as Jews by the Israelis?
Yes, but what people are also saying now is that they do not respect the [Ethiopian] rabbis as leaders. They respect the *kess*. The *kess* is still very strong and seen as the community leader.

Even among the younger people who were born in Israel?
Yes, there has been a change. Until the Blood Scandal, the young people wanted to be Israeli, and they respected the rabbis. They wanted to serve in the best army units and contribute to the country. But after this event, they said to themselves, "Israelis don't need us. They don't accept us, so we need to keep our own traditions." Now, many young people are returning

to their roots and they respect the *kess* more than they did before 1996. They are listening to more Amharic music. Ten years ago Ethiopians were marrying white Israelis more than they are now. Right now, almost all marriages are between Ethiopians.

I visited two Ethiopian synagogues recently and everyone was very welcoming. But most of the people in the traditional Ethiopian service were thirty-five or older. What will happen in two generations if there are no younger kessim being trained?
That is one of our big problems. Kess Avihu [in Ashkelon] is trying to train younger people. But in the next thirty to fifty years, I am afraid there will not be any more *kessim*.

In these synagogues, there was an Israeli Shabbat service that followed the traditional Ethiopian service. These people were teenagers and maybe up to age thirty praying in Hebrew.

There is a very big conflict between the yeshiva [religious school] students and the *kessim*. The *kessim* see the Ethiopian yeshiva students as not accepting Ethiopian Jewish tradition. Some of the younger *kessim*, like Kess Avihu, are very open. If they are open-minded, they say, "We came from Ethiopia because of our Jewish-ness, and therefore we need to learn to live with the other Jews." But there are other Ethiopians who live like the religious Israelis and leave our tradition. For example, Ethiopian men will study in the yeshiva, and when they visit their parents they won't eat what Mom cooks because it's not kosher enough. The mothers call our talk show and ask, "How can it be that we suffered in Ethiopia because we are Jews and we kept our tradition for two thousand years—how can it be that my own son, or my own daughter, won't eat what I cook?" The women are crying on the radio when they talk about this. It is so sad.

What about secular Ethiopian youth?

There is another group of young people who don't have the Ethiopian tradition, but they don't have an Israeli tradition either. They are not really Ethiopian, and they aren't really Israeli. So what they feel is only that they are black. They wear clothes to identify with the African Americans; they listen to hip-hop and rap [music]. Another thing that has changed is that women have suddenly become more educated than the men, and they are more likely to be working. They may be cleaners and security guards, but others are community leaders. In Ethiopia, the men were like kings, and now they are unemployed. Kids who are eleven or twelve years old speak Hebrew better than their parents, so the child has to take the parents to the doctor instead of the other way around. The whole community is very confused. That's the big problem—the community is confused.

I know this is another complicated issue, but what are people saying about the Falas Mura coming to Israel?

The community is divided. One group says, "Why didn't they come in the 1980s when we had to walk to Sudan?" The Ethiopian Jews were a religious community, so they think the Falas Mura only want to make *aliyah* because the life is better here. Other people in our community believe that since they [the ancestors of the Falas Mura] converted [to Christianity] more than a hundred years ago, they should still be considered Jews and should come. To make it more confusing, some Falas Mura married Christians, not other Falas Mura. So do we let their [Christian] families come too, under family reunification? You know, the Russian immigrants—not all of them are Jews. Why aren't people worried about the Jewish identity of the Russian *aliyah*? Well, they have political power. There are one million of them, and about 100,000 of us.

What is your own opinion about the Falas Mura? Should they come?

Right now there are 17,000 waiting in Addis Ababa and Gondar. But I will tell you, if you meet me here in three years, it could be many more. No one really knows. You know what I think? Israel is afraid of the reaction in the American Jewish community, because the Americans will ask Israel, "Is it because they are black that they are not being brought?" In Israel now there are about 30,000 Falas Mura [some say 20,000]. They all have families in Ethiopia, so where does it stop? It's very complicated.

It's very complicated to be an Ethiopian Israeli.

Yes, it is all very complicated. If we want to succeed, we have to work hard as a community. In that way, I can be a role model for other women. You can't just cry about discrimination. You can't cry about being black or being from Africa. And, another thing, you have to plan your family. Families have to have fewer children and make sure they get a good education.

"I think the next generation will have a good life. But our generation
has to work very hard, and we need a good education.
Family planning is something we have started doing here . . . .
I tell my kids, 'You have to believe you can succeed, and you have to work very hard.'
I remember when I was at the university, I worked three or four times
longer than the Israelis." —Tsega Melaku

Einat Asras

"There was an incident in the town of Hadera, where someone advertised an apartment building as 'Ethiopian-free,' meaning Ethiopians don't live here. It really hurt me. Behavior like that hurts the society. That's racism. It's racism in the workplace to say, 'We don't hire Ethiopian employees because our clients won't like it and won't come into our restaurant.' And it's not legal! It's a failure of the educational system. When I got to Israel I was taught about the Jews of the Middle East, of Spain, about the debates between the *Ashkenazim* and *Sephardim* on ritual slaughter and the dietary laws. But they don't teach children about the history of Ethiopian Jews. I know what happened during the immigration of other ethnic groups. I know what Zionist labor did, the pioneers of the state. I take my hat off to them and say *'kol hakavod'* [more power to them] for how they established the state. At the same time, I demand that the Ethiopian Jews also have a place in this educational system."

Many Ethiopian Israelis are outspoken about what they see as mistakes or inequities in their treatment by government ministries, the rabbinate, and municipal officials; but showing unmistakable anger is rare. We discovered Einat Asras through an interview she gave to an Israeli newspaper in which she blasted the unfair treatment of Ethiopians and especially the plight of her parents, whom she saw as relegated to the margins of their new society. A graduate of Bar Ilan University, Einat practices law and is studying for the bar exams. We met in her Tel Aviv office, where this photo was taken, and found her to be bubbly, outgoing, and, when her anger shows, as fiery as her reddish hair. We asked Einat if she would return to Ethiopia because of all the problems she describes. Her answer points to a feeling that runs very deep in the Ethiopian Israeli psyche and has been echoed in many interviews. "I wouldn't leave this country, and I don't know any Ethiopian Jews personally who would. I didn't come here thinking, 'If it's bad for me, I'm going to leave.' I came here because I am a Jew, and this is my country."

Itzik Dessie

"The Ministry of Education had a policy that there should be a quota for Ethiopian students in each school—

just the opposite of affirmative action. A maximum number, not a minimum. They said every school can accept only

twenty-five Ethiopian students, so when one of the children finished kindergarten and wanted to register for the first

grade, the [elementary] school said we have twenty-five Ethiopian children, and we don't want any more.

We asked, why not? He grew up here, his parents arrived in Israel twenty years ago, and he is an Israeli citizen like every

other student. The answer was, it creates a stigma for the school. The Minister of Education says that this citizen creates

a stigma for the school! We argued the case in the Supreme Court, and they ruled in our favor.

That policy was changed."

■

Although Itzik Dessie's story may sound like a self-serving invention of Hollywood, Israel's first Ethiopian lawyer really was attracted to the legal profession by the long-running television drama *L.A. Law*. The show was popular in Israel when Itzik was attending the University of Haifa. He recalls connecting emotionally with two of the main characters: "One of them was black, and the other one was a Jew. I loved both characters, and if you put them together, they were me." Itzik's legal career has taken on a seriousness that transcends its quirky inspiration. Recognizing the need for Ethiopian Israelis to have a legal resource, he was the founding director of Tebeka ("Justice-Maker" in Amharic), the Center for Legal Aid and Advocacy for the Ethiopian Israeli Community. Tebeka lawyers assist an average of fifty individuals per month, and they brought ten cases to court in 2005. Itzik is also involved in several programs to raise the standards and hone the skills of practicing Ethiopian Israeli lawyers and those in law school. In 2005, he took on another major responsibility when he was elected president of the board of the Ethiopian National Project, which includes seventeen Ethiopian-run nonprofits.

Itzik grew up in the Jewish town of Ambover and was taught to be strictly observant by his grandfather, who was a *kess*. When his father took a job working for the Organization for Rehabilitation and Training (ORT) in Addis Ababa, Itzik remained in Ambover with his grandfather, uncle, and siblings. In addition to working for ORT, his father secretly helped arrange for Jews to escape to Israel, an activity for which he served nine months in prison during 1983. After his release, Itzik's father was able to use his ORT connections to escape to Israel, and he arranged for Itzik, then fourteen years old, to be brought a few weeks later, in February 1985. Itzik is very careful about how he frames his arrival in Israel. "I would rather not speak of immigration; I prefer to speak about *aliyah*," he says, emphasizing the intentionality of the Ethiopian Jews. In our conversation, he talked about the problems of education for Ethiopian youth as well as the court cases that he has pursued for his community through his legal aid organization, Tebeka, which has several goals: it defends Ethiopian Israelis in cases of discrimination; it attempts to influence government policy through changes in civil law; and it cultivates

community empowerment. Because the Beta Israel were virtually a disenfranchised "caste" in Ethiopia, Itzik says that Ethiopian Israelis even today need to be reminded that they have civil rights and to demand that those rights be respected.

What was your schooling like when you first arrived in Israel?
Of course I studied Hebrew in the absorption center, and it was not difficult for me because I had a good education in my village. It was easier to learn Hebrew in 1985 because there were not as many Ethiopians here, so you could not get along with Amharic. You had to learn Hebrew. After the absorption center, I went to Yemin Orde, which gave me much more than formal education. Yemin Orde encouraged the students to help each other, not to be selfish, to respect everybody, and to treat everybody as equal. We learned some principles there that still accompany me everywhere I go. Yemin Orde was like a home for many Ethiopian children because at that time, most of us came without parents, without relatives, and had no one to live with. My father was here, but my mother remarried and did not have enough money to get out of Ethiopia, so she did not arrive until 1993.

Was it difficult to get into a university?
There was a unique program at the University of Haifa, something like affirmative action. Every applicant has to take the psychometric exam [a standard aptitude test]. Every immigrant group can take the exam in their own language, except for the Ethiopians. There is no Amharic exam, and the University of Haifa understood that this test is dependent on culture, so I was able to attend the school there. That's when I decided to study law. It was the *L.A. Law* show that made me think about becoming a lawyer.

You explained the case against the Ministry of Education and the illegal quotas for Ethiopian elementary school students. Are there other cases you've taken on?
Yes, another case that was about a very controversial subject: conversion. Back in 1984, when I arrived, the rabbinate said that we have to go through a special conversion to become a "real Jew." I laughed. I was more religious than most Israelis, so I was wondering, "How can you doubt that I'm a real Jew?" There was a demonstration for thirty days in Jerusalem to protest the policy, and it was changed because of that. The legal problem for my client began in May 2004. A woman who actually went through this

conversion process went to work in a restaurant, a falafel stand. One of the rabbis who checks to make sure that restaurants are kosher found out that there was an Ethiopian woman working there. He said to her, "Your religion is in doubt, so you have to stop working here. You can't cook." And she asked, "Why?" He told her, "Because you are Ethiopian, and you have to go through the conversion process." And she said, "I already did!" While this argument was going on, she was fired by the owner. I don't

blame the owner. If the rabbi wouldn't give him kosher certification, he could not stay in business. At this point, we have submitted the case to the court in Beersheva, but we don't have the decision yet.

So even though the conversions are no longer required, the attitude toward Jewish identity is still an obstacle to integration?
Religious status is very important for the Ethiopian community. If the rabbinate does not

accept us as they do every Jew, it will be difficult to feel that we belong here, that we are part of the society. I am not so religious now, and I don't care what the rabbis think of me. But for my father, my uncle, for the older people, it is still very important. I think some rabbis have a problem with the fact that there are black Jews.

Does this attitude present other practical problems for the community?
It has. In Yaffo we have an ordained Ethiopian

chief rabbi, Yosef Hadane. Every Ethiopian couple who wants to marry had to come to his office from wherever they live, in the north of Israel or in the south of Israel. They had to stop their work, spend their time, and come to Yaffo to get his approval. But Ethiopians are paying taxes and serving in the army like any other citizen, and we have the right to have that service [of marriage approval] near our homes, like everybody else. So we submitted a case to the Supreme Court in 2002, and on July 4, 2004, the Court finally decided that it's not right. Now Ethiopians can go to a local authority.

What do you think will happen to the Falas Mura? Are you involved in the effort to speed up their immigration, or aliyah?

Tebeka is focused on what is happening in Israel. But I am really disappointed by the government's handling of this Falas Mura issue. You have approximately 17,000 to 20,000 people in Addis and Gondar [these estimates are higher than others] who are waiting to come to Israel, but there are some government ministers who think we should bring only people who have money and are educated. Two weeks ago, immigrants came from France, and Israel welcomed them with flowers, with television cameras; and they had even asked these people to make *aliyah*. When Jews from Ethiopia say, "We want to come to Israel," the ministers don't accept them. They think bringing people from Ethiopia with no formal education and no money will be a burden to society. But I think the problem is

not money; it's the way that they see us.

If Israel were to bring all of the Falas Mura quickly, or even all at once, would that make the social and economic problems worse?

If the process is done correctly, it would make them better. Many mistakes have been made in the past, not by intention, but still mistakes. One mistake is that the Ethiopian community is concentrated in poor neighborhoods, which cannot offer employment. Over 60 percent of Ethiopian Israelis are unemployed. Then, some people don't want to work, because when the immigrants arrived the Ministry of Absorption put them all together for one or two years and gave them money. People got the idea that they can do nothing and still have money. These same people in Ethiopia worked hard, and they knew that if they did not work, they will not have money. But in Israel, they got the wrong idea. Another problem is that there is still prejudice. It is not nice to say that, but some people still have the idea that Ethiopians do not have enough talent, or that they are unable to work hard. We have to find a solution to these problems, but the solution is not to prevent Ethiopian Jews from coming to Israel.

What can be done to help solve the social problems in the community?

We have to give power back to the parents. One of the big mistakes the government made was saying to the parents, "We can educate your children [in boarding schools]; we know what is

good for them. Stand aside and do nothing." No, the parents and community must be part of the educational process.

Is there a program to encourage young Ethiopian students to become lawyers?

I don't encourage students to go to law school. But if they are going to law school, I want them to be among the best lawyers in Israel. There is a program called Israel at Heart, which sends Israeli young people abroad to talk about what Israel is like. Not what is in the newspapers, but the real Israel. We are trying to send Ethiopian law students overseas in the summer to study and to see how law firms in the U.S., Canada, or in England work. [In the summer 2005, Israel at Heart sent nine Ethiopian Israeli lawyers to the United States for two weeks.]

Chaim Peri [director of Yemin Orde] told me he thought Tebeka is helping to create a new style of leadership for the Ethiopian community, a non-political leadership. What did he mean by that?

We are using the power of our profession instead of political demonstrations. We are working with people who look at things professionally and use professional tools, such as bringing lawsuits, to solve problems. We have to take the community from dependence to independence. The way to do that is to nurture young leaders who can serve not only our community, but the whole Israeli society. Law school is the best training for leaders who can address not only legal problems, but the political areas too.

EPILOGUE

During our travels in Israel, my wife and I met a writer and translator in Kfar Haroe, a *moshav* of lush, dense flowering shrubs embracing white stone homes with orange-tiled roofs. The writer brought us to the home of a woman who was very ill at the time, but who agreed to see us because she sympathized with the goal of this project—to present life for the Ethiopian Jews of Israel from their perspective. She had spent years as a teacher of Ethiopian youngsters and shared her experiences generously. One memorable detail she related was that what Ethiopian children miss most about Ethiopia are the smells of the land and the cooking of food on open fires. More importantly, she recited for us a popular Ethiopian proverb: "Little by little, even the egg can stand on its legs and walk." After learning this proverb, I mentioned it to almost every Ethiopian Israeli I interviewed over the next year, and it invariably brought a smile to their lips. *Yes,* they agreed, *that is us.*

The Ethiopian Jews believe deeply in their ability to transform their lives in Israel, but only gradually. In the meantime, they struggle daily to build a better life. Poverty and unemployment are widespread, over 60 percent by most estimates. That their community is often perceived and characterized by the media as a burden to Israel is well known and unjust. Though their absorption requires support, the Ethiopian Jews are also an asset to Israeli society, as so many in this book demonstrate by their accomplishments. Their courage, fidelity to their Jewish tradition, and resourcefulness are what enabled them to reach Israel in the first place. Except for the Holocaust survivors, no group has suffered or sacrificed more to live as Jews in the Promised Land. Moreover, their cultural emphasis on patience, personal trust, and respect, especially for elders, offers a much-needed counterbalance to the often brash, impatient, aggressive, and youth-oriented society of Israel.

The people and government of Israel deserve praise for taking on the enormous challenge of absorbing a Jewish population so starkly different in background and culture from their own. But something is wrong when there is a widespread feeling among immigrants who arrived twenty years ago that they are second-class citizens and, even worse, as some admit to feeling, that they are seen as second-class Jews. In this context, what Shlomo Berihun said to me rings true: "Israel's attitude toward the Ethiopian Jews shows the attitude it has toward itself." Israel must help the Ethiopian Jews fulfill their potential in order to realize its own goal of being a multicultural, democratic, and open-hearted Jewish state.

Israel's policy toward completing the *aliyah* and funding programs to support the Ethiopian Jews already in Israel does, in fact, send a mixed message to the Ethiopian Jewish community. In 2005, the government agreed to increase immigration of the Falas Mura, those who linger in limbo in Ethiopia, from 300 to 600 per month. By mid-2006 there was still no increase in the rate, and a few months later, following the war in Lebanon, the government proposed reducing immigration to 150 per month, citing the cost of the war. After an angry outcry in both Israel and abroad, the government quickly reinstated the level to 300.

There are also paradoxical policies domestically. The Knesset approved a budget in the hundreds of millions over nine years for the Ethiopian National Project, but six years later, the ENP has received just over $12 million, virtually all of it from the United Jewish Communities (the Jewish Federations of North America). The Ethiopian Jews of Israel have nevertheless made great strides in education and employment. While their own community leaders reject affirmative action, which would mandate hiring Ethiopian Jews in the

mainstream economy, the government can help by creating incentives for employers to hire those on the lowest rung of the economic ladder.

That the Ethiopian Jews have persevered over the centuries and made *aliyah* almost in their entirety is a miracle of our own time. Even with substantial help from Jews around the world, the cost of completing the *aliyah* and the absorption of the Ethiopian Jews is daunting. But the cost of *not* seeing it through is also very high, not only to Israel's image of itself and to its mission as a Jewish nation, but also to the 100,000 Ethiopian Jews it has gone to great lengths to bring to the land. These are people who are working hard for their own futures and for their community. Their collective saga is one of dedication to living as Jews and commitment to living in Israel. Their individual stories show them to be a treasure that once fully claimed will enrich Judaism and Israeli society.

GLOSSARY

Abyssinia. A name for Ethiopia during the nineteenth and early-twentieth centuries.

Aksum. A city in Ethiopia. The Aksumite empire was an ancient kingdom that included geographical Ethiopia.

aliyah. Immigration to Israel; literally, "going up" to Israel.

American Jewish Joint Distribution Committee (JDC). Organization that assists Jewish communities in Israel and elsewhere in the world, including Ethiopia.

Amharic. The predominant language of modern Ethiopia.

Amidah. Standard Jewish prayer recited three times daily; literally, "Standing."

ayhud. Ge'ez term for non-Christian heretics during the Middle Ages in Ethiopia, referring specifically to Jews in some uses.

bagrut. Matriculation exam taken by Israeli students at the end of high school.

berakate. Bread that has been blessed by the priest, or *kess*, on the Sabbath. (Amharic)

Beta Israel. Name by which the Ethiopian Jews commonly referred to themselves; literally, "House of Israel."

Bet Din. Court of Jewish Law.

bet knesset. Synagogue. (Hebrew)

bet nida. A special house or hut where women are secluded during times of ritual impurity, such as during menstruation or following childbirth.

brit milah. Circumcision according to Jewish law.

buda. A derogatory term for Ethiopian Jews, meaning someone able to curse others with the "evil eye."

Cush. A biblical land south of Egypt sometimes interpreted to mean Ethiopia.

Derge. Committee that ruled Ethiopia following the communist takeover of 1974.

Diaspora. The dispersion of the Jews after the Babylonian exile; Jewish communities outside of Israel.

Ethiopian National Project (ENP). An Ethiopian-led organization in Israel supported by the Jewish federations in America, the Jewish Agency, and the state of Israel.

Ethiopic. Another term for Ge'ez, the classical Semitic language of Ethiopia, still used as the liturgical language of the Christian Church in Ethiopia.

Falasha. The name Ethiopian Jews were given by other Ethiopians. It was internationally accepted until outsiders realized it was intended to be derogatory. The Ethiopian Jews instead referred to themselves as Beta Israel.

Falas Mura. Ethiopian Jews who at one time lived as Christians and whose ancestors converted to Christianity.

ferenj. Amharic term used by Ethiopians for white Israelis. *Ferenj* means, roughly, "foreigner" (Hebrew plural, *ferenjim*).

Fidel. "Alphabet" in Amharic. The name of an organization that works with parents and teachers of Ethiopian schoolchildren.

Ge'ez. Classical Ethiopian language that preceded Amharic and other modern languages of the region. It is also the liturgical language for both Jews and Christians in Ethiopia.

Gondar. A city and province in northwest Ethiopia where most Ethiopian Jews lived before immigration to Israel.

halacha. Rabbinic Jewish law.

Hanukkah. Post-biblical holiday not known by Ethiopian Jews until the twentieth century.

hatafat dam. Literally, "a drop of blood." Symbolic circumcision required of Ethiopian Jewish males when they arrived in Israel. (Hebrew)

injerra. Ethiopian flat bread made from the indigenous grain tef.

Israel Association for Ethiopian Jews (IAEJ). An advocacy organization in Israel. Originally the American Association for Ethiopian Jews (AAEJ).

Jewish Agency. The Jewish Agency for Israel, created in 1929, which assists in all aspects of immigration to Israel.

kayla. Derogatory appellation for Ethiopian Jews, probably dating from the Middle Ages.

Kebra Negast. A volume of oral history and legends that comprise the saga of Ethiopia's development from biblical times.

kess. Priest; religious and spiritual leader.

Kiddush. A blessing or sanctification.

kippah. Yarmulke.

krar. A six-stringed lyre used in traditional Ethiopian music.

kushi. Derogatory name in Hebrew for black people, roughly equivalent to "nigger" in English, and deriving from the biblical land Cush (feminine, *kushit*).

Magen David Adom. Israel's equivalent of the Red Cross.

masgid. Synagogue. (Amharic)

mesob. Woven basket with a top that serves as a portable dining table. (Amharic)

mikveh. Immersion in water for religious purposes; a ritual cleansing. (Hebrew)

mitzvah. Commandment, in Hebrew (plural, *mitzvot*).

Mossad. Israel's intelligence agency.

North American Conference on Ethiopian Jewry (NACOEJ). An American-based advocacy organization that has been assisting Ethiopian Jews in Ethiopia and Israel since the 1980s.

olim. Immigrants to Israel.

Operation Joshua. Airlift brokered by American intervention to transport hundreds of Jews to Israel after Operation Moses was halted abruptly.

Operation Moses. Clandestine rescue of Ethiopian Jews from the refugee camps of Sudan from November 21, 1984, to January 5, 1985.

Operation Solomon. Airlift of May 24 and 25, 1991, when more than 14,000 Ethiopian Jews were flown from Addis Ababa to Israel in thirty-six hours.

Oral Law. Rabbinic Jewish law as contained in the Talmud.

Orit. The Ge'ez translation of the thirty-nine books of the Hebrew Bible, derived from the Greek Septuagint.

proteksia. Personal connections that give someone an advantage. (Hebrew)

psychometric exam. An aptitude test required of Israeli students before university study.

Quara. A remote region of Ethiopia where a Jewish community of 6,000 was discovered in 1992.

rabbinate. Official organization of Orthodox Judaism in Israel.

rabbinic Judaism. Jewish practice and law deriving from the Talmud, in contrast to biblical Judaism as practiced historically by the Ethiopian Jews.

Sanbat. Sabbath, in Amharic.

shemagleoch. Respected elders of the Ethiopian Jewish community.

shiftas. Bandits who robbed the Ethiopian Jews as they fled to Sudan during the 1980s. (Amharic)

Sigd. Annual hilltop festival of the Ethiopian Jews based on the Book of Nehemia. Observed in Ethiopia and Israel.

Talmud. The Oral Law and foundation of rabbinic Judaism. The Talmud was unknown to the Ethiopian Jews until the twentieth century.

Te'ezaza Sanbat. *Commandments of the Sabbath*, a book written centuries ago by Ethiopian Jews and still read in Israel in the synagogue.

tef. A grain indigenous to Ethiopia that is the basic ingredient of *injerra*, a staple of the diet.

tela. Homemade beer that contains less alcohol than commercial beer. (Amharic)

Tigray. A northern province of Ethiopia, east of Gondar, from which the Ethiopian Jews fled in the 1970s. Tigrayan Jews were the first Ethiopian Israelis.

tukul. An Ethiopian village home, usually a circular hut of straw, mud, and sticks.

Yom Hazkarah. A holiday inaugurated in Israel in 1985 to memorialize the 4,000 to 5,000 Ethiopian Jews who perished in the flight from Ethiopia and in the refugee camps of Sudan.

NOTES

From King Solomon to Operation Solomon

1. Steven Kaplan, *The Beta Israel (Falasha) in Ethiopia: From Earliest Times to the Twentieth Century* (New York: New York University Press, 1992), p. 19. Kaplan cites his source as *The Journal of Semitic Studies* 9, (1964): 1–10.

2. The Getatchew Haile citation appears in James Quirin, *The Evolution of the Ethiopian Jews: A History of the Beta Israel to 1920* (Pittsburgh: University of Pennsylvania Press, 1992), p. 18.

3. James Quirin, *The Evolution of the Ethiopian Jews: A History of the Beta Israel to 1920* (Pittsburgh: University of Pennsylvania Press, 1992), p. 18.

4. Kaplan, *Beta Israel,* p. 8.

5. The study was conducted by Gerard Lucotte and Pierre Smets and published in *Human Biology,* vol. 71 (December 1999), pp. 989–993.

6. According to David Kessler, Eldad Ha-Dani died in the year 890. *The Falashas: The Forgotten Jews of Ethiopia* (New York: Schocken Books, 1985), p. 74.

7. There is some controversy about the text of the quotation. See Kaplan, *Beta Israel,* footnote 22, p. 183.

8. The argument for this conclusion is set forth in a volume of research in the field of ethnomusicology. See Kay Kaufman Shelemay, *Music, Ritual, and Falasha History* (East Lansing: Michigan State University Press, 1989). The author's revolutionary conclusions about the influence of ex-Christian monks of the fourteenth century on Beta Israel religious liturgy has for the most part been accepted by Steven Kaplan, James Quirin, and other historians who describe Beta Israel development as an Ethiopian, rather than as a Jewish, phenomenon.

9. Kessler, *Falashas,* p. 85.

10. Kaplan, *Beta Israel,* p. 128.

11. Kessler, *Falashas,* p. 93. Also see note 134 in Kaplan, *The Beta Israel,* p. 287.

12. Kaplan, *Beta Israel,* p. 136.

13. Kessler, *Falashas,* p. 151.

Chapter One: Reliving the Exodus

1. See interview with Dr. Seffefe Aycheh in Chapter Eight.

2. Nigist Mengesha, the director of the Ethiopian National Project, is interviewed in Chapter Seven.

Chapter Three: The New People of the Book

1. Comedian Yossi Wassa tells his expanded version of the story in Chapter Six.

2. See interview with Rikki Tegeba in Chapter One.

3. For a discussion of KEDMA, see interview with Shlomo Molla in Chapter Seven.

Chapter Five: In God We Trust

1. See interview with Sirak Sabahat in Chapter Six.

Chapter Six: Singing a New Song in a New Land

1. See interview with Batia Eyob in Chapter Seven.

2. See interview with Shlomo Akale in Chapter Seven.

3. The Blood Scandal of 1996 is discussed in the introduction to Chapter Four and in the interview with Adissu Mesele in Chapter Seven.

4. For information about Fidel, see interview with Takele Mekonen in Chapter One.

5. See interview with Takele Mekonen in Chapter One.

Chapter Seven: Getting Organized

1. The Blood Scandal of 1996 is discussed in the introduction to Chapter Four.

Chapter Eight: Professionally Speaking

1. See interview with Nigist Mengesha in Chapter Seven.

2. See interview with Shlomo Berihun in Chapter One.

3. Gidon Ayech is interviewed in Chapter Four.

4. For a further description of KEDMA, see the interview in Chapter Seven with Shlomo Molla.

5. See interview with Takele Mekonen in Chapter One.

SELECTED BIBLIOGRAPHY

BenEzer, Gadi. *The Ethiopian Jewish Exodus: Narratives of the Migration Journey to Israel, 1977–1985.* Memory and Narrative, vol. 9. London: Routledge, 2002.

Kaplan, Steven. *The Beta Israel (Falasha) in Ethiopia: From Earliest Times to the Twentieth Century.* New York: New York University Press, 1992.

Kaplan, Steven, and Ruth Westheimer. *Surviving Salvation: The Ethiopian Jewish Family in Transition.* New York: New York University Press, 1992.

Kessler, David. *The Falashas: The Forgotten Jews of Ethiopia.* New York: Schocken Books, 1985.

Leslau, Wolf. *Falasha Anthology: The Black Jews of Ethiopia.* New York: Schocken Books, 1951.

Marcus, Harold G. *A History of Ethiopia.* Berkeley and Los Angeles: University of California Press, 2002.

Messing, Simon D. *The Story of the Falashas: "Black Jews" of Ethiopia.* Hamden, Connecticut: Simon Messing, 1982.

Pankhurst, Richard. *A Social History of Ethiopia.* Trenton: Red Sea Press, 1992.

Parfitt, Tudor. *Operation Moses: The Untold Story of the Secret Exodus of the Falasha Jews from Ethiopia.* New York: Stein and Day Publishers, 1985.

Parfitt, Tudor, and Emanuela Trevisan Semi, eds. *Beta Israel in Ethiopia and Israel: Studies on Ethiopian Jews.* Surrey, England: Curzon Press, 1998.

Quirin, James. *The Evolution of the Ethiopian Jews: A History of the Beta Israel to 1920.* Pittsburgh: University of Pennsylvania Press, 1992.

Salamon, Hagar. *The Hyena People: Ethiopian Jews in Christian Ethiopia.* Berkeley and Los Angeles: University of California Press, 1999.

Shelemay, Kay Kaufman. *A Song of Longing: An Ethiopian Journey.* Chicago: University of Illinois Press, 1991.

———. *Music, Ritual, and Falasha History.* East Lansing: Michigan State University Press, 1989.

Spector, Stephen. *Operation Solomon: The Daring Rescue of the Ethiopian Jews.* New York: Oxford University Press, 2005.

Wagaw, Teshome G. *For Our Soul: Ethiopian Jews in Israel.* Detroit: Wayne State University Press, 1993.

The Ethiopian Jews of Israel: Personal Stories of Life in the Promised Land

2007 First printing
Text copyright © 2007 Len Lyons
Photographs copyright © Ilan Ossendryver, unless otherwise noted.

For information regarding permission to reprint material from this book, please e-mail the author using the web site *www.ethiopianisraelisproject.org.*

All photographs in this book are by Ilan Ossendryver, unless otherwise indicated here: pages 6, 32, 141, 165, the color photographs of Jews in Ethiopia are by Lieman/Minkin, courtesy of Mike Lieman and the North American Conference on Ethiopian Jewry in New York; the black and white photographs of Jews in Ethiopia are printed courtesy of Beth Hatefutsoth in Tel Aviv, Israel; pages 21, 24, 26, 29, 31, photographs by Doron Bacher; page 18, photograph by Moshe Bar Yehuda; page 205, photograph by Art Leipzig and reproduced by permission; pages 50, 67 (lower right), 137 (bottom), photographs by Len Lyons; page 22, the original map was created for this book by Tagist Yosef of Tel Aviv, Israel, and is reproduced by permission.

Library of Congress Cataloging-in-Publication Data

Lyons, Leonard.
    The Ethiopian Jews of Israel : personal stories of life in the Promised Land / Len Lyons ; with photography by Ilan Ossendryver.
        p. cm.
    Includes bibliographical references.
    ISBN-13: 978-1-58023-323-1 (hardcover)
    ISBN-10: 1-58023-323-6 (hardcover)
    1. Jews, Ethiopian—Israel. 2. Israel—Ethnic relations. I. Ossendryver, Ilan. II. Title.
DS113.8.F34L96 2007
304.8'5694063—dc22

2006034488
CIP

Book and cover design by Kari Finkler
Edited by Karyn Slutsky
Copyedited by Elizabeth S. Shanley

For People of All Faiths, All Backgrounds
Published by Jewish Lights Publishing
A Division of Longhill Partners, Inc.
Sunset Farm Offices, Route 4, P.O. Box 237
Woodstock, VT 05091
Tel: (802) 457-4000   Fax: (802) 457-4004
www.jewishlights.com

Developed and produced by Verve Editions, Burlington, Vermont

VERVE
E D I T I O N S

www.verveeditions.com

10 9 8 7 6 5 4 3 2 1

Printed in China